PRACTICAL DRAFTING™

APPLIED ENGINEERING GRAPHICS

WORK BOOK

WRITTEN AND ILLUSTRATED BY MELVIN G. PETERMAN

First Edition: 1999 ©

IMPORTANT NOTICE

Though all the information in this book has been carefully compiled and checked, there is no warranty of any kind expressed or implied. No responsibility for any errors or omissions is assumed.

ISBN: 0-9722058-3-7

Melvin G. Peterman

INSIGHT™ TECHNICAL EDUCATION™

TOLL FREE: 877.640.2256 ✪ WWW.INSIGHTTECHED.COM

A Personal note:

Thank you for your purchase! If you find items that need to be corrected or you want to make suggestions, please contact me on the phone or on the web.

— Melvin G. Peterman

Dedicated to:

My King who has blessed without bounds. My family who has supported me at every turn and without limits. My parents who taught me to look on the bright side of everything and who taught me to have faith, to work hard, and to never give up.

My books are not a personal endeavor. They are the work of a family following God in the pursuit of liberty.

Thanks to:

A special thanks to Brad, for his support, friendship, & proofing of this work.

Thoughts for consideration:

Patrick Henry, after he had witnessed a minister in Culpeper, Va. being scourged to death for not taking a license to preach, wrote the words that were later included in his famous speech: "What is it that Gentlemen wish? What would they have? Is life so dear, or peace so sweet, as to be purchased at the price of chains and slavery? Forbid it, Almighty God! I know not what course others may take, but as for me, give me liberty or give me death!"

Psalms 118:9

 It is better to trust in the LORD than to put confidence in princes.

2 Chronicles 7:14

If my people, who are called by my name, shall humble themselves, and pray, and seek my face, and turn from their wicked ways; then will I hear from heaven, and will forgive their sin, and will heal their land.

A brief note of introduction:

This Practical Drafting series is a natural extension of the Complete-A-Sketch™ series. This book will expose the student to many types of drafting and standards. This volume is intended to be an overview of many different applications of drafting. Drafting is the language of engineering. In the engineering field today it is imperative that all participants, drafters, designers, engineers, machinists, electricians, builders, etc. must understand this language. The drawings created are used to assure that a product, part, or building can be built and checked for quality. A drawing is considered a living document and can be revised and updated at any time to adapt to changing needs.

This study is geared to be used by students without outside instruction. The study is built with the intent of helping to promote the use of hand and computer drafting skills. All the lessons in this book may be accomplished both by hand and on the computer. It is my strong recommendation that the student do the lessons by hand using tools of the trade. Then, after being comfortable with manual drafting, complete the lessons on the computer.

Tools and supplies required:

Small drafting board	Triangle 30° x 60° x 90°	Mechanical pencil, .3mm
T-square	Bow compass with center adjust	Eraser, white for paper
2 Scales, English & Metric	Dividers	Eraser shield
Isometric circle template	Mechanical pencil, .9mm	Drafting tape
Triangle 45° x 45° x 90°	Mechanical pencil, .7mm	8 ½" x 11" paper
Dictionary	Mechanical pencil, .5mm	11" x 17" paper

Types of CAD Programs:

Start with the simple and inexpensive. Consider the type of computer you own and the amount of money in your budget. There are many products to choose from; they range in price from free (download from the Internet) to several thousands of dollars. Choose one that suits you and learn it. It is my recommendation that you learn one or two programs. If you want to know which CAD programs to focus on, you need to figure out what features are important to you. If you are looking to be in a specific field and you want to prepare yourself for a job or career, look in the help wanted section of the news paper or look at some job web sites like www.monster.com, www.boeing.com, and www.ceweekly.com; this will tell you the program or programs you want to learn.

About the author:

In addition to being an author, publisher & business owner, I am a mechanical designer. As it has turned out, I have worked in almost every type of commercial environment imaginable from construction to nuclear to high tech to factories that produce food, extrude plastic, and make shoe parts. I have been working since about 1975 in technical fields. As a youth in 1975, I wanted to help my father and I wanted to do the type of work my father did so I started drawing ductwork systems for him. Since then, I have worked as a mechanical, piping, electrical, and architectural drafter, and as a tooling, machinery, and mechanical designer and patent developer for myself and others. I am proficient in manual and computer drafting, design, and CAD customizing. Additionally, I am proficient in most types of computer software including programming, databases, etc.

Instructions:

First let me state that you, the owner of this book, may make as many copies of noted pages for personal use as you wish. However, you may not sell, transmit, or give away copies in any form.

1. Make as many practice copies as you wish of noted pages.
2. Follow the instructions for each lesson.
3. Refer back to previous lessons as required.

CONTENTS

FORWARD

This book is intended to be a guide and an introduction to the world of engineering graphics. There are many books that will tell you how everything should be. This book is more about strong suggestions, standards, guidelines, and building your foundation and giving you the tools you need to do your own in depth studies. There are few absolutes in engineering as a whole and this is what allows innovation and progress. Learn to ask why. Learn to question the way things are done. Every organization runs differently and has different standards. Learn to adapt without personal compromise.

Drafting is the language of engineering of all types, a method of documentation. Most science and engineering disciplines require a level of drawing skill that allows easy communication. That is why virtually all science and engineering schools require courses in drafting. Documenting ideas is imperative. This allows for design, thought, and improvements prior to work occurring. This documentation also allows for the work to be done again. A technical drawing is intended to convey complex concepts with brevity, simplicity, and clarity. There are industry standards for producing drawings and it is the intent of this book to demonstrate adherence to those standards. Most of the standards that will be followed in this book are ANSI (American National Standards Institute, section Y14) or standards that have occurred due to compromises associated with the use of CAD.

In drafting as in most professions, neatness counts. Presentation is not everything; however, it can mean selling an idea or getting a job. First impressions of a drawing are extremely important. The presentation of your drawings tells the viewer the type of person you are. From personal experience I would share with you that it is great to have a customer, boss, or co-worker say "these are great looking drawings." Drafting is an art and even when you use CAD, the spacing, balance, and overall presentation is still critical.

The skills you will learn in this book will benefit you for life regardless of your final career choices. You will probably not produce manual drawings for a living; however, learning manually is the best way to learn. The concepts and principles in this book apply to drafting & design not just to manual or CAD work. It is intended that this book focus on the most critical areas only. It is not the purpose of this book to have you become a professional manual drafter. The goal is to assist you in mastering some drafting concepts and the art of drafting. These concepts will apply to using CAD and in other professional and personal projects. Completing this book is only the first step.

Housekeeping and neatness count. Keep your tools organized, your work space tidy, and your work in order. For manual drafting for right handers, work from top to bottom and from left to right. For left handers, work from right to left. Keep your hands, papers, and tools clean and do not push your tools across the paper. Pick up the tools and place them where you need them to be. Stay relaxed. Sit in a comfortable position and have fun.

LESSON 1.00
LINES & LETTERING

NOTE:
LINE WEIGHTS ARE IMPORTANT TO EVERY DRAWING. LINE WEIGHTS HELP THE READER OF THE DRAWING. IT IS AN IMPORTANT PART OF THE DRAFTING LANGUAGE. THIS APPLIES TO BOTH CAD & MANUAL DRAFTING.

———————————————————— .3mm, CONSTRUCTION & GUIDELINES, DRAW LIGHTLY

———————————————————— .9mm OR .7mm, OBJECT LINES

– – – – – – – – – – – – – – – .5mm, HIDDEN LINES

———————— 1.000 ———————— .5mm, EXTENSION, DIMENSION, AND LEADER LINES

——— – ——— – ——— – ——— .5mm, CENTER LINES

——— – – ——— – – ——— .3mm, PHANTOM LINES

———— ■ ———— ■ ———— .9mm TO 1.8mm MAX., CUTTING PLANE LINES

〜〜〜〜〜〜 .9mm OR .7mm, BREAK LINES

/ // // // // /. .3mm, SECTION LINES

INSTRUCTIONS:
DRAW 4 SETS OF LINES FREE HAND BELOW. USE THE DOTTED LINE IN THE FIRST BOX AS A GUIDE.

1.000	

LESSON 1.01
LINES & LETTERING

NOTE:
ENGINEERING DRAWINGS CLEARLY DESCRIBE A PART, PROCESS, & PROCEDURE. BELOW IS A TYPICAL 3 VIEW ORTHOGRAPHIC PROJECTION THAT IS USED FOR SUCH A PURPOSE. THE 3 VIEW DRAWING IS USED EXTENSIVELY IN ENGINEERING.

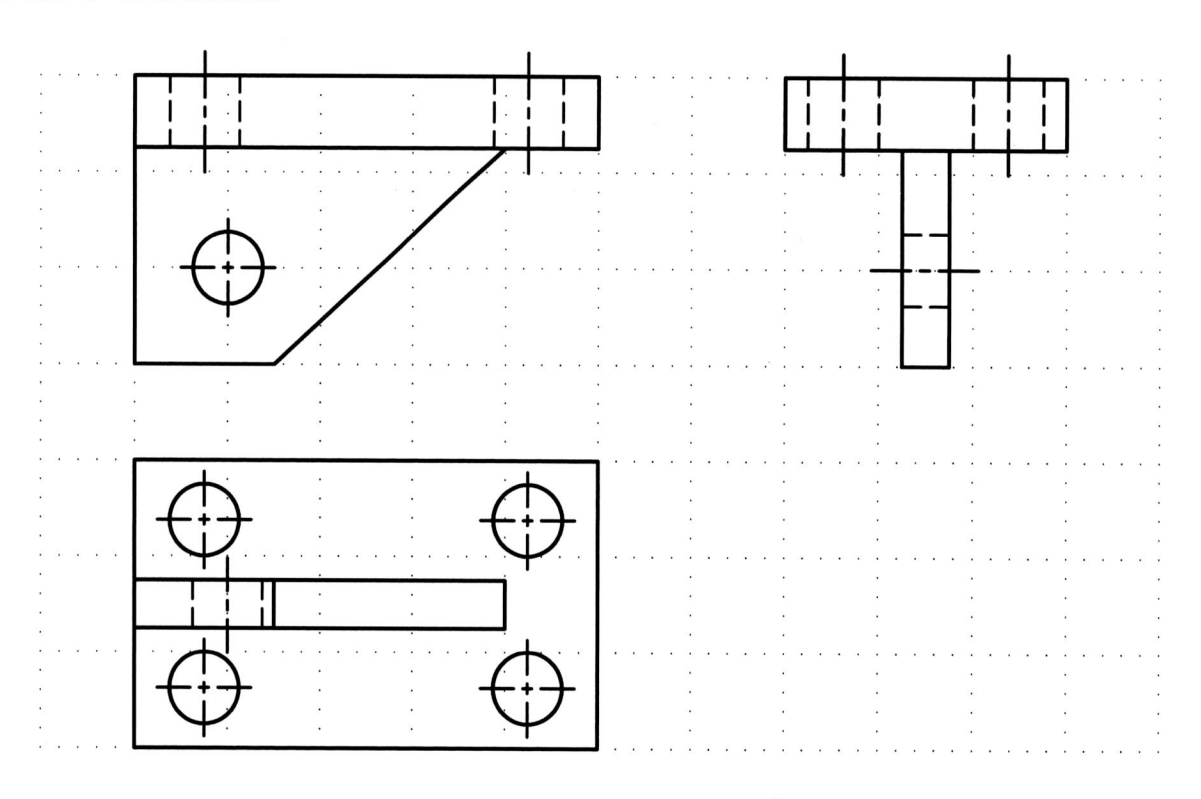

INSTRUCTIONS:
USING THE CORRECT LINE WEIGHTS, DRAW THE THREE FACES OF THE ABOVE OBJECT FREE HAND ON THE GRID BELOW. ENSURE THAT THE THREE VIEWS ARE ALIGNED AND IN THE SAME RELATIVE LOCATION.

LESSON 1.02
LINES & LETTERING

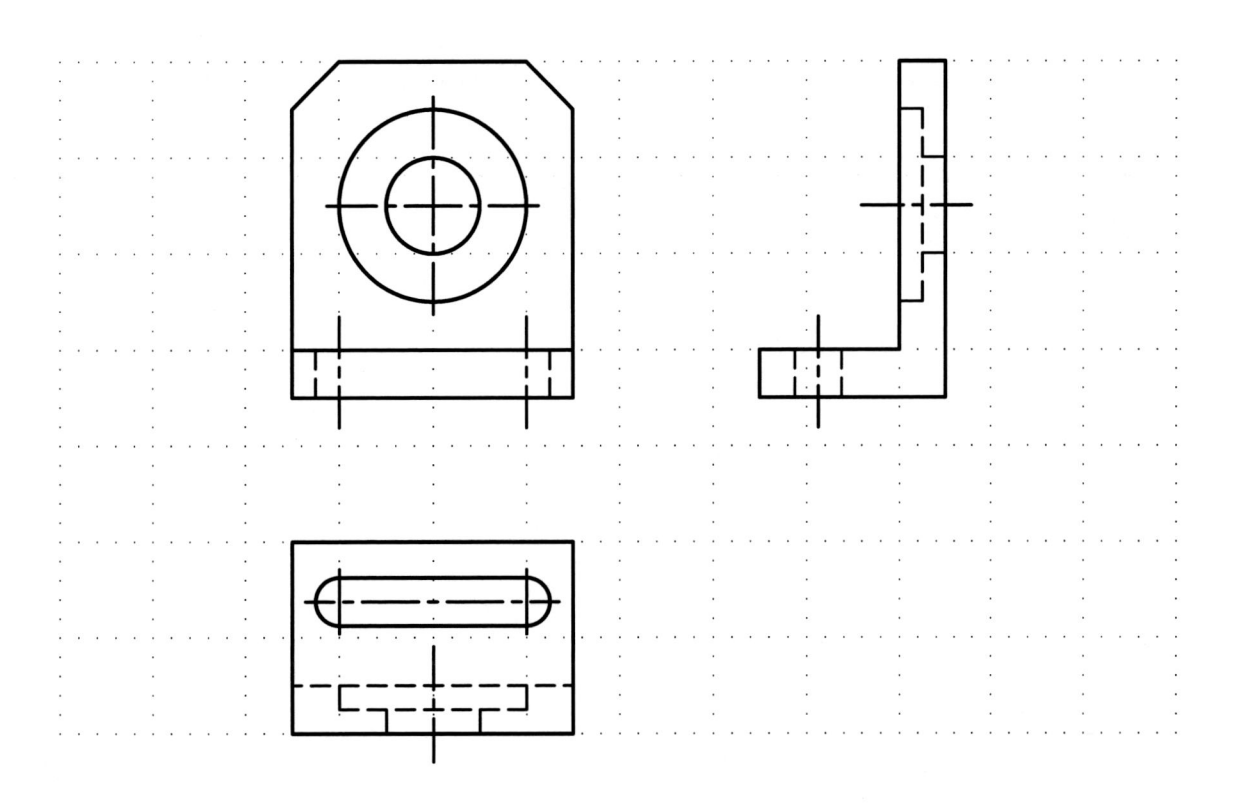

INSTRUCTIONS:
USING THE CORRECT LINE WEIGHTS, DRAW THE THREE FACES OF THE ABOVE OBJECT FREE HAND ON THE GRID BELOW. ENSURE THAT THE THREE VIEWS ARE ALIGNED AND IN THE SAME RELATIVE LOCATION.

LESSON 1.03
LINES & LETTERING

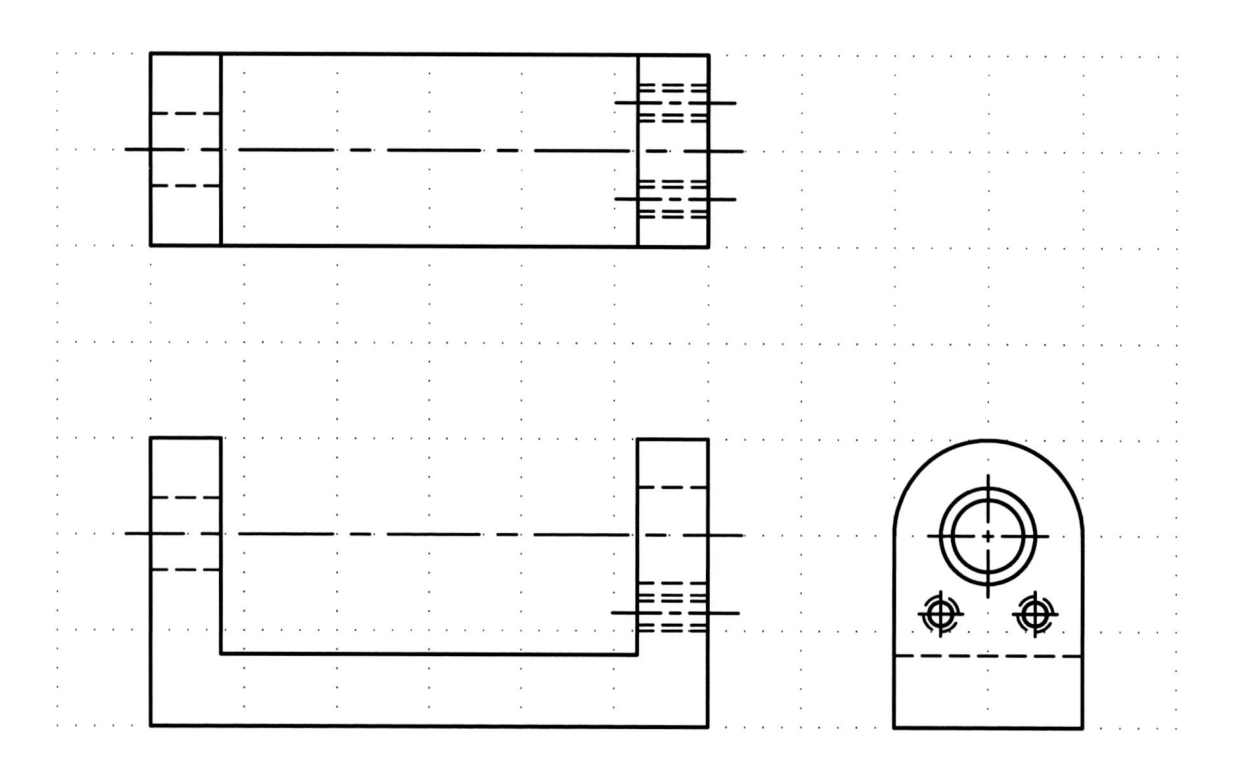

INSTRUCTIONS:
USING THE CORRECT LINE WEIGHTS, DRAW THE THREE FACES OF THE ABOVE OBJECT FREE HAND ON THE GRID BELOW. ENSURE THAT THE THREE VIEWS ARE ALIGNED AND IN THE SAME RELATIVE LOCATION.

LESSON 1.04
LINES & LETTERING

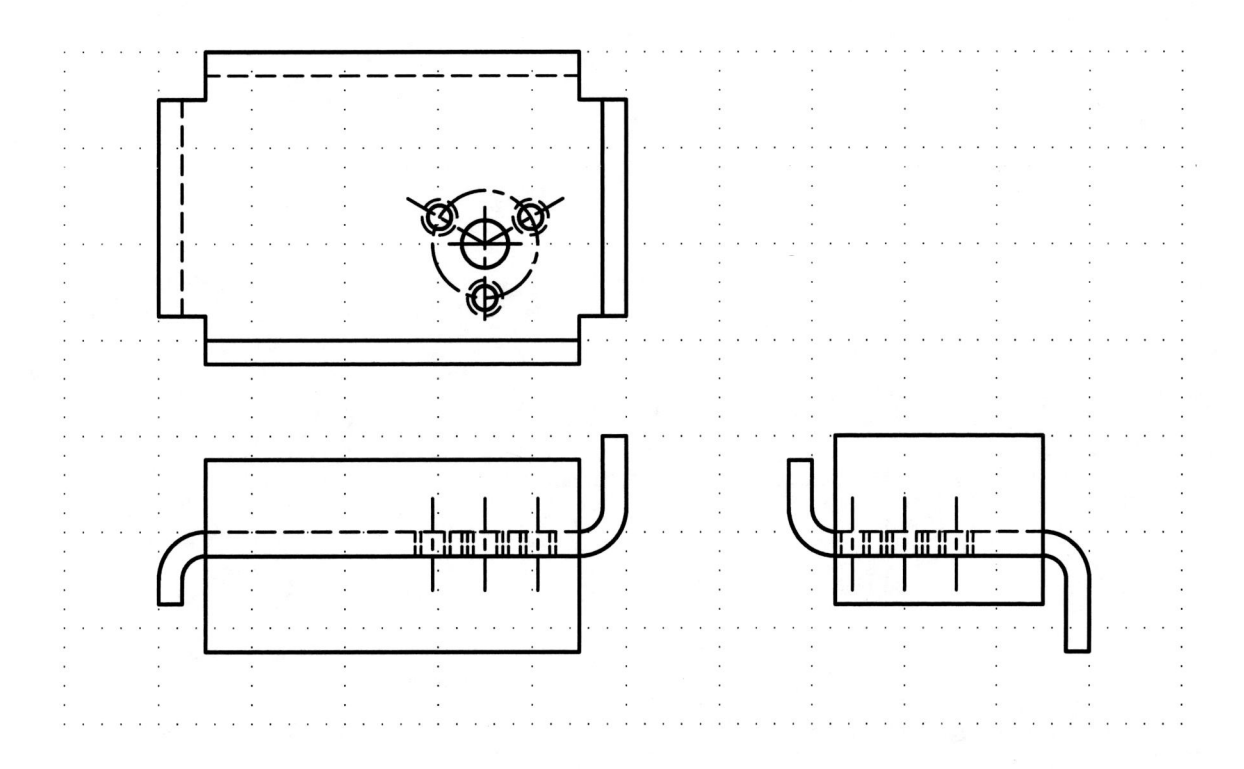

INSTRUCTIONS:
USING THE CORRECT LINE WEIGHTS, DRAW THE THREE FACES OF THE ABOVE OBJECT FREE HAND ON THE GRID
BELOW. ENSURE THAT THE THREE VIEWS ARE ALIGNED AND IN THE SAME RELATIVE LOCATION.

LESSON 1.05
LINES & LETTERING

NOTE:
LETTERING IS AN INDIVIDUAL EXPRESSION. THE INTENT IS TO DESCRIBE TWO LETTERING METHODS AND THEN YOU CAN DEVELOP YOUR OWN STYLE. COMPOSITION OF EACH LETTER IS IMPORTANT AND REQUIRES CARE, PROPER SPACING, & THE CORRECT AMOUNT OF LEAD DENSITY OR OPAQUENESS. THE FIRST FONT OR STYLE IS THE MOST COMMON. THE FONT STYLE IS CALLED A SAN SERIF, A PLAIN GOTHIC FONT OR STYLE. THIS CHARACTER SET IS LIKE THE ONE USED TO CREATE THESE LESSONS.

TEXT MUST BE PLAIN, SIMPLE, EASY TO READ AND FOR THE PURPOSES OF THIS LESSON, 1/8" HIGH FOR TEXT, 3/16" FOR SUBTITLES, AND 1/4" FOR TITLES. THIS LESSON DEMONSTRATES THE END RESULT OF ACCEPTABLE CHARACTERS; THE EXACT STEPS TO FORM THE FONT YOU USE IS NOT IMPORTANT. THE LETTERS YOU USE MUST BE WELL FORMED AND ALL CAPS.

VERTICAL TEXT

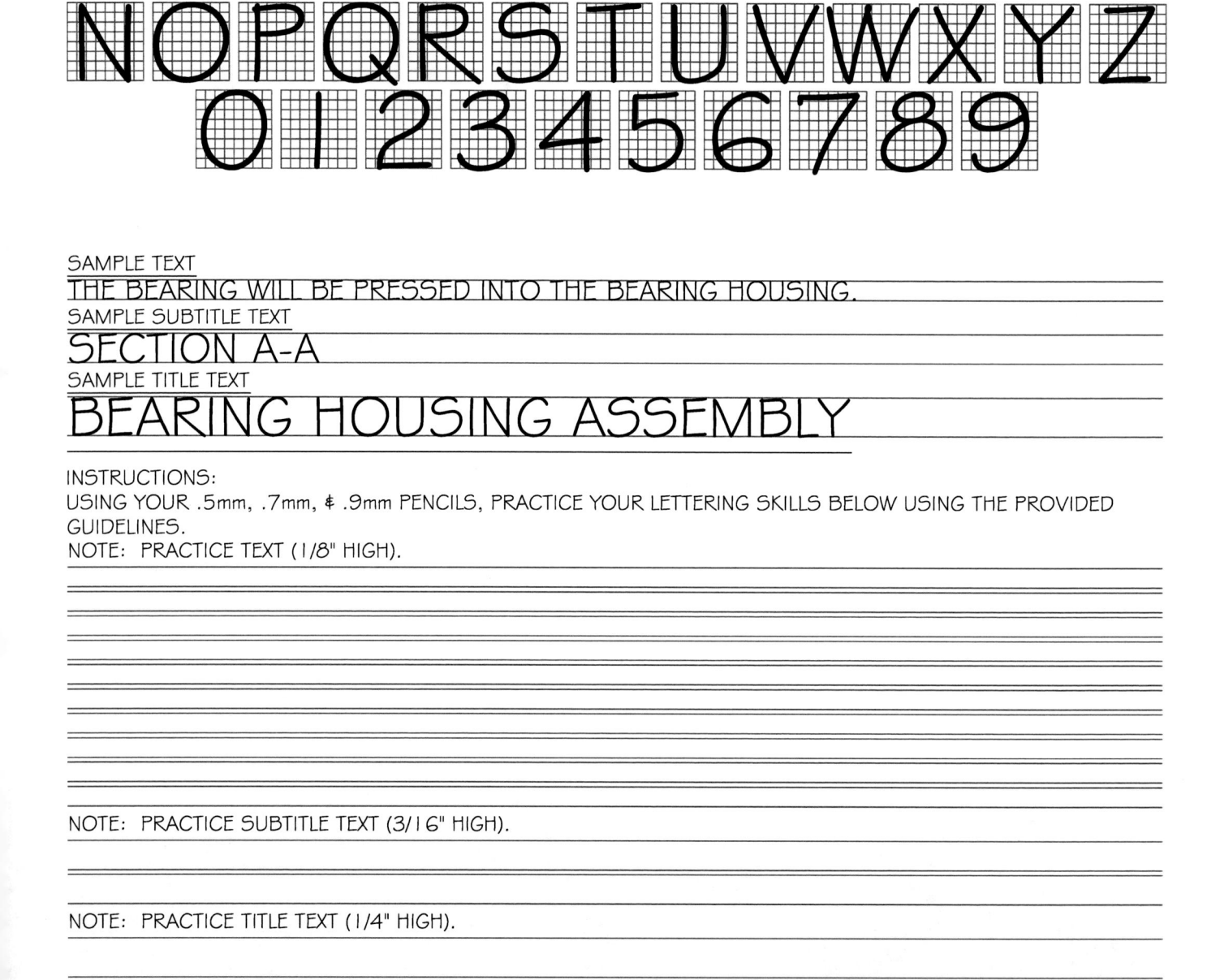

SAMPLE TEXT
THE BEARING WILL BE PRESSED INTO THE BEARING HOUSING.
SAMPLE SUBTITLE TEXT
SECTION A-A
SAMPLE TITLE TEXT
BEARING HOUSING ASSEMBLY

INSTRUCTIONS:
USING YOUR .5mm, .7mm, & .9mm PENCILS, PRACTICE YOUR LETTERING SKILLS BELOW USING THE PROVIDED GUIDELINES.
NOTE: PRACTICE TEXT (1/8" HIGH).

NOTE: PRACTICE SUBTITLE TEXT (3/16" HIGH).

NOTE: PRACTICE TITLE TEXT (1/4" HIGH).

LESSON 1.06
LINES & LETTERING

NOTE:
NOW TRY SOME ITALIC LETTERS. THIS LETTERING STYLE IS LEANING TO THE THE RIGHT 10°.

TO RESTATE AGAIN, ANY TEXT USED IN DRAFTING MUST BE PLAIN, SIMPLE, EASY TO READ AND FOR THE PURPOSES OF THIS LESSON, 1/8" HIGH FOR TEXT, 3/16" FOR SUBTITLES, AND 1/4" FOR TITLES. THIS LESSON DEMONSTRATES THE END RESULT OF ACCEPTABLE CHARACTERS; THE EXACT STEPS TO FORM THE FONT YOU USE IS NOT IMPORTANT. THE LETTERS YOU USE <u>MUST BE WELL FORMED AND ALL CAPS.</u>

ITALIC TEXT

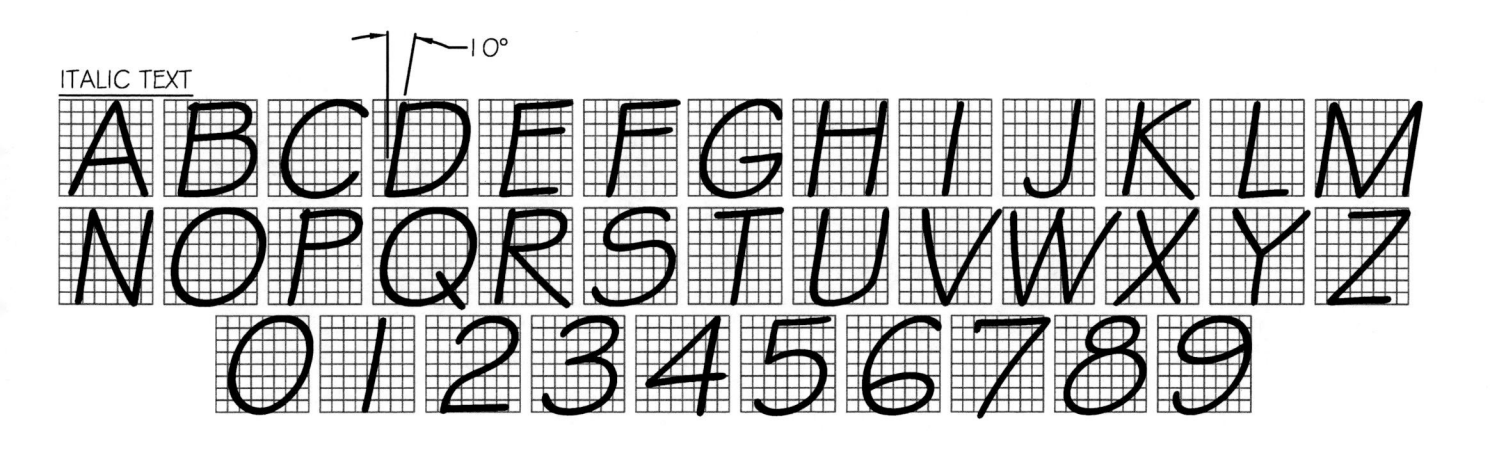

SAMPLE TEXT
THE BEARING WILL BE PRESSED INTO THE BEARING HOUSING.
SAMPLE SUBTITLE TEXT
SECTION A-A
SAMPLE TITLE TEXT
BEARING HOUSING ASSEMBLY

INSTRUCTIONS:
USING YOUR .5mm, .7mm, & .9mm PENCILS, PRACTICE YOUR LETTERING SKILLS BELOW USING THE PROVIDED GUIDELINES.
NOTE: PRACTICE TEXT (1/8" HIGH).

NOTE: PRACTICE SUBTITLE TEXT (3/16" HIGH).

NOTE: PRACTICE TITLE TEXT (1/4" HIGH).

LESSON 1.07
LINES & LETTERING

NOTE:
TEXT JUSTIFICATION (HORIZONTAL TEXT POSITION) IS ALSO IMPORTANT. THIS LESSON IS TO REINFORCE THAT LINES OF TEXT NEED TO BE JUSTIFIED UNIFORMLY TO HELP MAINTAIN THE CRISP CHARACTER OF THE DRAFTING DOCUMENT. TEXT JUSTIFICATION CAN ADD BALANCE TO THE DRAWING AND IT CAN KEEP THE DRAWING FROM BEING CLUTTERED AND UNCLEAR.

NOTE:
THIS TEXT IS LEFT JUSTIFIED. THAT MEANS THAT ALL THE LINES OF TEXT IN THIS BODY OF TEXT ARE LINED UP ON THE LEFT SIDE.

NOTE:
THIS TEXT IS CENTER JUSTIFIED. THAT MEANS THAT ALL THE LINES OF TEXT IN THIS BODY OF TEXT ARE LINED UP ON THE CENTER LINE OF THE TEXT BODY.

NOTE:
THIS TEXT IS RIGHT JUSTIFIED. THAT MEANS THAT ALL THE LINES OF TEXT IN THIS BODY OF TEXT ARE LINED UP ON THE RIGHT SIDE.

EXAMPLES:

INSURE THAT ALL
WELDING IS
COMPLETE PRIOR
TO FINAL ASSEMBLY

SECTION A-A
SCALE: 2X

NOTE:
ALL SURFACES
TO BE CLEAN &
FREE OF ALL
OIL & RUST

INSTRUCTIONS:
USING YOUR .5mm, .7mm, & .9mm PENCILS, PRACTICE YOUR LETTERING SKILLS BELOW USING THE PROVIDED GUIDELINES.
NOTE: PRACTICE LEFT JUSTIFIED TEXT.

NOTE: PRACTICE RIGHT JUSTIFIED TEXT.

NOTE: PRACTICE CENTER JUSTIFIED TEXT. CENTER ON PROVIDED CENTER LINE.

LESSON 2.00
DRAFTING TOOLS

NOTE:

DRAFTING TOOLS FOR THE EXERCISES IN THIS BOOK ARE KEPT TO A MINIMUM. IT IS MY INTENTION TO USE ONLY THE MOST COMMON AND AVAILABLE TOOLS. IT IS MY GOAL TO INTRODUCE THE TOOLS AND METHODS, NOT TO MAKE YOU A PROFESSIONAL MANUAL DRAFTER. HENCE, THE FOLLOWING EXERCISES WILL HELP YOU TO UNDERSTAND CONCEPTS THAT YOU WILL USE IN CAD, SHOULD YOU PURSUE A CAREER IN A TECHNICAL FIELD.

TYPES OF TRIANGLES:

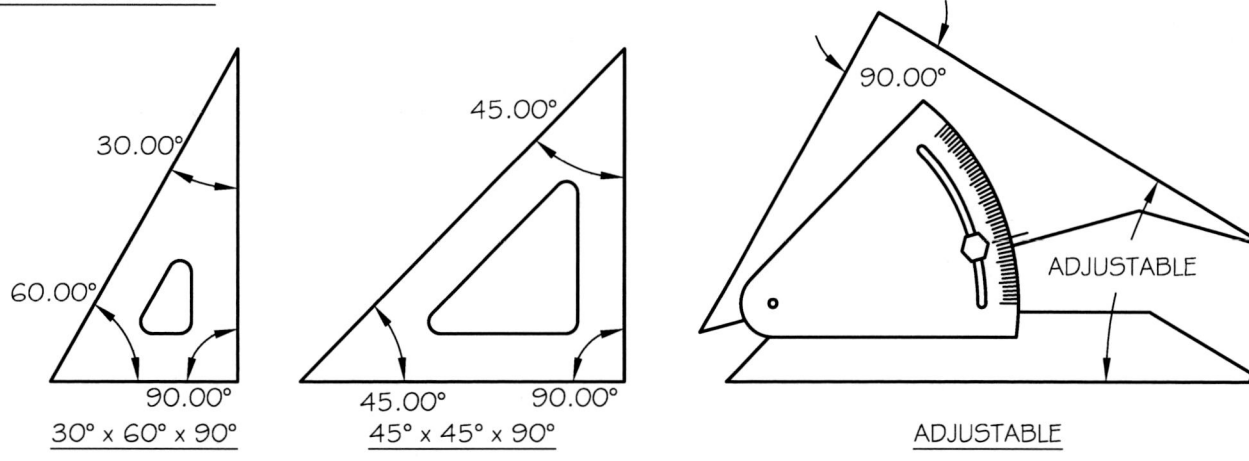

30° x 60° x 90°   45° x 45° x 90°   ADJUSTABLE

SCALES & RULES:

SCALES ARE SPECIALIZED RULERS. THERE ARE 2 SIDED SCALES, 3 SIDED SCALES, ARCHITECTURAL SCALES, ENGINEERING SCALES, AND METRIC SCALES. EVERY TYPE OF SCALE HAS ITS BENEFITS AND DRAW BACKS. THE BENEFITS OF THE 2 SIDED RULE IS THAT IT HAS A VERY LOW PROFILE. THE BENEFIT OF THE 3 SIDED RULE IS THAT IT HAS MORE SCALES ON IT. ENGINEERING RULES BREAK THE STANDARD INCH INTO 10, 20, 30, 40, AND 50 UNITS. THE METRIC SCALE, DEPENDING ON THE TYPE YOU ACQUIRE, MAY SHOW ALL THE COMMON METRIC DRAWING SCALES 1:2.5, 1:5, 1:10, 1:20, 1:50, 1:100. THE TYPE OF RULE YOU CHOOSE TO USE IS UP TO YOU. THERE WILL BE PROBLEMS USING BOTH ENGLISH AND METRIC IN THIS BOOK! IT DOES NOT MATTER WHERE YOU LIVE IN THE WORLD, KNOWING BOTH ENGLISH AND METRIC SYSTEMS OF MEASUREMENT IS IMPORTANT.

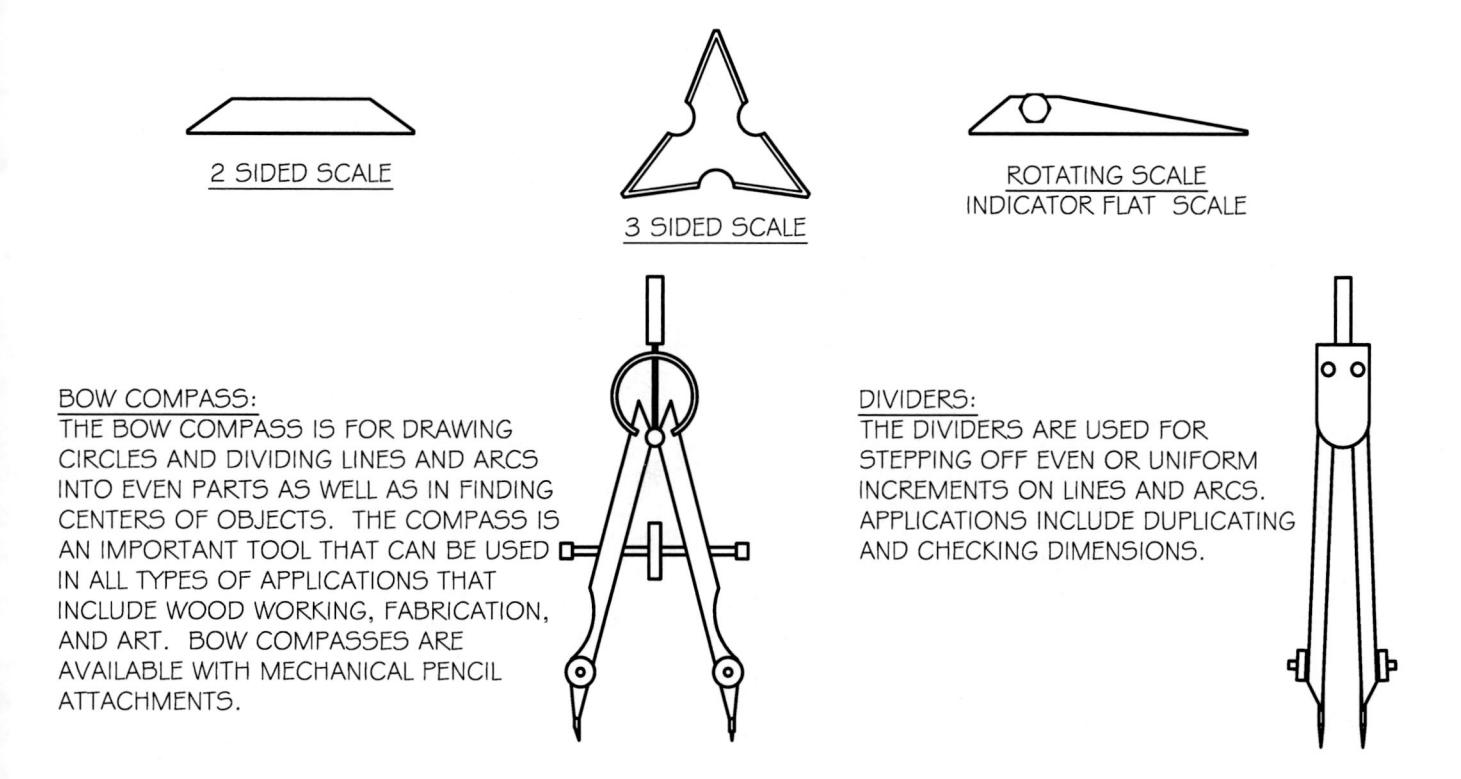

2 SIDED SCALE

3 SIDED SCALE

ROTATING SCALE
INDICATOR FLAT SCALE

BOW COMPASS:

THE BOW COMPASS IS FOR DRAWING CIRCLES AND DIVIDING LINES AND ARCS INTO EVEN PARTS AS WELL AS IN FINDING CENTERS OF OBJECTS. THE COMPASS IS AN IMPORTANT TOOL THAT CAN BE USED IN ALL TYPES OF APPLICATIONS THAT INCLUDE WOOD WORKING, FABRICATION, AND ART. BOW COMPASSES ARE AVAILABLE WITH MECHANICAL PENCIL ATTACHMENTS.

DIVIDERS:

THE DIVIDERS ARE USED FOR STEPPING OFF EVEN OR UNIFORM INCREMENTS ON LINES AND ARCS. APPLICATIONS INCLUDE DUPLICATING AND CHECKING DIMENSIONS.

LESSON 2.01
DRAFTING TOOLS

TYPES OF TEMPLATES:
THERE ARE MANY TYPES OF TEMPLATES AVAILABLE. THEY START WITH THE SIMPLE AND RANGE TO THE COMPLEX.
EXAMPLES INCLUDE CIRCLE, SQUARE, HEX, ELLIPSE, STEEL SHAPES, ELECTRONIC, ARCHITECTURAL, LETTER GUIDES, ARROW HEADS, ETC.

TEMPLATES:

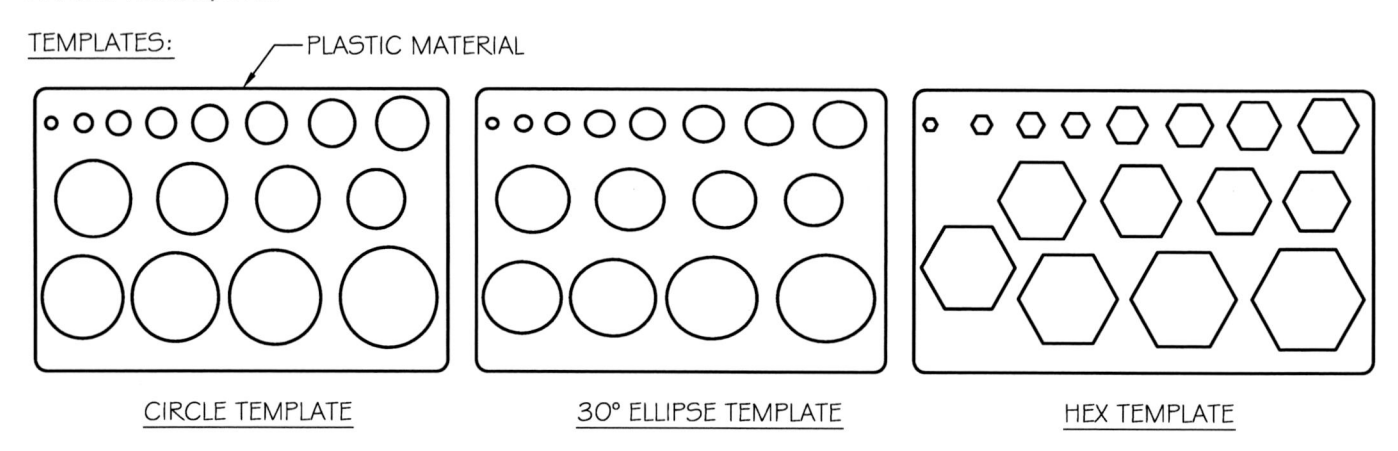

CIRCLE TEMPLATE   30° ELLIPSE TEMPLATE   HEX TEMPLATE

OTHER TOOLS:

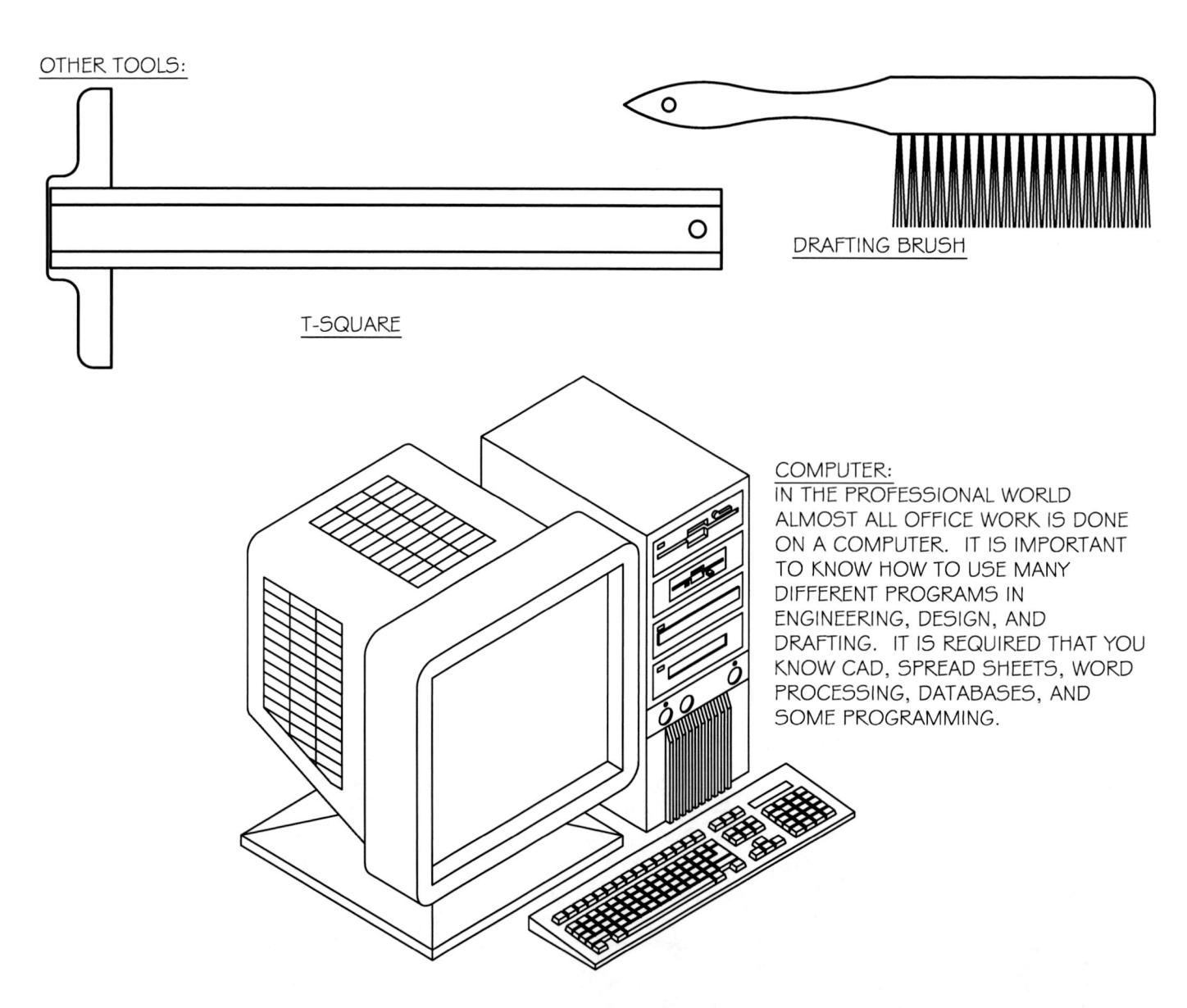

T-SQUARE

DRAFTING BRUSH

COMPUTER:
IN THE PROFESSIONAL WORLD ALMOST ALL OFFICE WORK IS DONE ON A COMPUTER. IT IS IMPORTANT TO KNOW HOW TO USE MANY DIFFERENT PROGRAMS IN ENGINEERING, DESIGN, AND DRAFTING. IT IS REQUIRED THAT YOU KNOW CAD, SPREAD SHEETS, WORD PROCESSING, DATABASES, AND SOME PROGRAMMING.

LESSON 3.00
GEOMETRIC SHAPES & CONSTRUCTIONS
SPECIAL NOTE: WHEN NO DIMENSIONS ARE SPECIFIED IN THIS SECTION, MAKE UP YOUR OWN.

NOTE:
GEOMETRY IS THE BASIS OF ALL ENGINEERING DRAWINGS; DEMONSTRATED BY THE DRAWINGS BELOW.

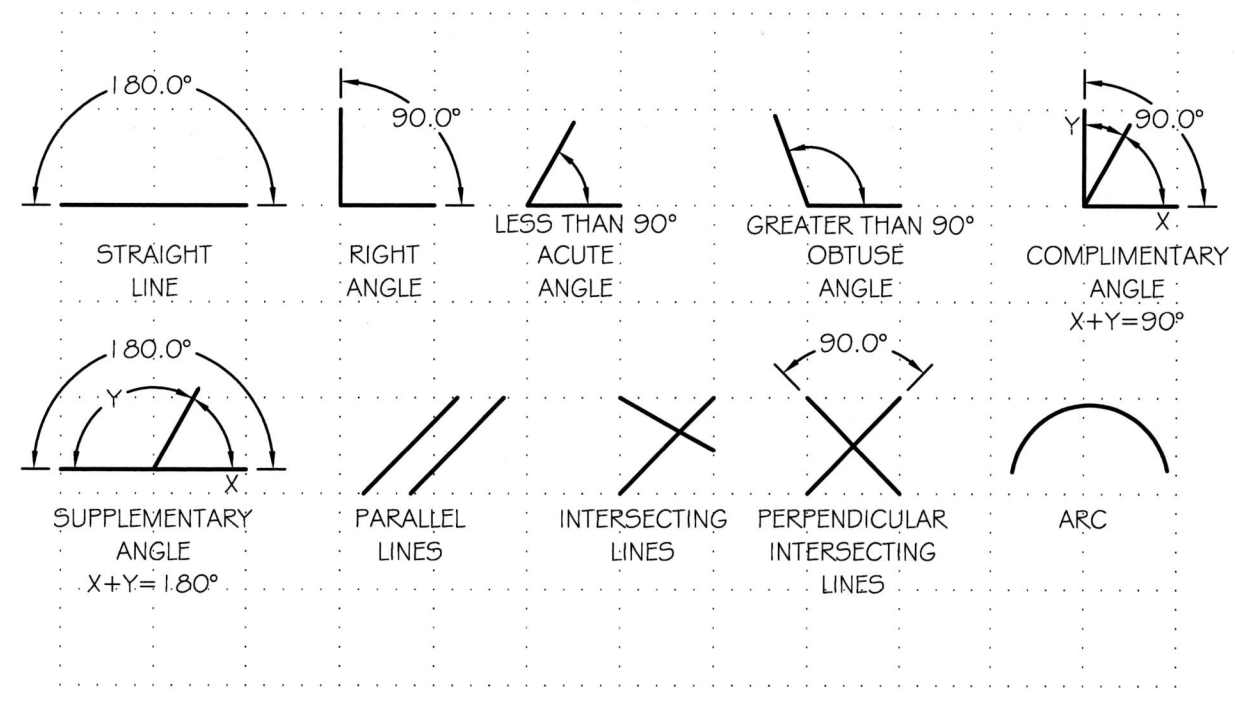

INSTRUCTIONS:
FREE HAND DRAW & LETTER THE ITEMS FROM ABOVE. USING & LEAVING LIGHT GUIDELINES FOR LETTERING IS
ACCEPTABLE. REFER TO LESSON 1.06 FOR LETTERING INFORMATION.

LESSON 3.01
GEOMETRIC SHAPES & CONSTRUCTIONS

NOTE:
BELOW ARE TRIANGLES. A RULE TO REMEMBER: THE SUM OF ALL INTERNAL ANGLES OF ANY TRIANGLE ALWAYS EQUALS 180°.

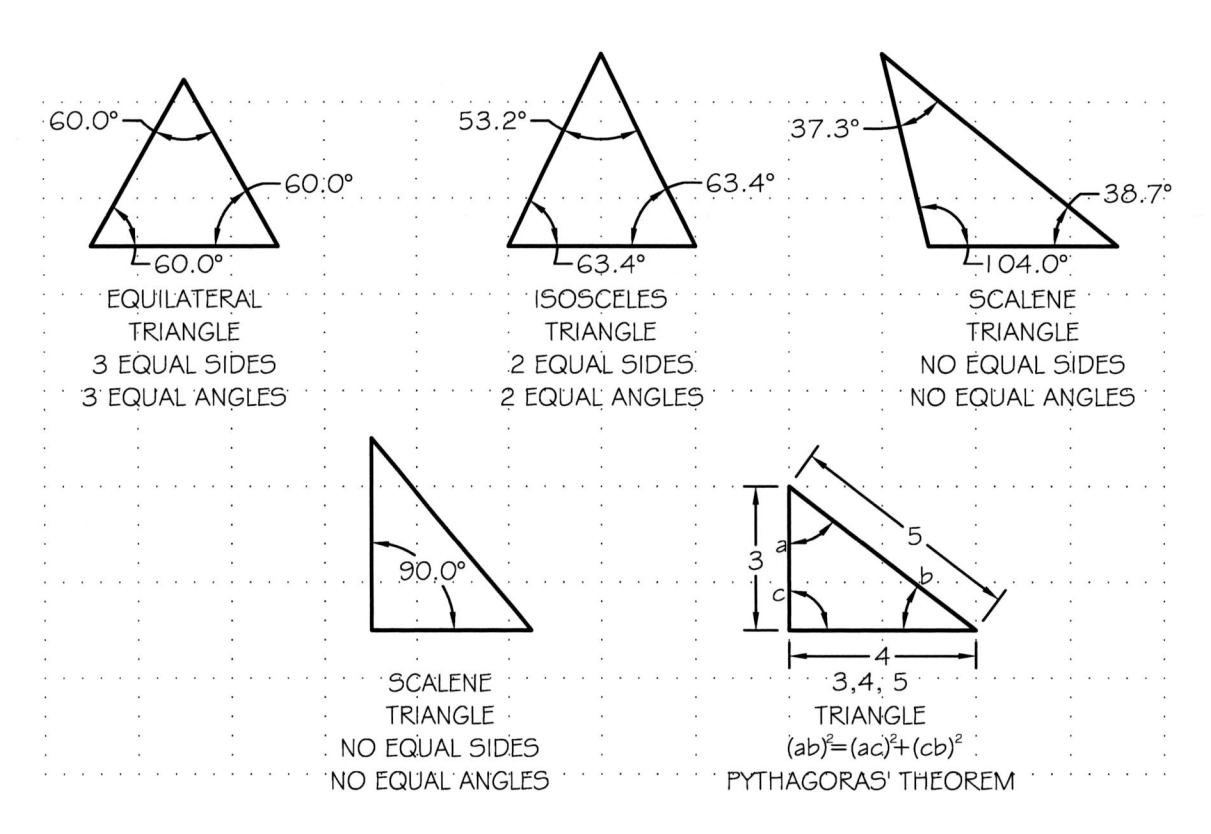

EQUILATERAL
TRIANGLE
3 EQUAL SIDES
3 EQUAL ANGLES

ISOSCELES
TRIANGLE
2 EQUAL SIDES
2 EQUAL ANGLES

SCALENE
TRIANGLE
NO EQUAL SIDES
NO EQUAL ANGLES

SCALENE
TRIANGLE
NO EQUAL SIDES
NO EQUAL ANGLES

3, 4, 5
TRIANGLE
$(ab)^2 = (ac)^2 + (cb)^2$
PYTHAGORAS' THEOREM

INSTRUCTIONS:
FREE HAND DRAW & LETTER THE ITEMS FROM ABOVE. USING & LEAVING LIGHT GUIDELINES FOR LETTERING IS ACCEPTABLE.

LESSON 3.02
GEOMETRIC SHAPES & CONSTRUCTIONS

NOTE:
BELOW ARE QUADRILLES. A QUADRILLE IS ANY SHAPE THAT CONSISTS OF 4 STRAIGHT LINES. RULES TO
REMEMBER: 1.) IF THE SIDES ARE PARALLEL & THE ANGLES ARE 90°, THEN IT IS A SQUARE OR RECTANGLE.
REMEMBER: 2.) IF BOTH PAIR OF OPPOSITE LINES ARE PARALLEL, THE SHAPE IS A PARALLELOGRAM.

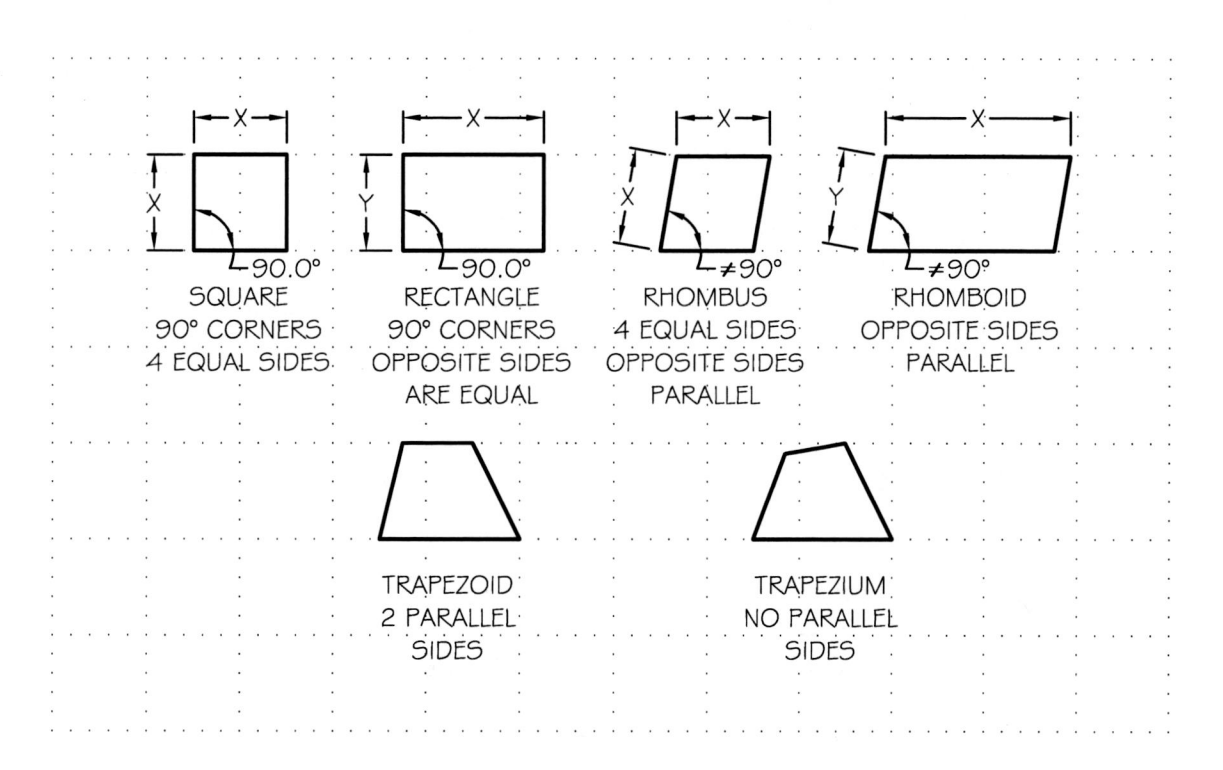

INSTRUCTIONS:
FREE HAND DRAW & LETTER THE ITEMS FROM ABOVE. USING & LEAVING LIGHT GUIDELINES FOR LETTERING
IS ACCEPTABLE.

LESSON 3.03
GEOMETRIC SHAPES & CONSTRUCTIONS

NOTE:
BELOW ARE POLYGONS. A RULE TO REMEMBER: IF THE SIDES ARE OF EQUAL LENGTH & CAN BE INSCRIBED OR CIRCUMSCRIBED AROUND A CIRCLE, IT IS A REGULAR POLYGON.

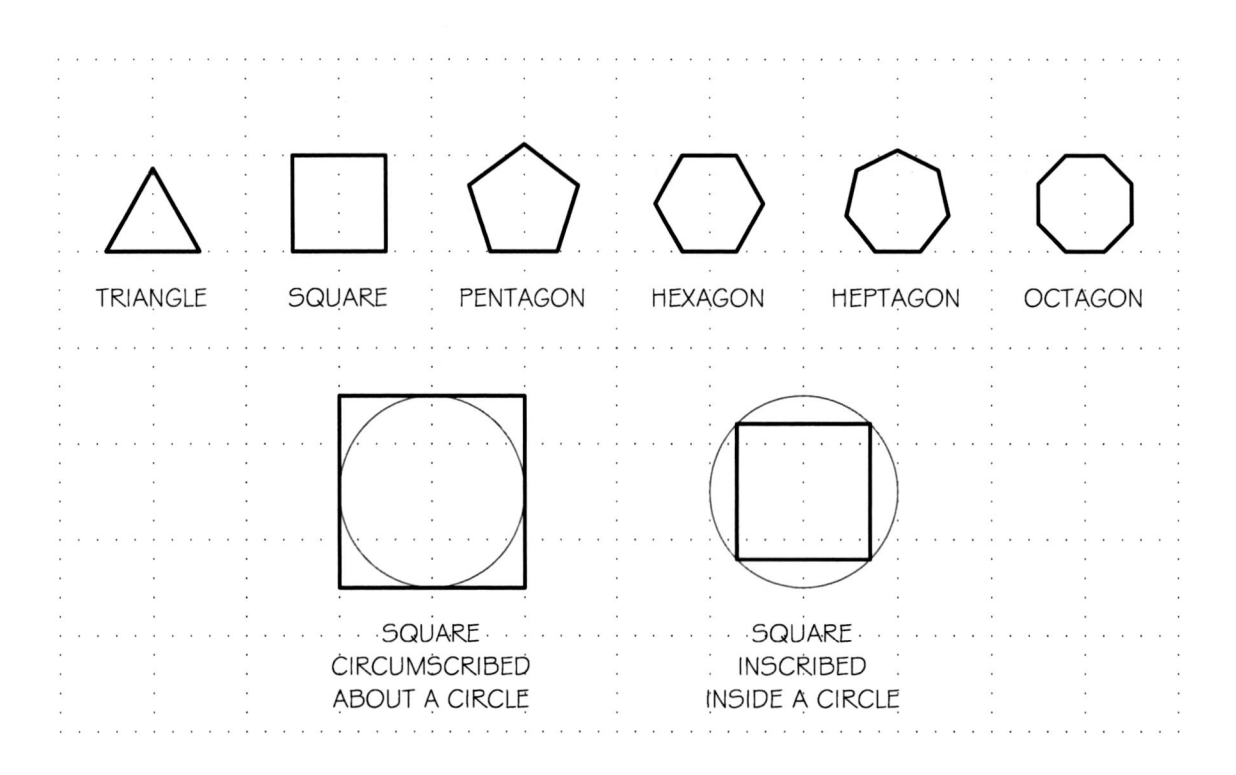

INSTRUCTIONS:
FREE HAND DRAW & LETTER THE ITEMS FROM ABOVE. USING & LEAVING LIGHT GUIDELINES FOR LETTERING IS ACCEPTABLE.

LESSON 3.04
GEOMETRIC SHAPES & CONSTRUCTIONS

NOTE:
BELOW IS A CIRCLE WITH ALL OF ITS PARTS DENOTED & DIAGRAMMED. A RULE TO REMEMBER: A CIRCLE IS AN ARC OF 360°. AN ARC IS ANY PART OF A CIRCLE.

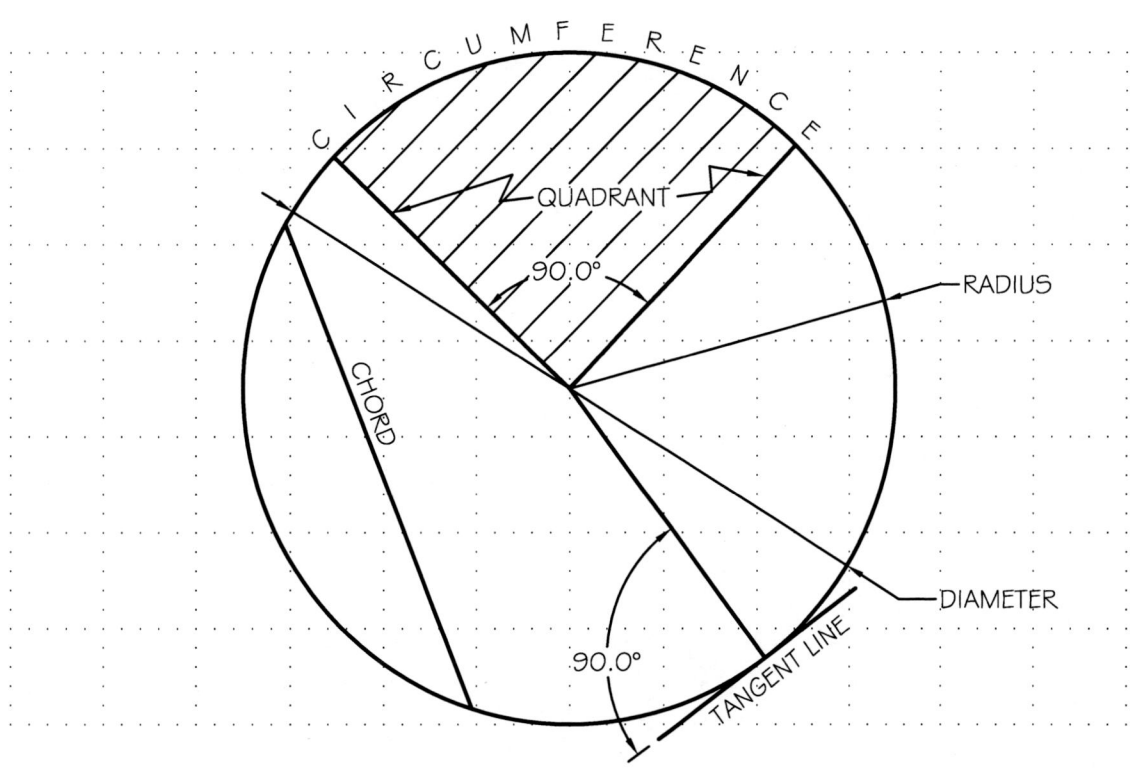

INSTRUCTIONS:
FREE HAND DRAW & LETTER THE ITEMS FROM ABOVE. USING & LEAVING LIGHT GUIDELINES FOR LETTERING IS ACCEPTABLE.

LESSON 3.05
GEOMETRIC SHAPES & CONSTRUCTIONS

NOTE:
BISECTING LINE, ARC, & ANGLE USING ARCS.

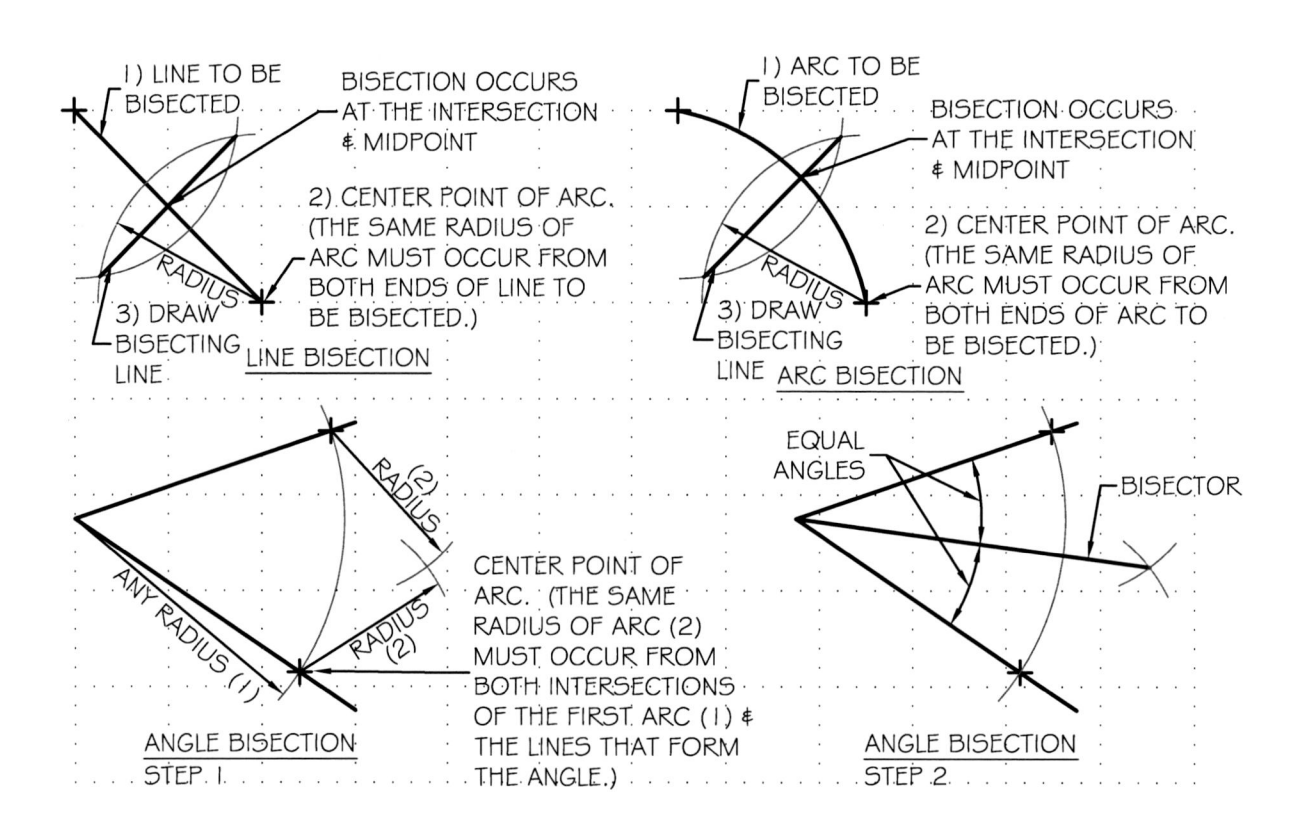

1) LINE TO BE BISECTED

BISECTION OCCURS AT THE INTERSECTION & MIDPOINT

2) CENTER POINT OF ARC. (THE SAME RADIUS OF ARC MUST OCCUR FROM BOTH ENDS OF LINE TO BE BISECTED.)

3) DRAW BISECTING LINE

RADIUS

LINE BISECTION

1) ARC TO BE BISECTED

BISECTION OCCURS AT THE INTERSECTION & MIDPOINT

2) CENTER POINT OF ARC. (THE SAME RADIUS OF ARC MUST OCCUR FROM BOTH ENDS OF ARC TO BE BISECTED.)

3) DRAW BISECTING LINE

RADIUS

ARC BISECTION

RADIUS (2)

ANY RADIUS (1)

RADIUS (2)

CENTER POINT OF ARC. (THE SAME RADIUS OF ARC (2) MUST OCCUR FROM BOTH INTERSECTIONS OF THE FIRST ARC (1) & THE LINES THAT FORM THE ANGLE.)

ANGLE BISECTION STEP 1

EQUAL ANGLES

BISECTOR

ANGLE BISECTION STEP 2

INSTRUCTIONS:
USING TOOLS OR CAD, REPRODUCE THE ABOVE RESULTS OF THE EXERCISE. SPECIAL CAD NOTE: USE THE EXACT POINTS OF OBJECTS (EX. END POINTS, MID POINT, CENTER) TO INSURE THAT ALL GEOMETRY IS CONSTRUCTED EXACTLY WHERE IT NEEDS TO BE.
CAD COMMANDS TO CONSIDER: ARC, CIRCLE, LINE.

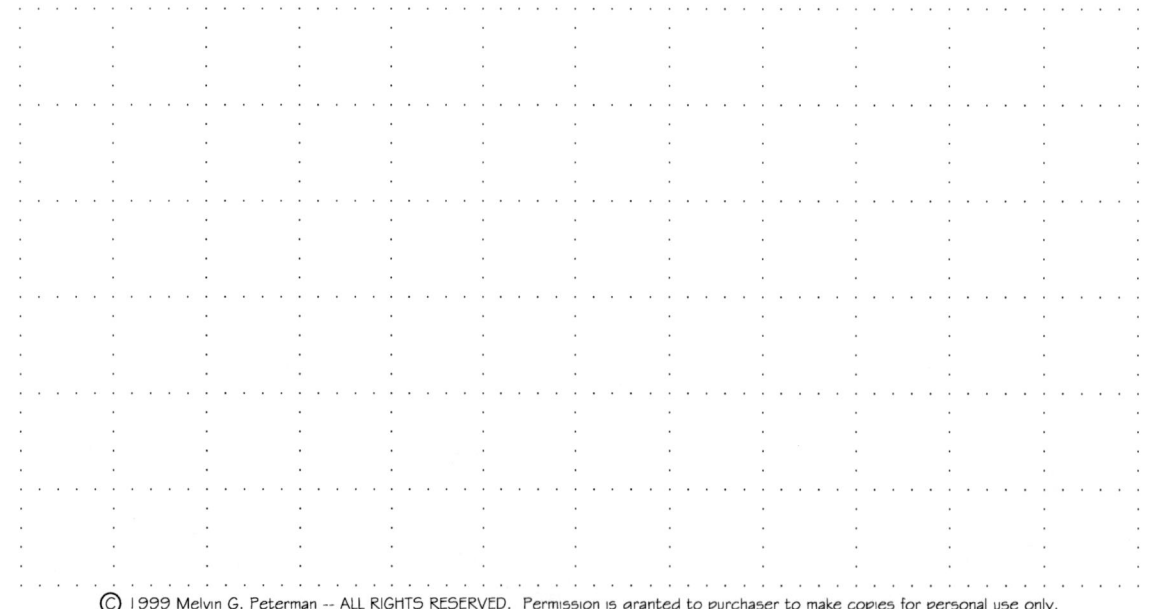

LESSON 3.06
GEOMETRIC SHAPES & CONSTRUCTIONS

NOTE:
CREATE PARALLEL LINES USING ARCS & STRAIGHT EDGES.

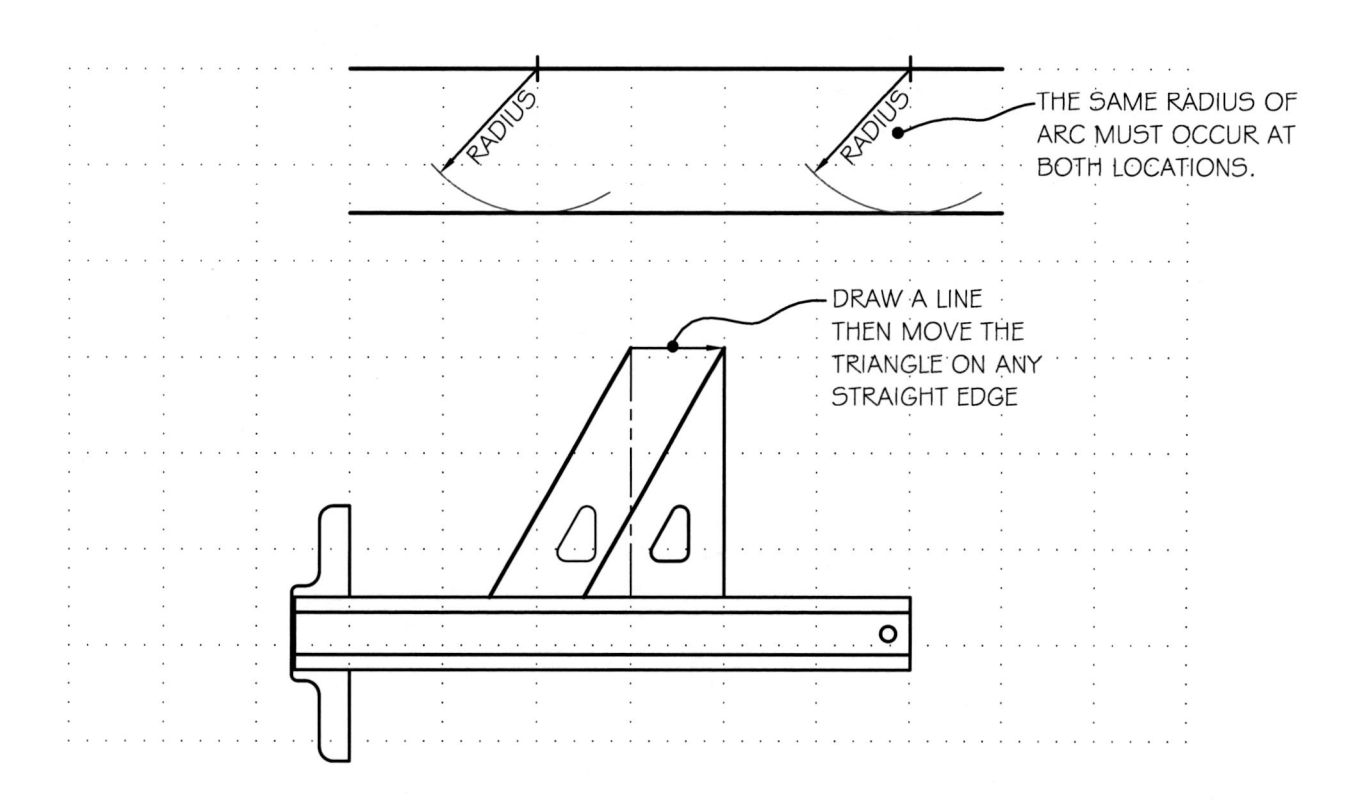

THE SAME RADIUS OF
ARC MUST OCCUR AT
BOTH LOCATIONS.

DRAW A LINE
THEN MOVE THE
TRIANGLE ON ANY
STRAIGHT EDGE

INSTRUCTIONS:
USING TOOLS OR CAD, REPRODUCE THE ABOVE RESULTS OF THE EXERCISE.
CAD COMMANDS TO CONSIDER: OFFSET, COPY

LESSON 3.07
GEOMETRIC SHAPES & CONSTRUCTIONS

NOTE:
USING A RULE TO DIVIDE LINES INTO EQUAL PARTS.

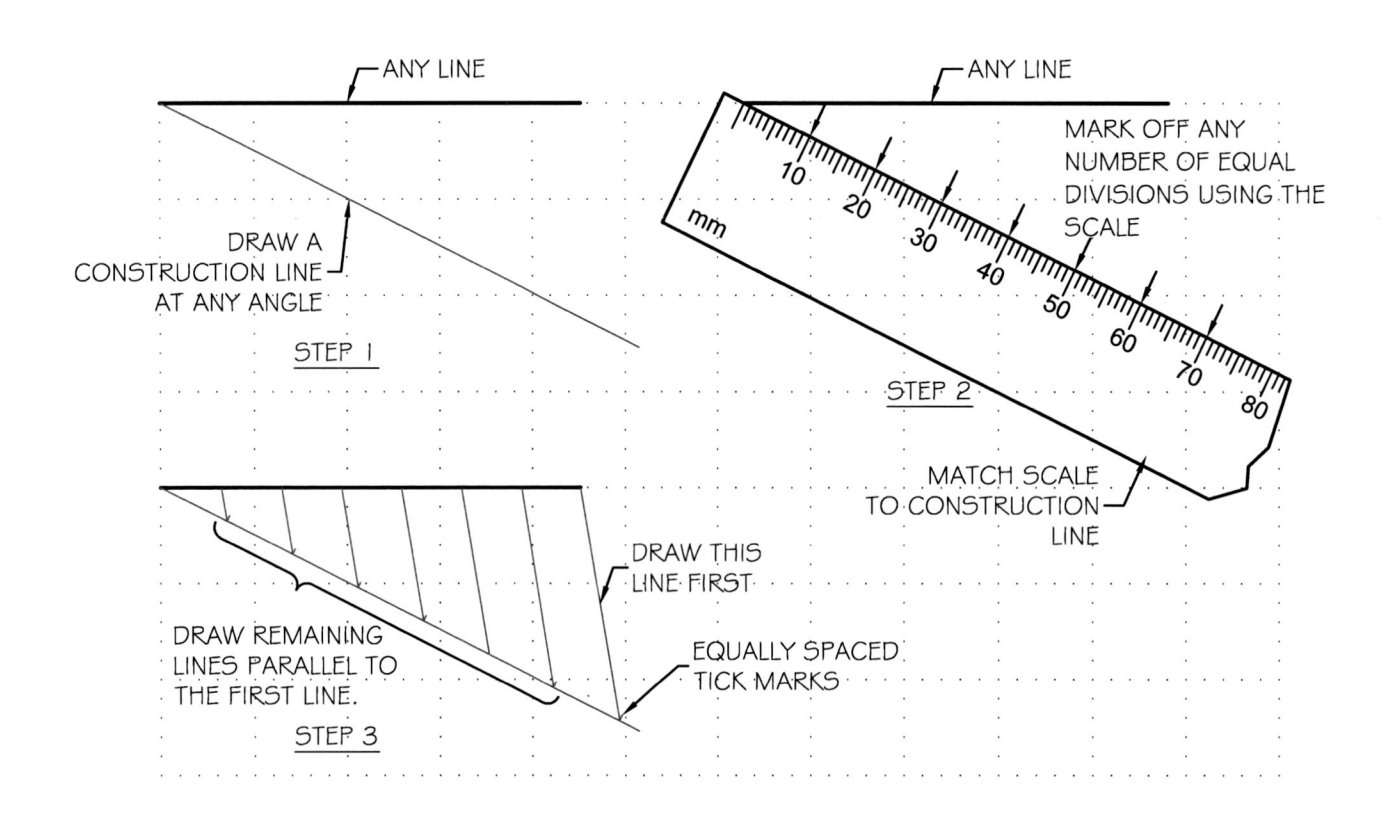

INSTRUCTIONS:
USING TOOLS OR CAD, REPRODUCE THE ABOVE RESULTS OF THE EXERCISE.
CAD COMMANDS TO CONSIDER: DIVIDE, COPY, OFFSET, ARRAY

LESSON 3.08
GEOMETRIC SHAPES & CONSTRUCTIONS

NOTE:
USING A RULE TO DIVIDE LINES INTO EQUAL PARTS.

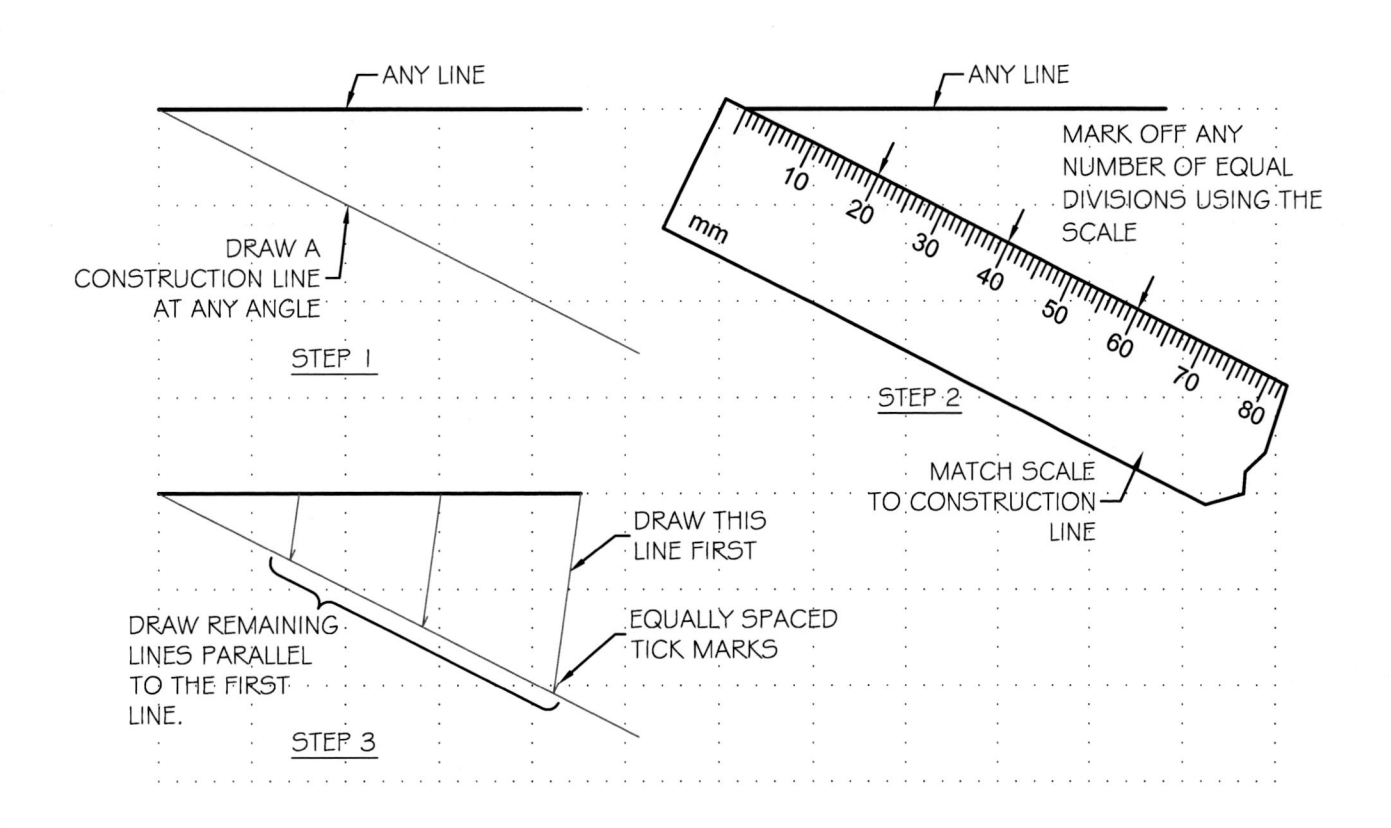

DRAW A CONSTRUCTION LINE AT ANY ANGLE

ANY LINE

STEP 1

ANY LINE

MARK OFF ANY NUMBER OF EQUAL DIVISIONS USING THE SCALE

STEP 2

MATCH SCALE TO CONSTRUCTION LINE

DRAW REMAINING LINES PARALLEL TO THE FIRST LINE.

DRAW THIS LINE FIRST

EQUALLY SPACED TICK MARKS

STEP 3

INSTRUCTIONS:
USING TOOLS OR CAD, REPRODUCE THE ABOVE RESULTS OF THE EXERCISE.
CAD COMMANDS TO CONSIDER: DIVIDE, COPY, OFFSET, ARRAY

LESSON 3.09
GEOMETRIC SHAPES & CONSTRUCTIONS

NOTE:
PRACTICAL APPLICATION OF EQUAL DIVISIONS.

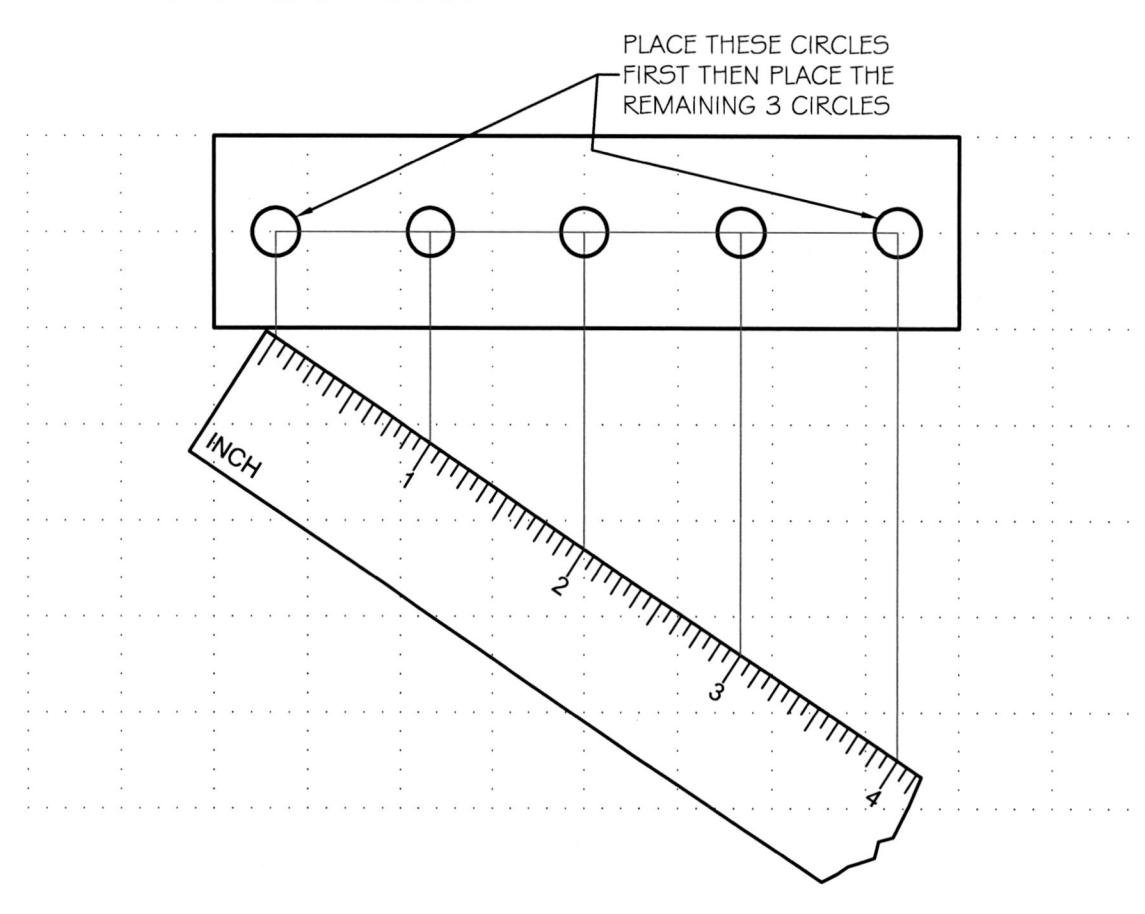

INSTRUCTIONS:
USING TOOLS OR CAD, REPRODUCE THE ABOVE RESULTS OF THE EXERCISE.
CAD COMMANDS TO CONSIDER: DIVIDE, COPY, OFFSET, ARRAY

LESSON 3.10
GEOMETRIC SHAPES & CONSTRUCTIONS

NOTE:
DRAWING A TRIANGLE WITH PREDETERMINED OR "GIVEN" SIDES.

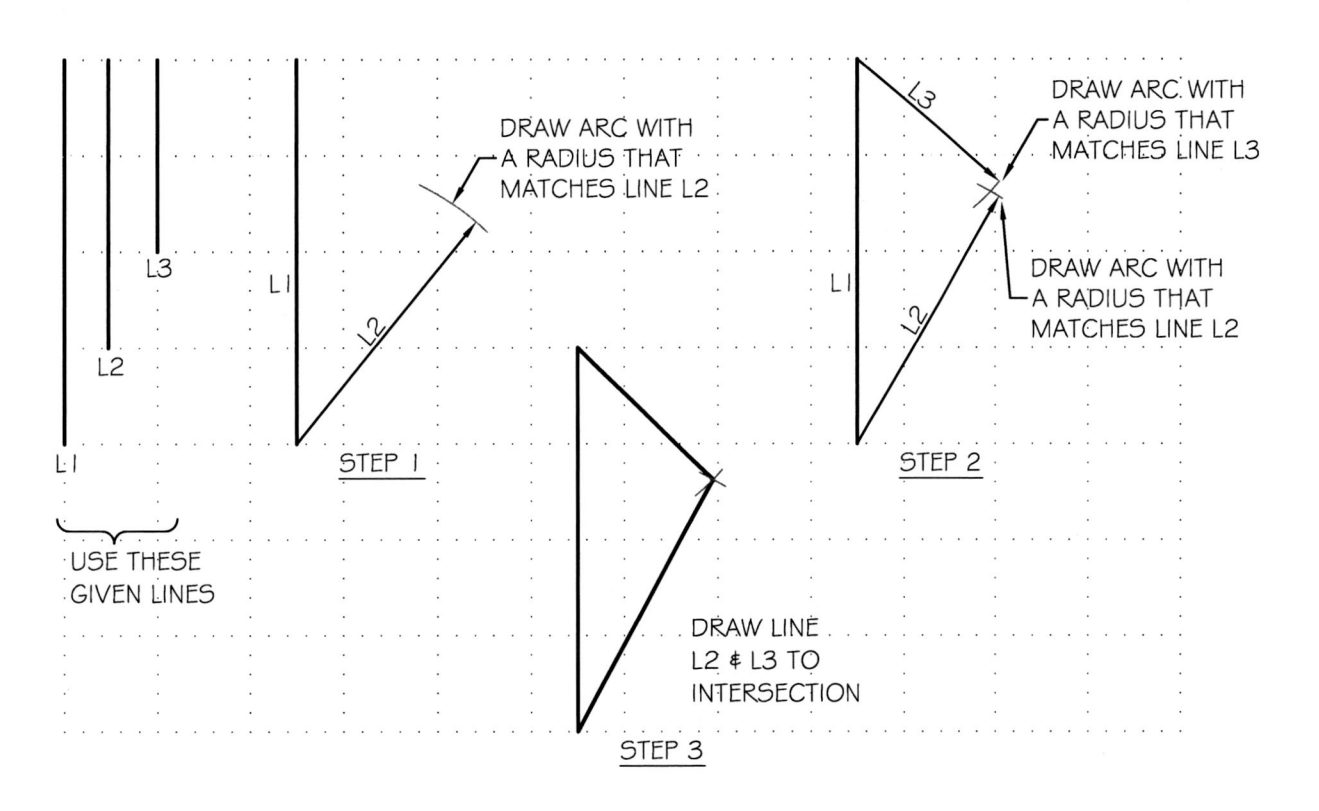

DRAW ARC WITH A RADIUS THAT MATCHES LINE L2

DRAW ARC WITH A RADIUS THAT MATCHES LINE L3

DRAW ARC WITH A RADIUS THAT MATCHES LINE L2

STEP 1

STEP 2

STEP 3

DRAW LINE L2 & L3 TO INTERSECTION

USE THESE GIVEN LINES

INSTRUCTIONS:
USING TOOLS OR CAD, REPRODUCE THE ABOVE RESULTS OF THE EXERCISE.
CAD COMMANDS TO CONSIDER: CIRCLE, ARC, COPY, OFFSET, ARRAY, ROTATE

LESSON 3.11
GEOMETRIC SHAPES & CONSTRUCTIONS

NOTE:
DRAW EQUILATERAL TRIANGLE USING 2 METHODS.

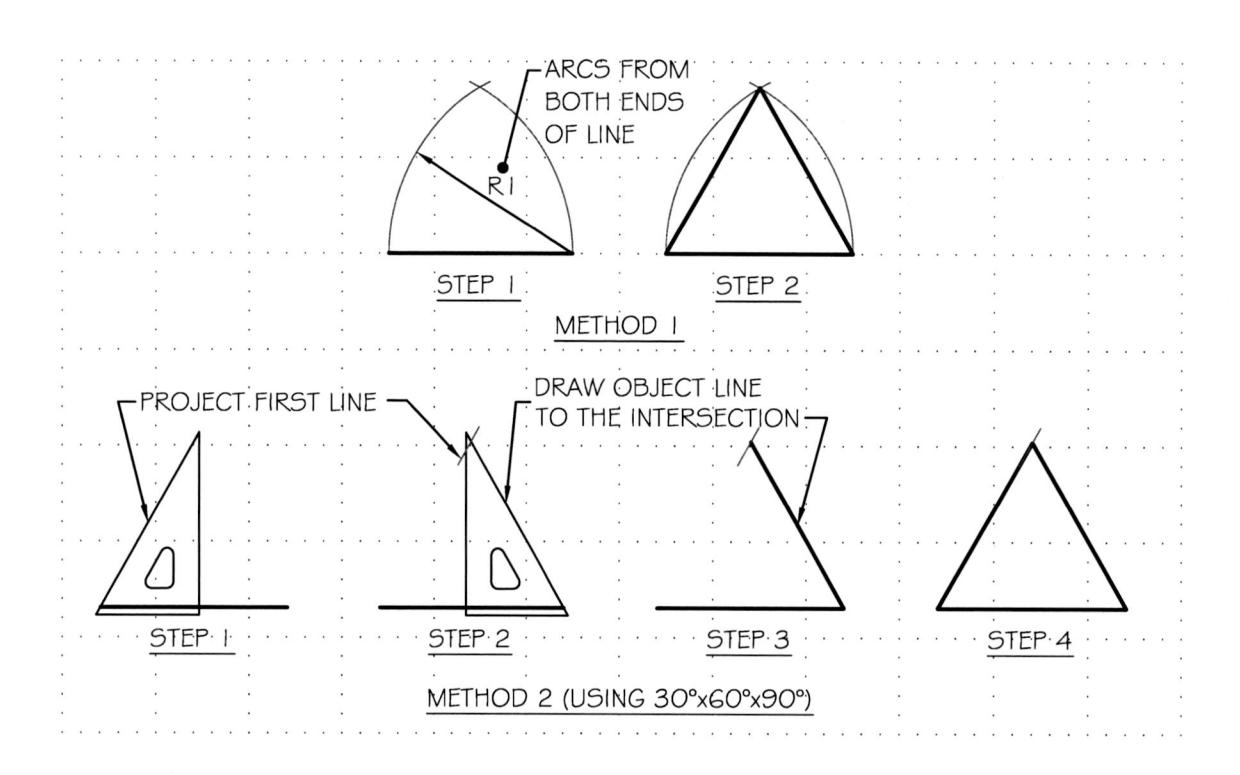

METHOD 1

METHOD 2 (USING 30°x60°x90°)

INSTRUCTIONS:
USING TOOLS OR CAD, REPRODUCE THE ABOVE RESULTS OF THE EXERCISE.
CAD COMMANDS TO CONSIDER: LINE, ARC, CIRCLE, POLYGON, RELATIVE COORDINATE, ABSOLUTE COORDINATE

LESSON 3.12
GEOMETRIC SHAPES & CONSTRUCTIONS

NOTE:
DRAW SQUARE USING 2 METHODS.

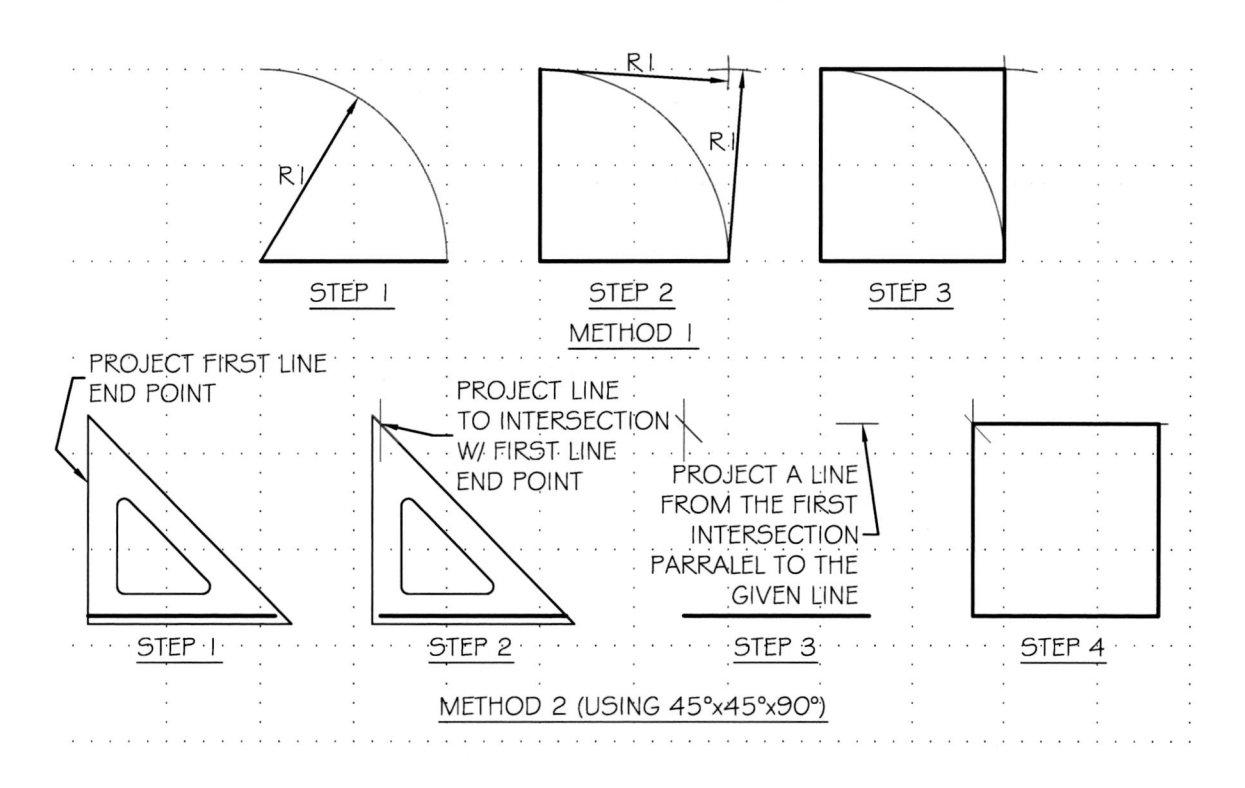

STEP 1   STEP 2   STEP 3
METHOD 1

PROJECT FIRST LINE END POINT

PROJECT LINE TO INTERSECTION W/ FIRST LINE END POINT

PROJECT A LINE FROM THE FIRST INTERSECTION PARRALEL TO THE GIVEN LINE

STEP 1   STEP 2   STEP 3   STEP 4

METHOD 2 (USING 45°x45°x90°)

INSTRUCTIONS:
USING TOOLS OR CAD, REPRODUCE THE ABOVE RESULTS OF THE EXERCISE.
CAD COMMANDS TO CONSIDER: LINE, ARC, CIRCLE, OFFSET, POLYGON, COORDINATES

LESSON 3.13
GEOMETRIC SHAPES & CONSTRUCTIONS

NOTE:
FINDING THE CENTER OF A CIRCLE. THIS SAME CONCEPT WORKS FOR SQUARES, RECTANGLES, & MOST REGULAR POLYGONS.

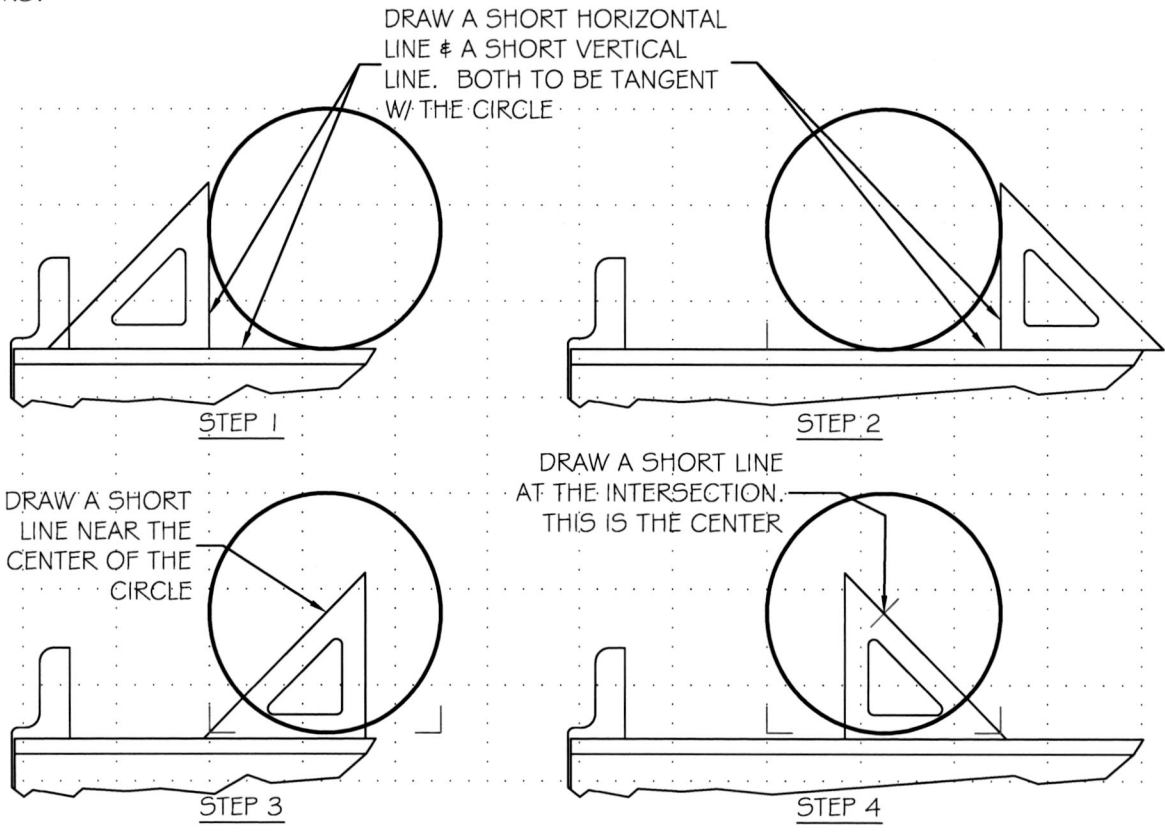

DRAW A SHORT HORIZONTAL LINE & A SHORT VERTICAL LINE. BOTH TO BE TANGENT W/ THE CIRCLE

STEP 1

STEP 2

DRAW A SHORT LINE NEAR THE CENTER OF THE CIRCLE

DRAW A SHORT LINE AT THE INTERSECTION. THIS IS THE CENTER

STEP 3

STEP 4

INSTRUCTIONS:
USING TOOLS OR CAD, REPRODUCE THE ABOVE RESULTS OF THE EXERCISE.
CAD COMMANDS TO CONSIDER: LINE, CIRCLE

LESSON 3.14
GEOMETRIC SHAPES & CONSTRUCTIONS

NOTE:
INSCRIBING AND CIRCUMSCRIBING A SQUARE ABOUT A CIRCLE.

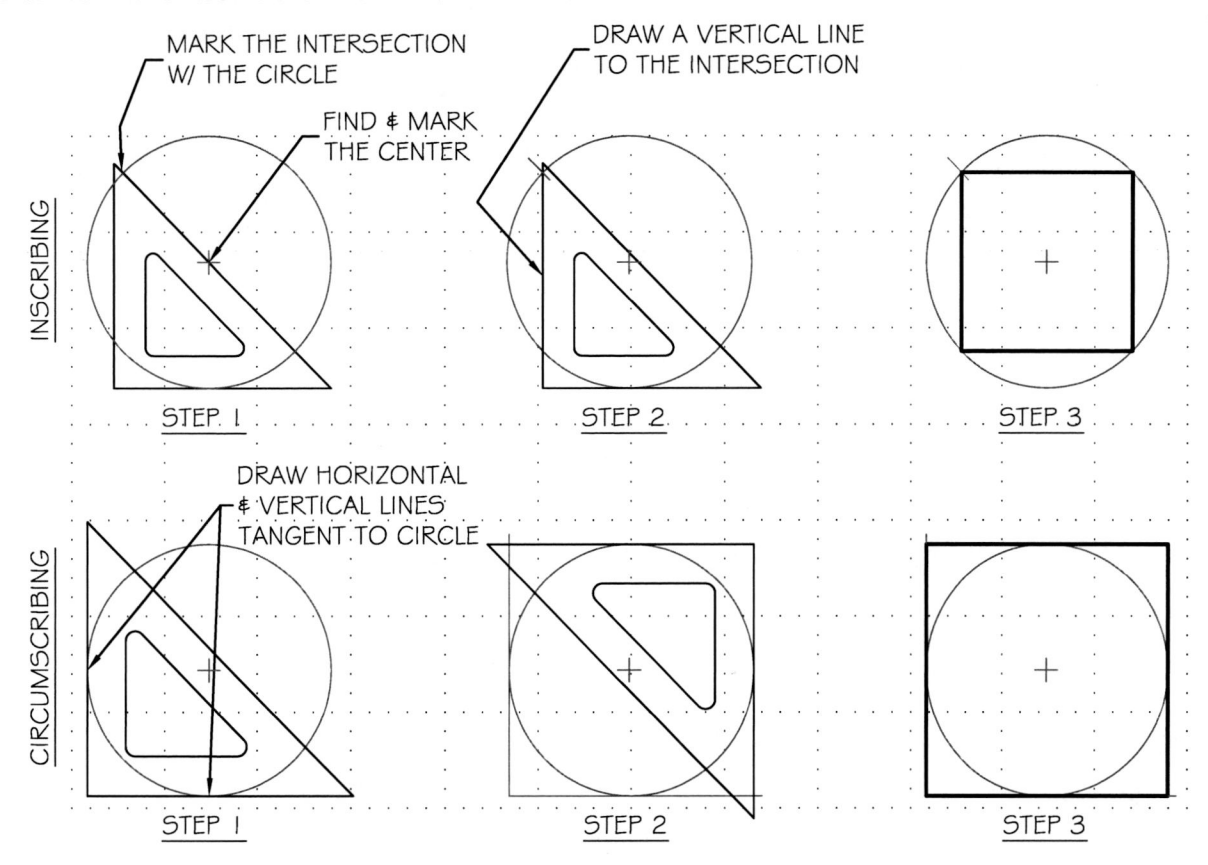

INSTRUCTIONS:
USING TOOLS OR CAD, REPRODUCE THE ABOVE RESULTS OF THE EXERCISE.
CAD COMMANDS TO CONSIDER: POLYGON, COPY, OFFSET, ARRAY

LESSON 3.15
GEOMETRIC SHAPES & CONSTRUCTIONS

NOTE:
INSCRIBING A PENTAGON ABOUT A CIRCLE.

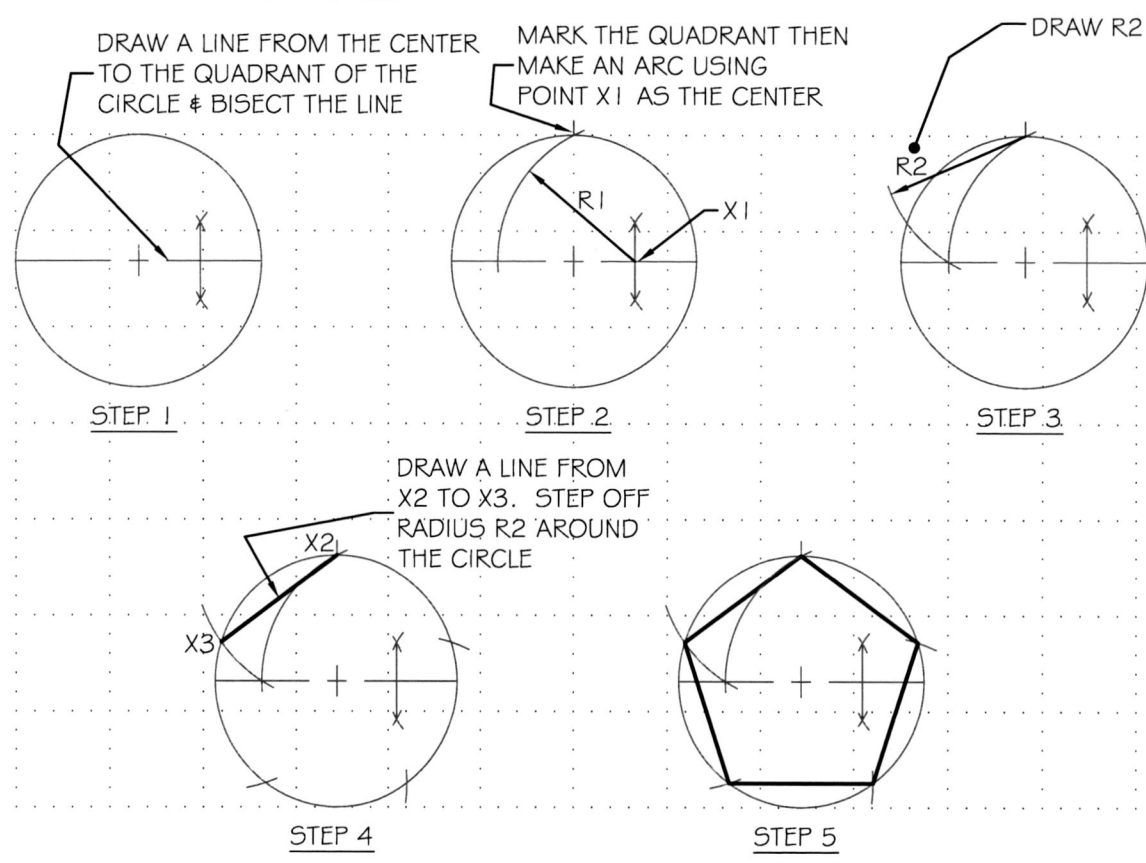

DRAW A LINE FROM THE CENTER TO THE QUADRANT OF THE CIRCLE & BISECT THE LINE

MARK THE QUADRANT THEN MAKE AN ARC USING POINT X1 AS THE CENTER

DRAW R2

STEP 1   STEP 2   STEP 3

DRAW A LINE FROM X2 TO X3. STEP OFF RADIUS R2 AROUND THE CIRCLE

STEP 4   STEP 5

INSTRUCTIONS:
USING TOOLS OR CAD, REPRODUCE THE ABOVE RESULTS OF THE EXERCISE.
CAD COMMANDS TO CONSIDER: POLYGON, ARRAY

LESSON 3.16
GEOMETRIC SHAPES & CONSTRUCTIONS

NOTE:
INSCRIBING A HEXAGON & CIRCUMSCRIBING AN OCTAGON ABOUT A CIRCLE.

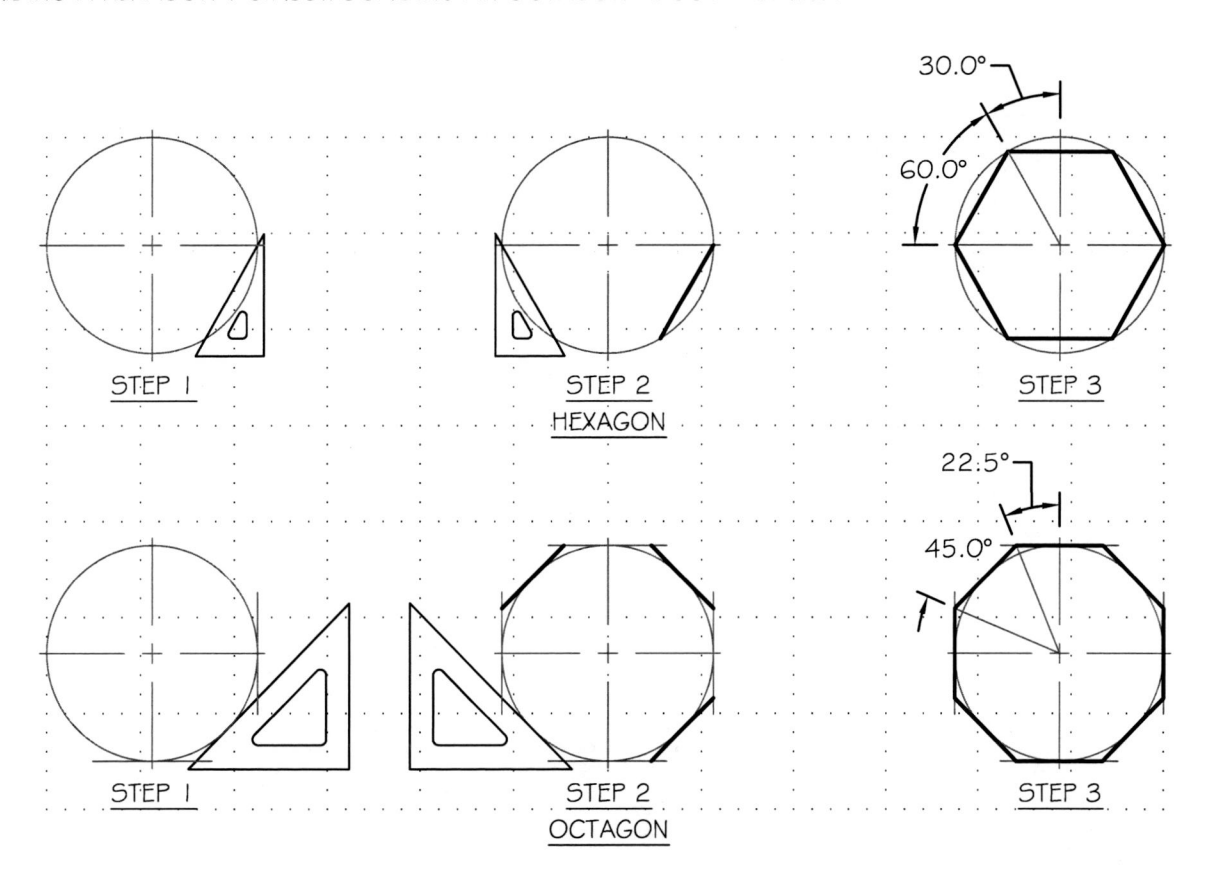

INSTRUCTIONS:
USING TOOLS OR CAD, REPRODUCE THE ABOVE RESULTS OF THE EXERCISE.
CAD COMMANDS TO CONSIDER: POLYGON, ARRAY

LESSON 3.17
GEOMETRIC SHAPES & CONSTRUCTIONS

NOTE:
LINES TANGENT TO 2 CIRCLES.

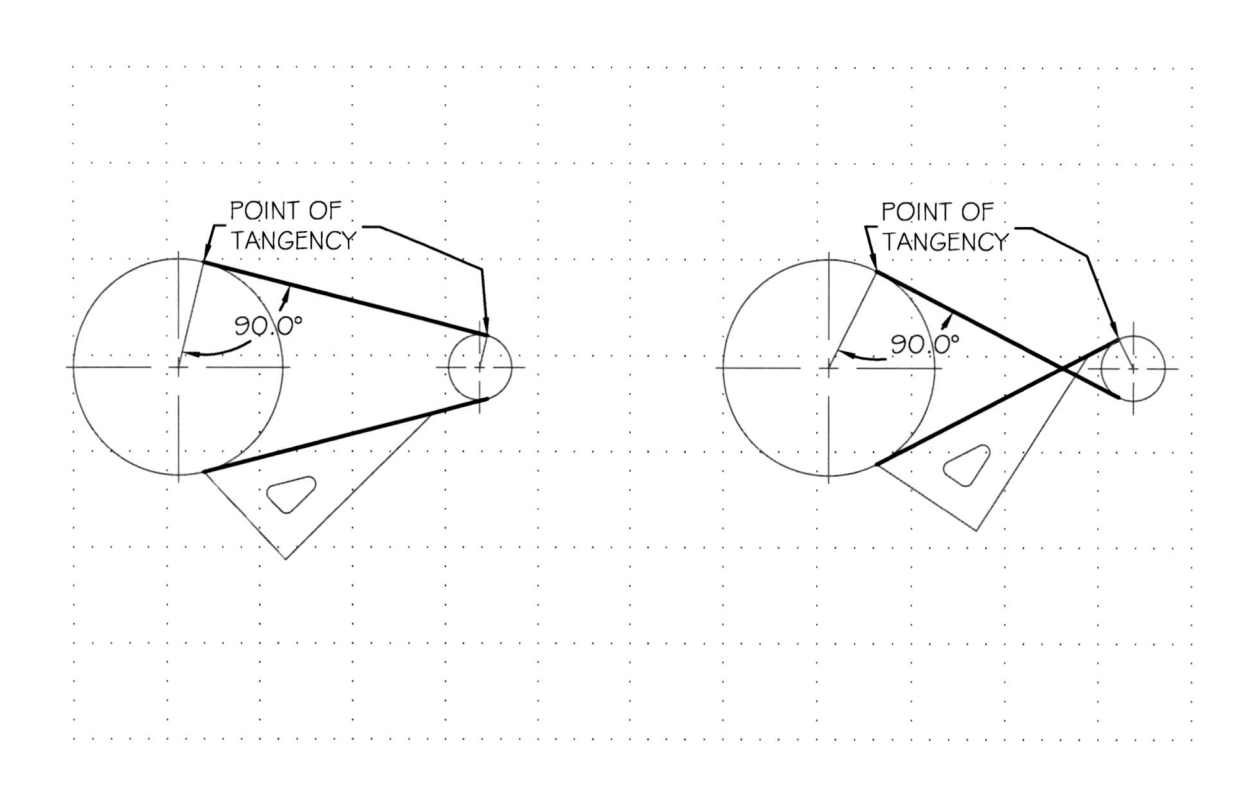

INSTRUCTIONS:
USING TOOLS OR CAD, REPRODUCE THE ABOVE RESULTS OF THE EXERCISE.
CAD COMMANDS TO CONSIDER: CIRCLE, LINE

LESSON 3.18
GEOMETRIC SHAPES & CONSTRUCTIONS

NOTE:
ARC TANGENT TO 2 LINES. THIS IS CALLED A FILLET IF IT IS ON THE INSIDE CORNER & IT IS CALLED A
RADIUS IF IT IS ON THE OUTSIDE CORNER.

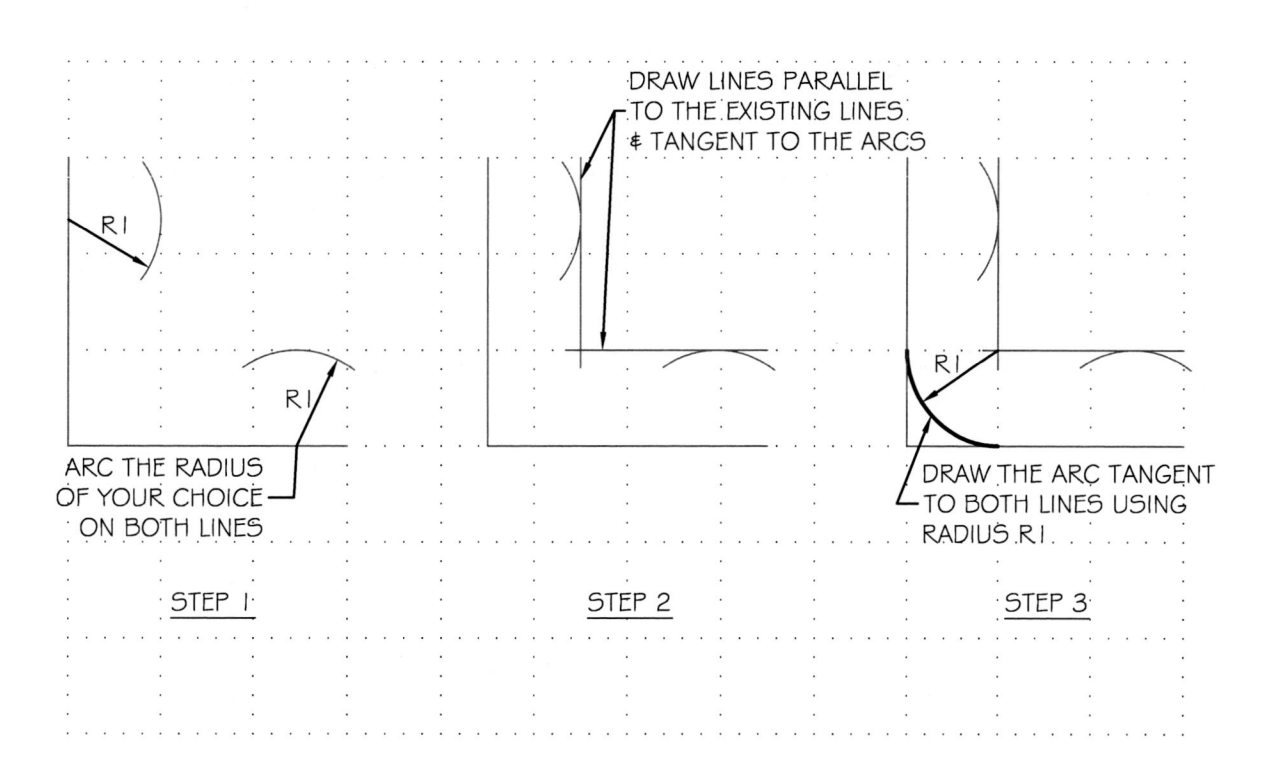

INSTRUCTIONS:
USING TOOLS OR CAD, REPRODUCE THE ABOVE RESULTS OF THE EXERCISE.
CAD COMMANDS TO CONSIDER: LINE, ARC, CIRCLE, FILLET, TRIM, EXTEND

LESSON 3.19
GEOMETRIC SHAPES & CONSTRUCTIONS

NOTE:
ARC TANGENT TO 2 LINES. THIS IS CALLED A FILLET IF IT IS ON THE INSIDE CORNER & IT IS CALLED A RADIUS IF IT IS ON THE OUTSIDE CORNER.

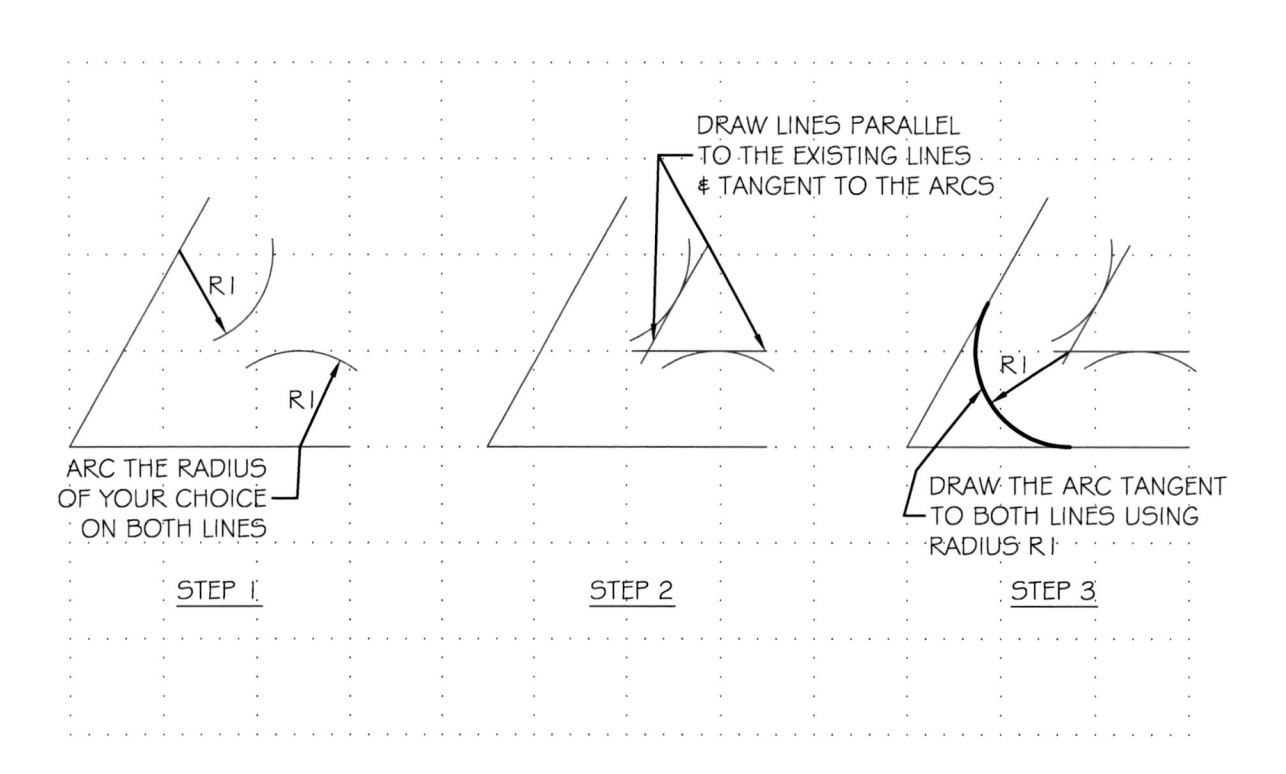

INSTRUCTIONS:
USING TOOLS OR CAD, REPRODUCE THE ABOVE RESULTS OF THE EXERCISE.
CAD COMMANDS TO CONSIDER: LINE, ARC, CIRCLE, FILLET, TRIM, EXTEND

LESSON 3.20
GEOMETRIC SHAPES & CONSTRUCTIONS

NOTE:
ARC TANGENT TO 2 LINES. THIS IS CALLED A FILLET IF IT IS ON THE INSIDE CORNER & IT IS CALLED A RADIUS IF IT IS ON THE OUTSIDE CORNER.

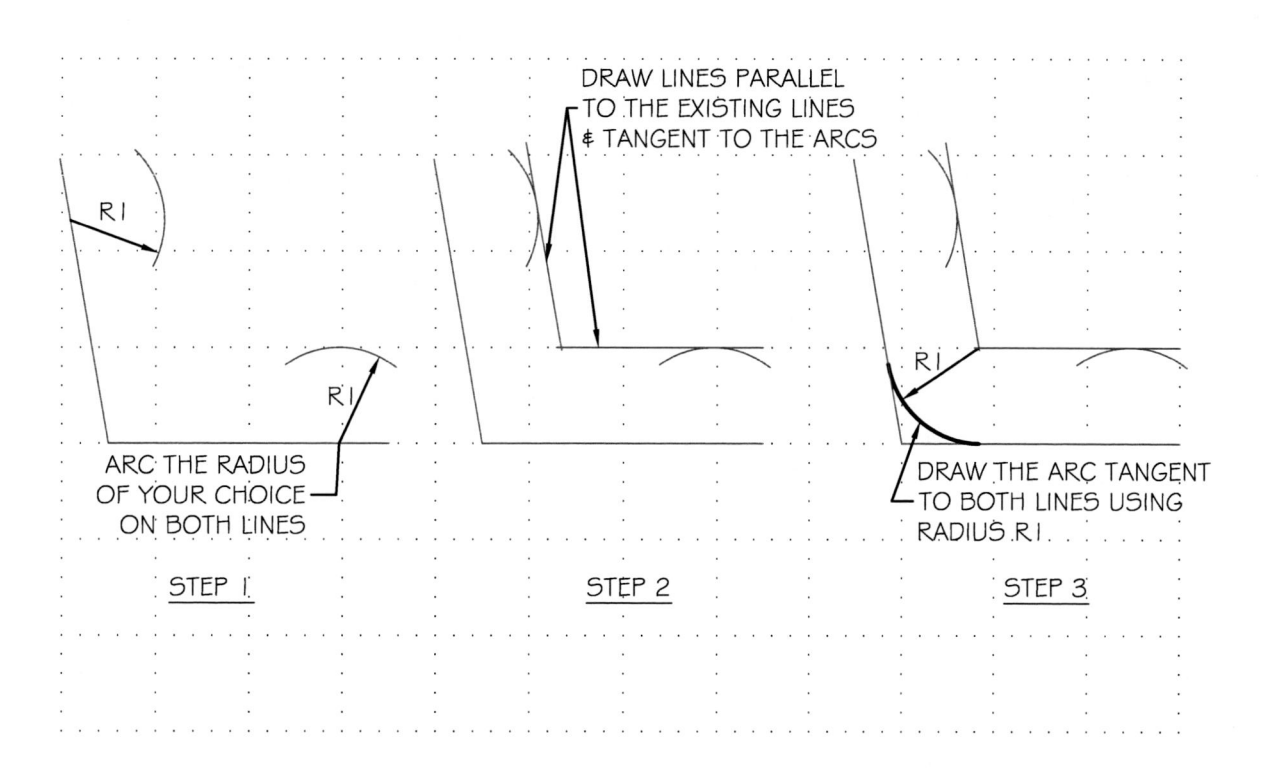

INSTRUCTIONS:
USING TOOLS OR CAD, REPRODUCE THE ABOVE RESULTS OF THE EXERCISE.
CAD COMMANDS TO CONSIDER: LINE, ARC, CIRCLE, FILLET, TRIM, EXTEND

LESSON 3.21
GEOMETRIC SHAPES & CONSTRUCTIONS

NOTE:
ARC TANGENT TO 2 CIRCLES.

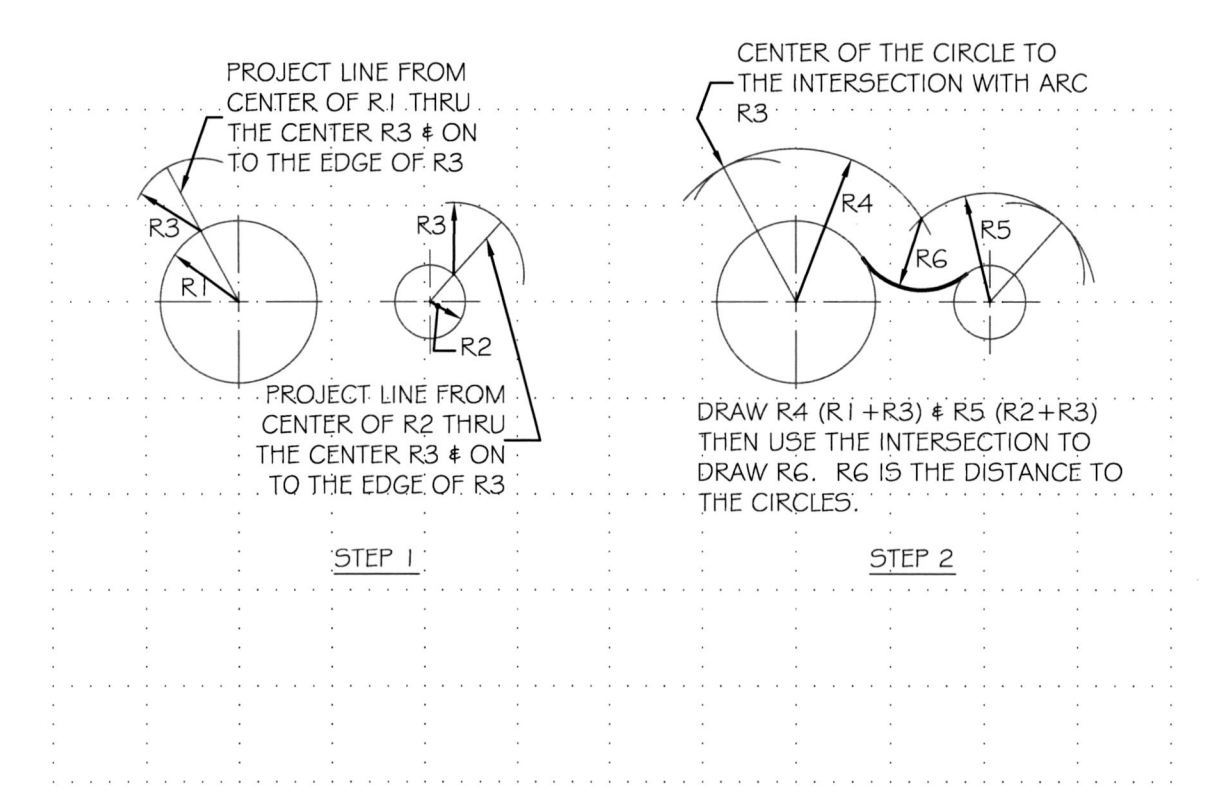

PROJECT LINE FROM
CENTER OF R1 THRU
THE CENTER R3 & ON
TO THE EDGE OF R3

PROJECT LINE FROM
CENTER OF R2 THRU
THE CENTER R3 & ON
TO THE EDGE OF R3

STEP 1

CENTER OF THE CIRCLE TO
THE INTERSECTION WITH ARC
R3

DRAW R4 (R1+R3) & R5 (R2+R3)
THEN USE THE INTERSECTION TO
DRAW R6. R6 IS THE DISTANCE TO
THE CIRCLES.

STEP 2

INSTRUCTIONS:
USING TOOLS OR CAD, REPRODUCE THE ABOVE RESULTS OF THE EXERCISE.
CAD COMMANDS TO CONSIDER: LINE, ARC, CIRCLE, FILLET, TRIM, EXTEND

LESSON 3.22
GEOMETRIC SHAPES & CONSTRUCTIONS

NOTE:
ARC TANGENT TO 2 CIRCLES. R1 = ANY RADIUS OF YOUR CHOICE. R2 = ANY RADIUS OF YOUR CHOICE. R3 = ANY RADIUS OF YOUR CHOICE, THAT IS LARGER THAN R1 & R2.

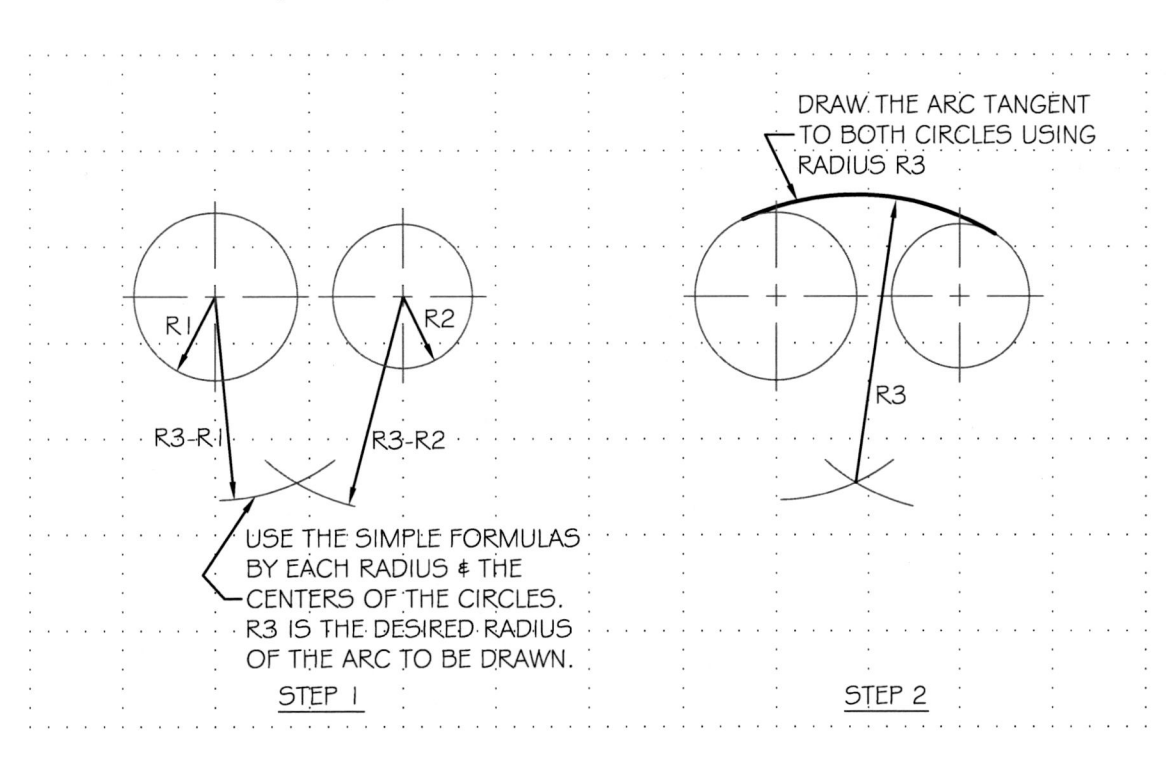

INSTRUCTIONS:
USING TOOLS OR CAD, REPRODUCE THE ABOVE RESULTS OF THE EXERCISE.
CAD COMMANDS TO CONSIDER: LINE, ARC, CIRCLE, FILLET, TRIM, EXTEND

LESSON 3.23
GEOMETRIC SHAPES & CONSTRUCTIONS -- TEST

NOTE:
THIS TEST REPRESENTS THE SKILLS THAT HAVE BEEN PRESENTED TO THIS POINT. REVIEW PAST LESSONS AS REQUIRED. DIMENSIONING IS OPTIONAL; IT IS GOOD PRACTICE. SIMPLY DUPLICATE THE DIMENSIONING AS WELL.
HINT: WHEN THERE IS A NUMBER & THEN AN X (4X) THAT REPRESENTS THE FACT THAT THE SPECIFIC FEATURE OCCURS THAT MANY TIMES ON THE PART. 4X MEANS THAT ITEM OCCURS 4 TIMES.

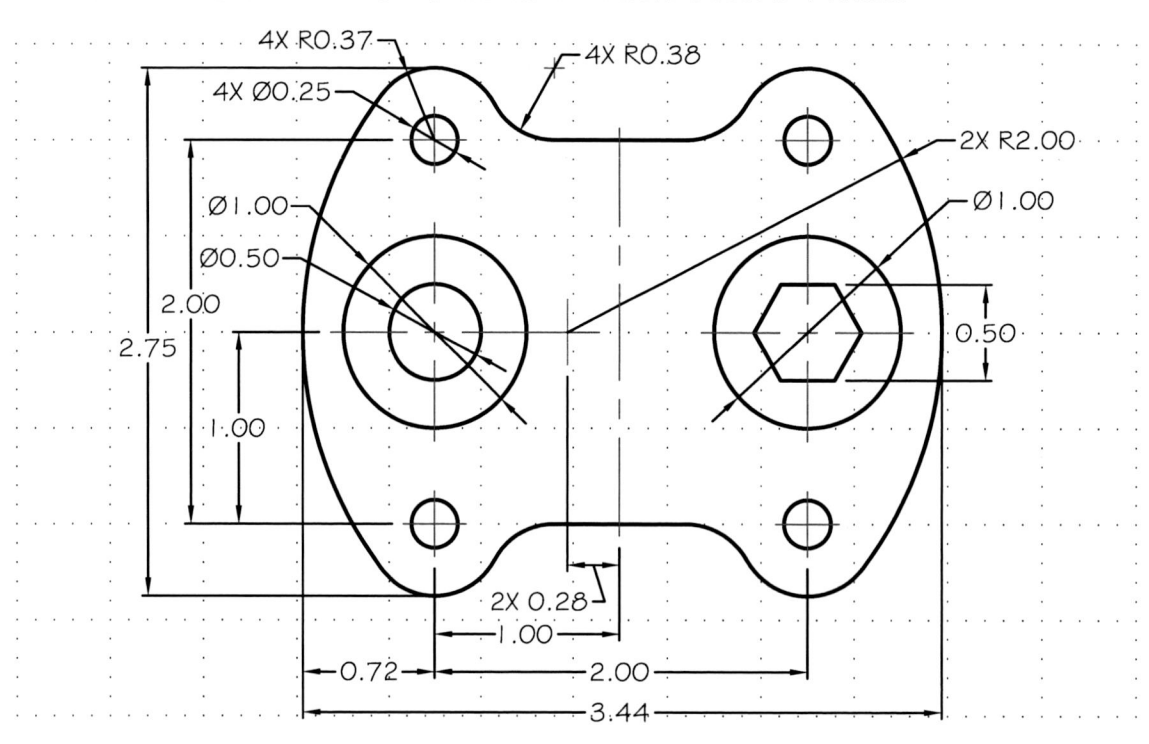

INSTRUCTIONS:
USING TOOLS OR CAD, REPRODUCE THE ABOVE RESULTS OF THE TEST.

LESSON 4.00
SKETCHING

NOTE:
MOST OF THE LINES USED IN SKETCHING ARE STRAIGHT.

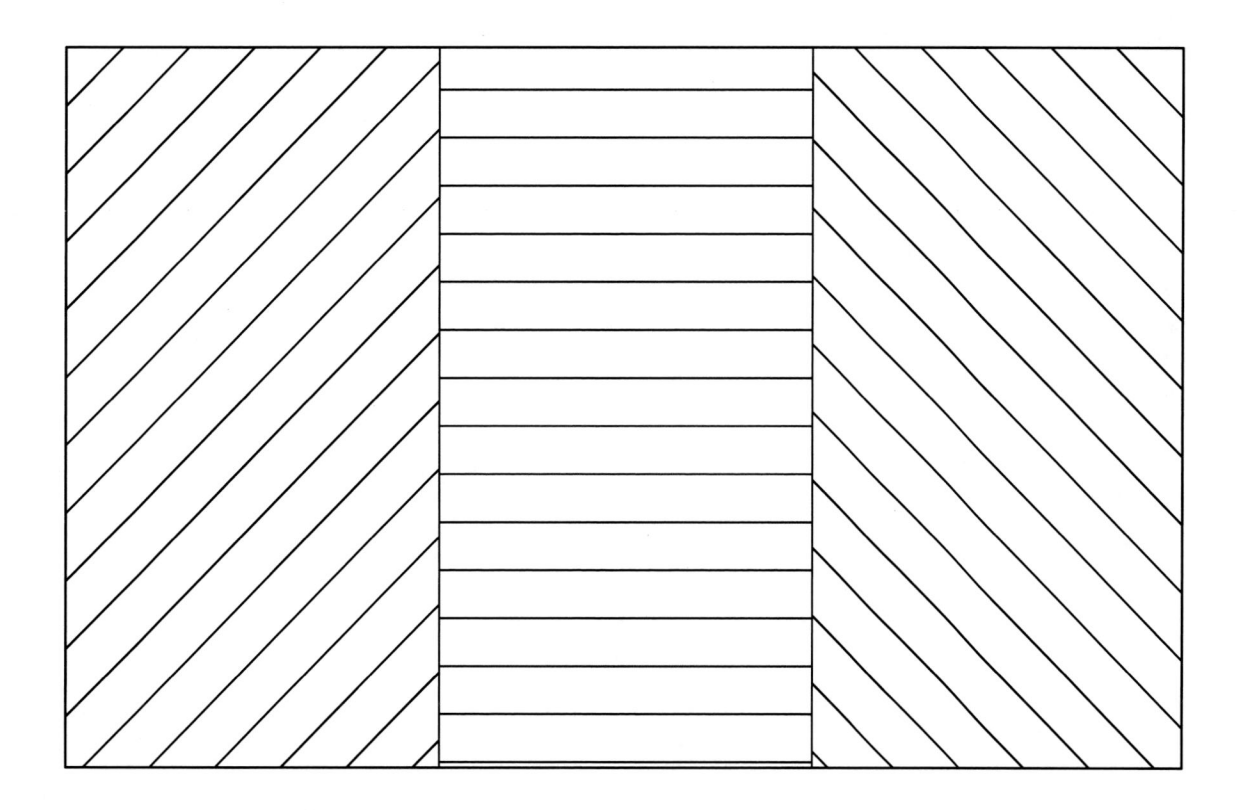

INSTRUCTIONS:
USING FREE HAND SKETCHING, REPRODUCE THE ABOVE RESULTS OF THE EXERCISE.

LESSON 4.01
SKETCHING

NOTE:
CIRCLES & ARCS ARE THE MOST DIFFICULT. BREAK THEM INTO SMALLER ARCS & THEY BECOME MUCH EASIER.
THERE ARE TWO METHODS THAT CAN BE USED. THESE METHODS ARE REFERRED TO AS "BLOCKING" IT IN.

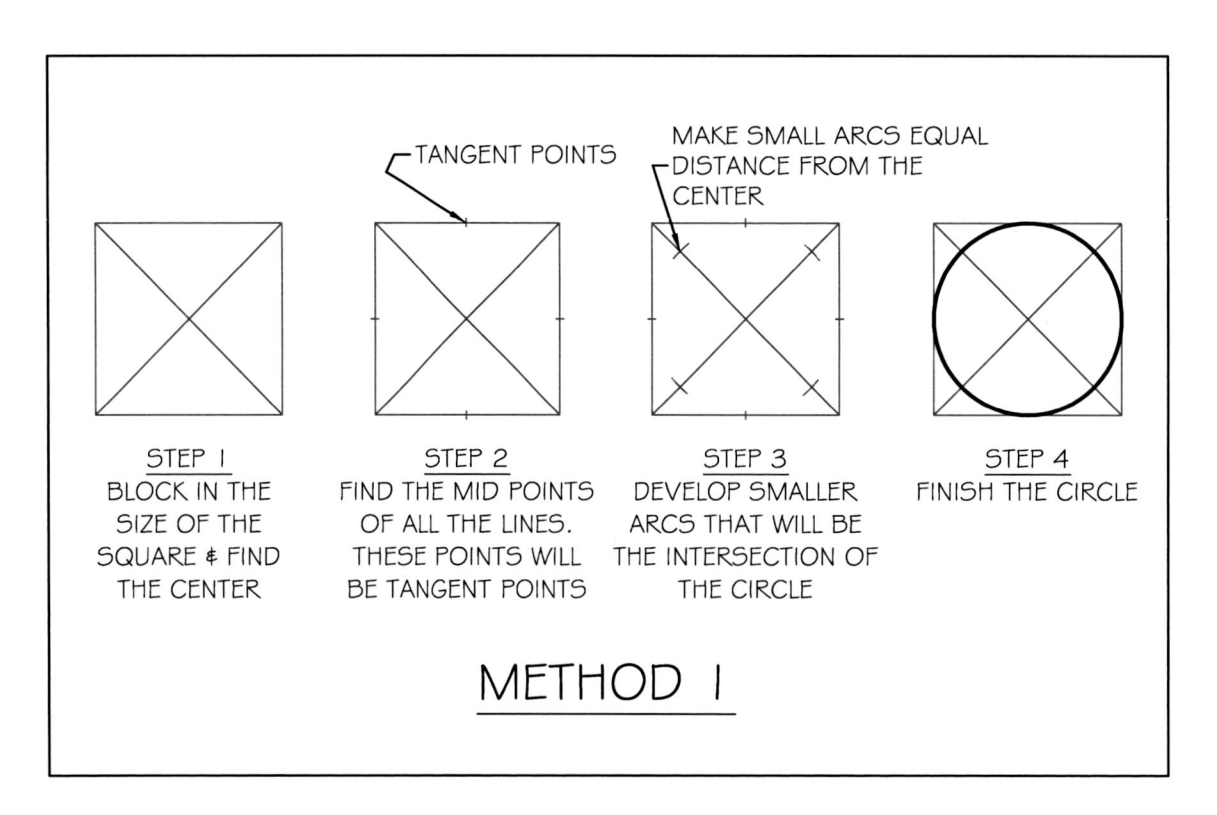

STEP 1
BLOCK IN THE
SIZE OF THE
SQUARE & FIND
THE CENTER

STEP 2
FIND THE MID POINTS
OF ALL THE LINES.
THESE POINTS WILL
BE TANGENT POINTS

STEP 3
DEVELOP SMALLER
ARCS THAT WILL BE
THE INTERSECTION OF
THE CIRCLE

STEP 4
FINISH THE CIRCLE

METHOD 1

INSTRUCTIONS:
USING FREE HAND SKETCHING, REPRODUCE THE ABOVE RESULTS OF THE EXERCISE.

LESSON 4.02
SKETCHING

NOTE:
CIRCLES & ARCS ARE THE MOST DIFFICULT. BREAK THEM INTO SMALLER ARCS & THEY BECOME MUCH EASIER.
THERE ARE TWO METHODS THAT CAN BE USED. THESE METHODS ARE REFERRED TO AS "BLOCKING" IT IN.

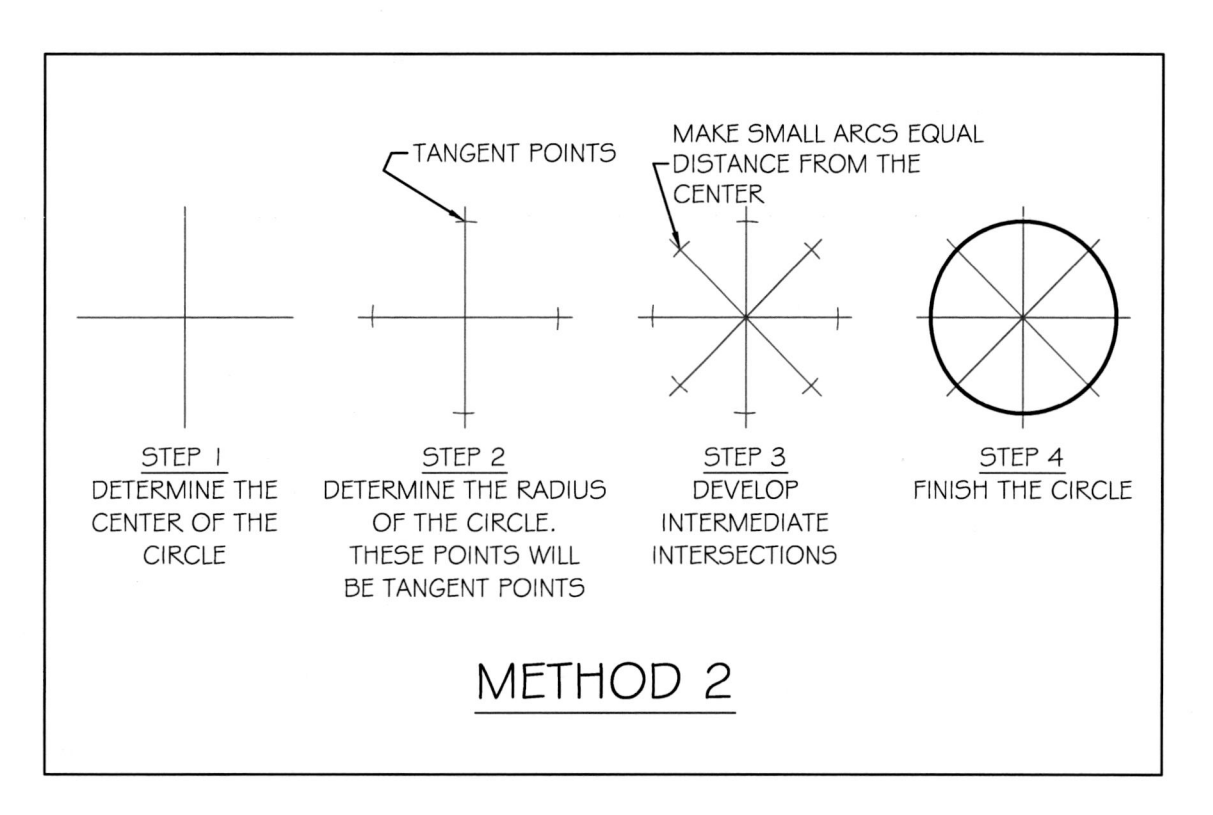

STEP 1
DETERMINE THE
CENTER OF THE
CIRCLE

STEP 2
DETERMINE THE RADIUS
OF THE CIRCLE.
THESE POINTS WILL
BE TANGENT POINTS

STEP 3
DEVELOP
INTERMEDIATE
INTERSECTIONS

STEP 4
FINISH THE CIRCLE

METHOD 2

INSTRUCTIONS:
USING FREE HAND SKETCHING, REPRODUCE THE ABOVE RESULTS OF THE EXERCISE.

LESSON 4.03
SKETCHING

NOTE:
ELLIPSES ARE A SPECIAL CHALLENGE. WHEN DRAWING ELLIPSES REMEMBER THAT THEY ARE REPRESENTING AN OBLIQUE VIEW OF A CIRCLE.

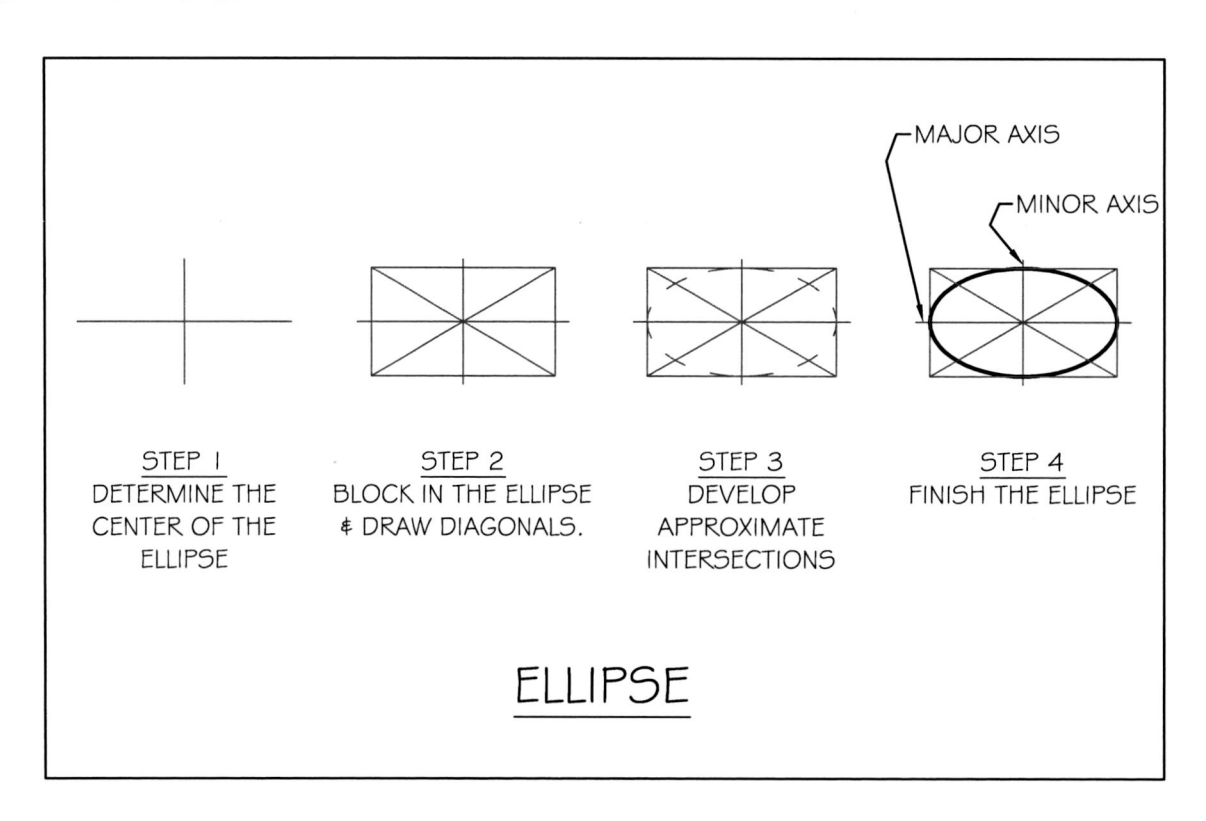

STEP 1
DETERMINE THE
CENTER OF THE
ELLIPSE

STEP 2
BLOCK IN THE ELLIPSE
& DRAW DIAGONALS.

STEP 3
DEVELOP
APPROXIMATE
INTERSECTIONS

STEP 4
FINISH THE ELLIPSE

ELLIPSE

INSTRUCTIONS:
USING FREE HAND SKETCHING, REPRODUCE THE ABOVE RESULTS OF THE EXERCISE.

LESSON 4.04
SKETCHING

NOTE:
SKETCHING IS AN IMPORTANT PART OF THE ENGINEERING & DOCUMENTATION PROCESS. SKETCHING IS AN IMPORTANT SKILL THAT IS USED EVERYDAY. ANY KIND OF PAPER IS ADEQUATE. THERE HAS BEEN MORE THAN ONE MAJOR BREAKTHROUGH ON A NAPKIN IN A RESTAURANT. THE EASIEST PAPER TO USE IS GRID OR SECTIONAL PAPER THAT IS AVAILABLE IN DIFFERENT GRID SIZES & COLORS. SKETCHING IS A VALUABLE METHOD OF STUDYING THE PART OR ASSEMBLY BEING CONSIDERED. COMPUTERS ARE NOT ALWAYS AVAILABLE & BEING ABLE TO CONVEY THOUGHTS & IDEAS ON PAPER OR WHITE BOARD CAN MAKE YOU A BETTER COMMUNICATOR. SKETCHING DOES NOT MEAN IT CAN BE SLOPPY. ALL ENGINEERING SKETCHES MUST BE NEAT.

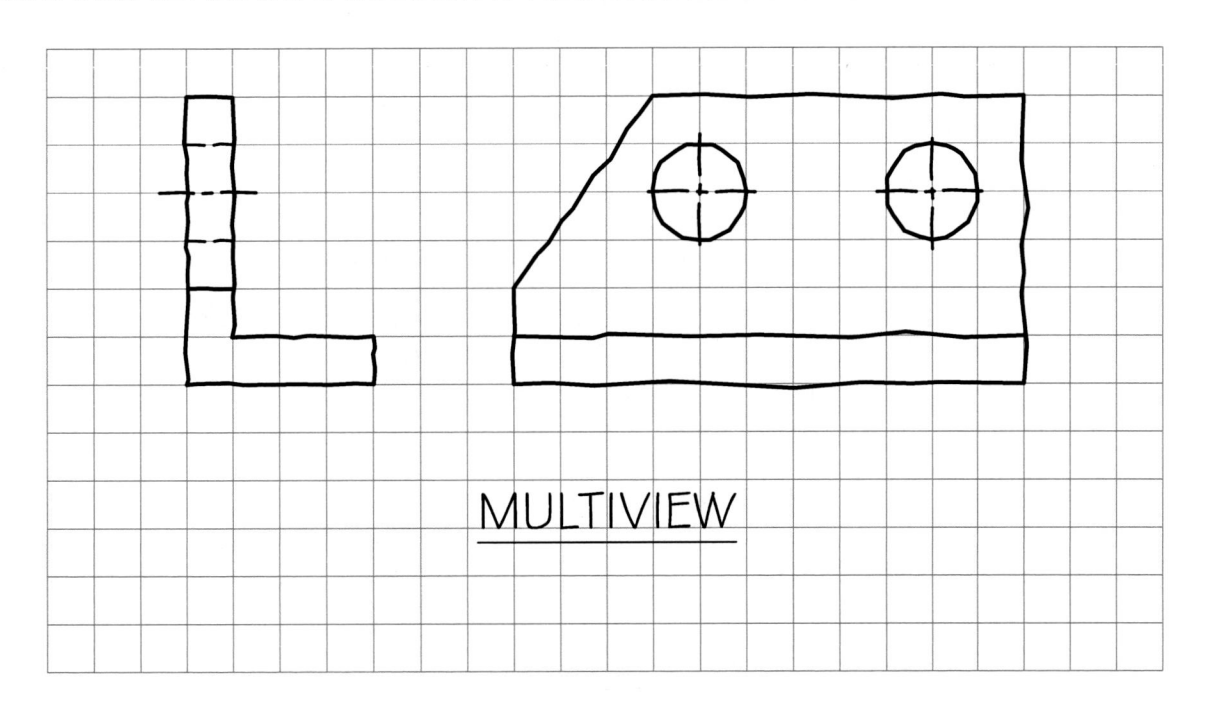

MULTIVIEW

INSTRUCTIONS:
USING FREE HAND SKETCHING, REPRODUCE THE ABOVE RESULTS OF THE EXERCISE.

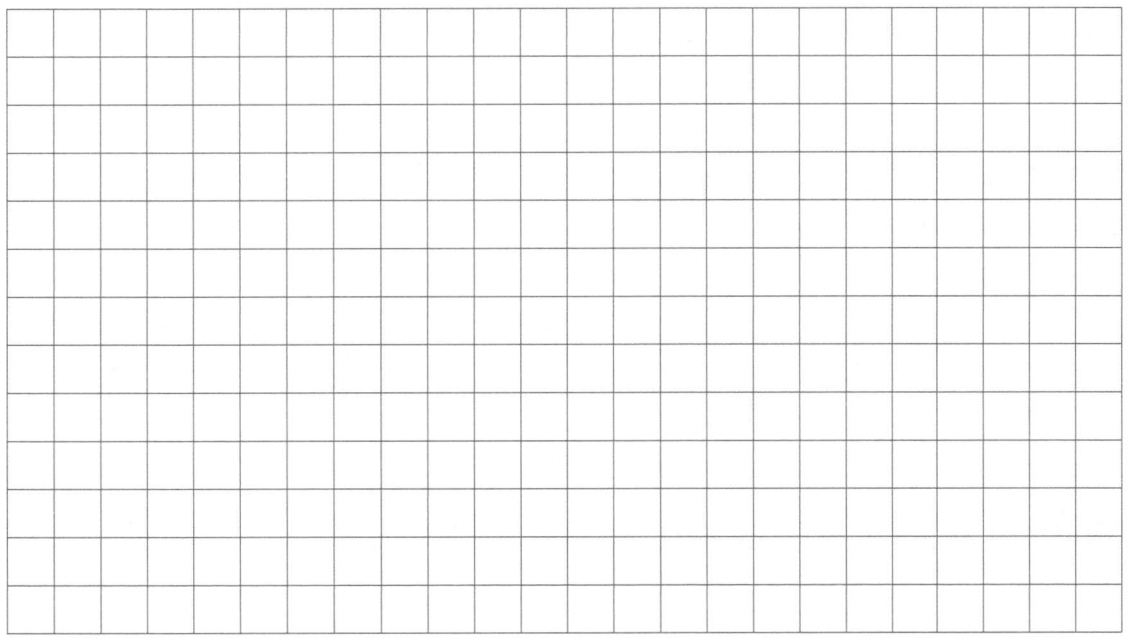

LESSON 4.05
SKETCHING

NOTE:
SKETCHES ARE NOT REQUIRED TO BE TO SCALE, THOUGH THEY SHOULD BE PROPORTIONAL. THE LINES SHOULD BE AS STRAIGHT & UNIFORM IN DARKNESS AS POSSIBLE. SOME SKETCHES ARE DONE IN INK & THERE IS NOT A SECOND CHANCE TO MAKE IT LOOK GOOD OR READABLE.

ISOMETRICS USE A TYPE OF ELLIPSE THAT IS SHAPED TO MATCH THE ANGLE OR FACE THAT IT IS ON. AN ISOMETRIC CIRCLE IS INTENDED TO REPRESENT CIRCLES SEEN AT AN ANGLE.

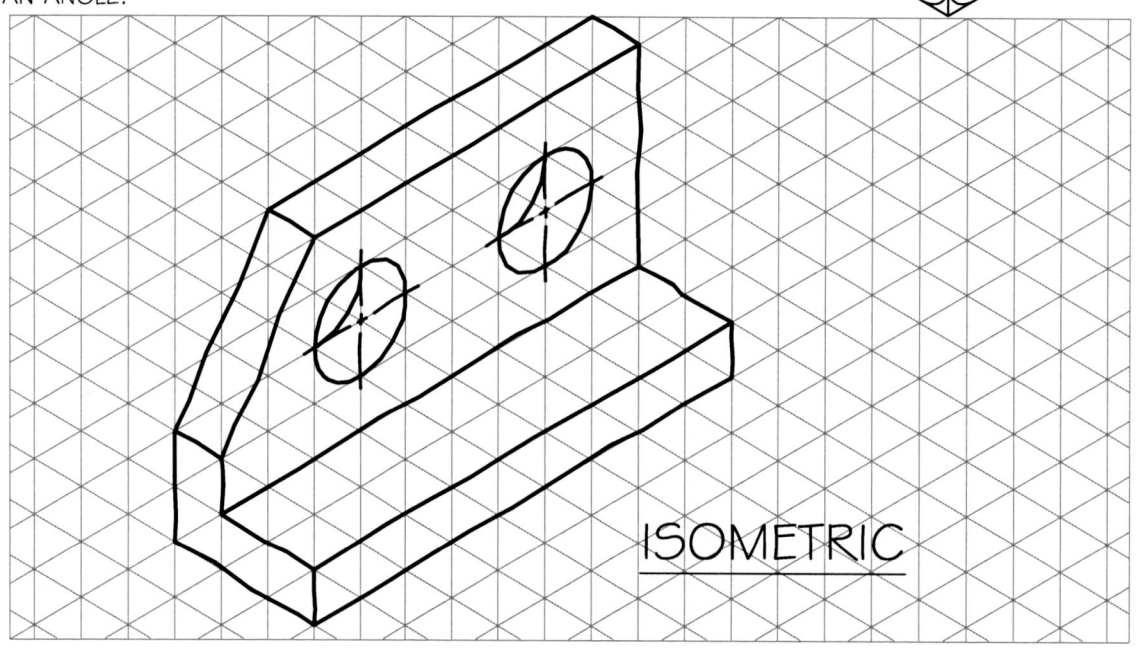

INSTRUCTIONS:
USING FREE HAND SKETCHING, REPRODUCE THE ABOVE RESULTS OF THE EXERCISE.

LESSON 4.06
SKETCHING

NOTE:
SOME TYPES OF SKETCHES ARE SIMPLER TO USE & SOME ARE MORE COMPLEX. USE THE METHOD THAT OFFERS THE BEST VALUE FOR THE TIME USED TO PRODUCE & THE REQUIREMENTS OF THE SITUATION.

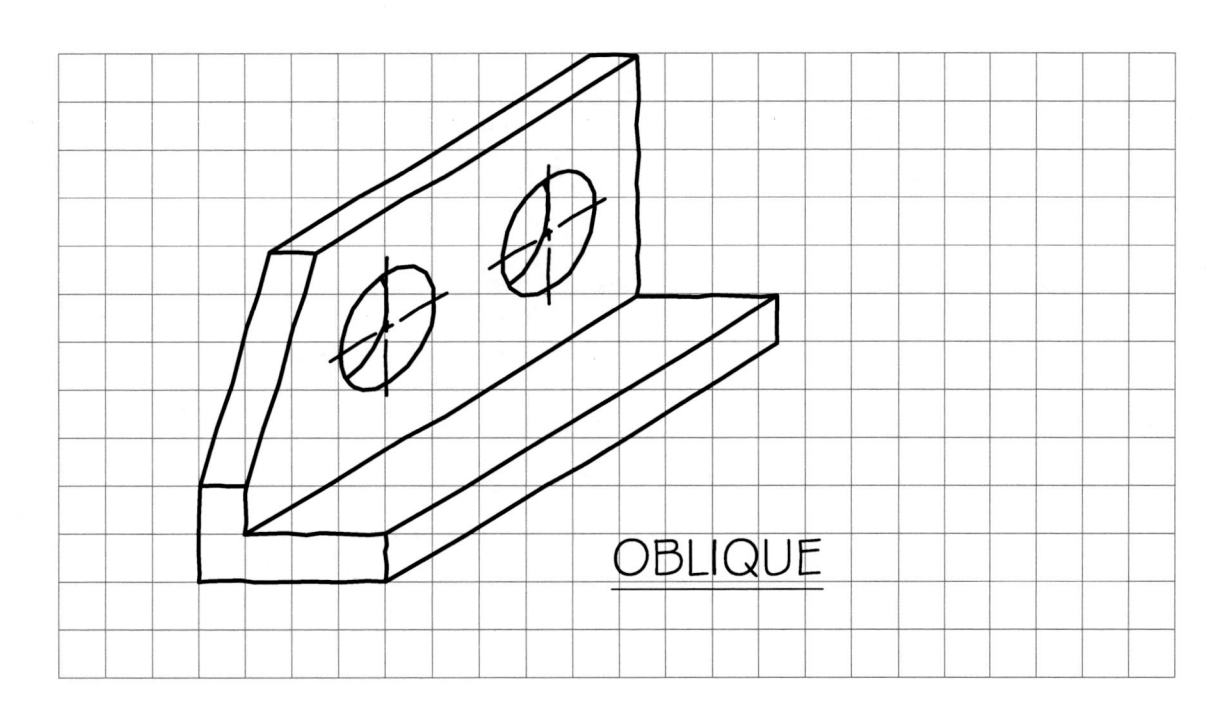

OBLIQUE

INSTRUCTIONS:
USING FREE HAND SKETCHING, REPRODUCE THE ABOVE RESULTS OF THE EXERCISE.

LESSON 4.07
SKETCHING

NOTE:
PERSPECTIVE SKETCHES LOOK GOOD BUT REQUIRE SIGNIFICANT TIME TO PRODUCE WELL.

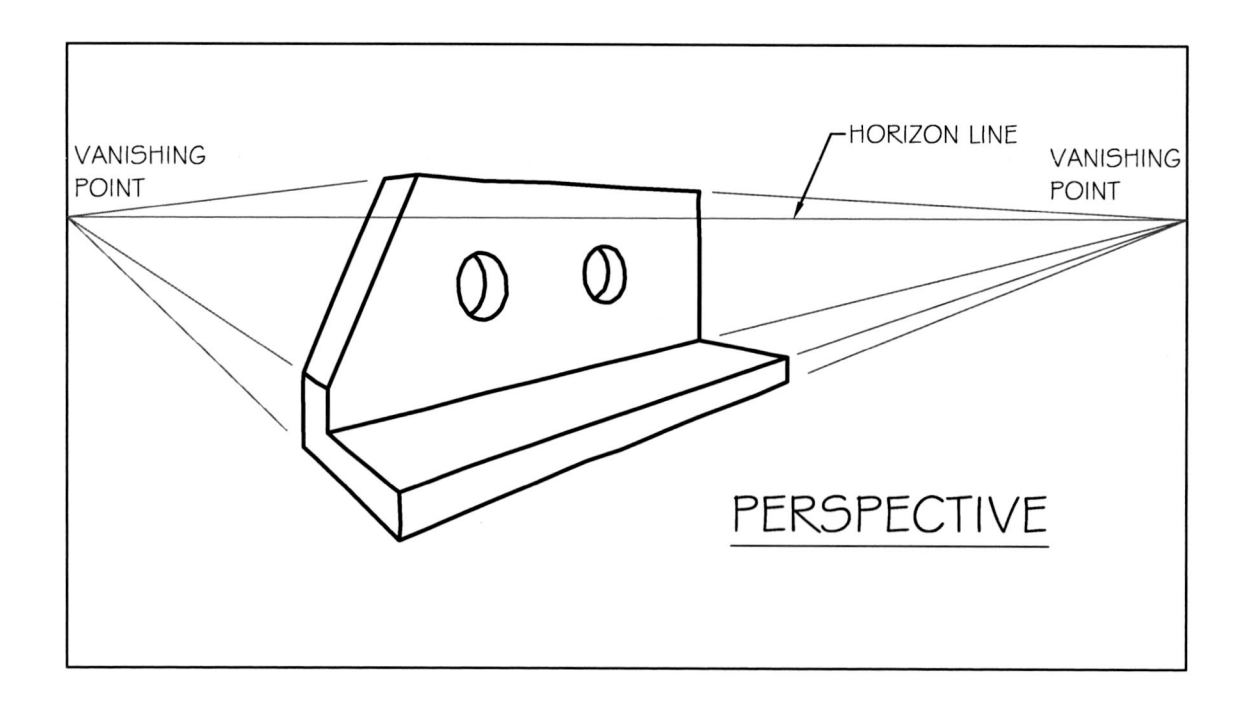

INSTRUCTIONS:
USING FREE HAND SKETCHING, REPRODUCE THE ABOVE RESULTS OF THE EXERCISE.

LESSON 4.08
SKETCHING -- MULTIVIEW

NOTE:
THE 3 NORMAL VIEWS OF ANY OBJECT ARE THE FRONT, TOP, & RIGHT SIDE. IF THE LEFT VIEW SHOWS A FEATURE MORE CLEARLY, THEN SHOW IT. IF YOU NEED THE 6 NORMAL VIEWS OF ANY OBJECT TO CLARIFY IT, THEN SHOW THEM ALL. THIS IS AN OVER VIEW OF THE 6 NORMAL VIEWS OF ANY OBJECT.

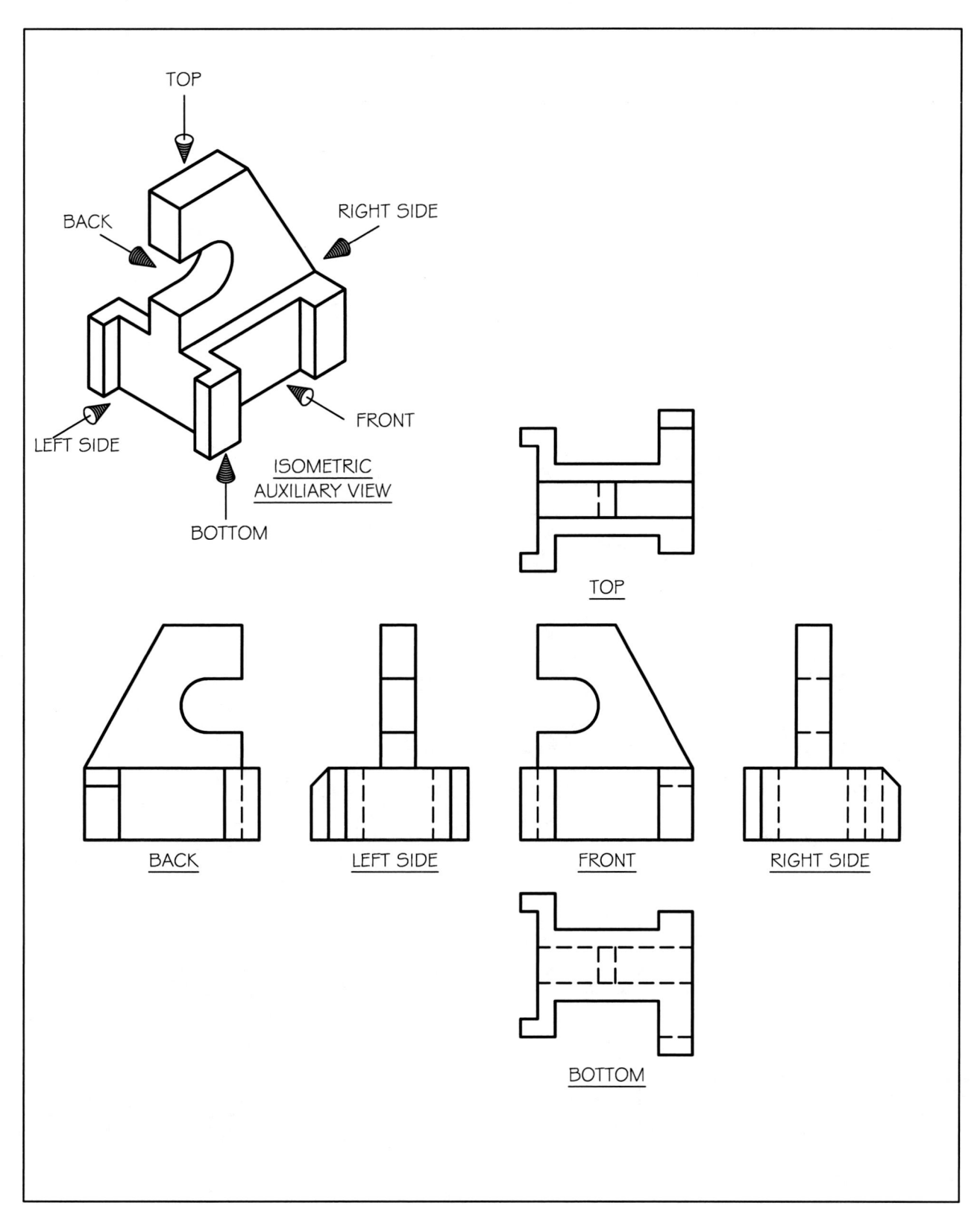

LESSON 4.09
SKETCHING -- MULTIVIEW

NOTE:
THE NUMBER OF VIEWS REQUIRED FOR A PART IS DICTATED BY THE PART & THE ORGANIZATION IT IS BEING PRODUCED FOR. THERE ARE MANY APPLICATIONS WHERE A SINGLE VIEW IS PERFECTLY ADEQUATE. OTHER PARTS WILL REQUIRE MORE VIEWS. DRAW ONLY WHAT IS NEEDED & NO MORE. THIS IS PRODUCTION WORK. IN THE EVENT THE WORK IS BEING DONE IN A 3D MODELING PACKAGE, THE PART WILL BE COMPLETE. HOWEVER, THE ACTUAL 2D REPRESENTATION OF THE PARTS SHOULD BE KEPT TO A MINIMUM. MORE WORK EQUALS MORE TIME WHICH EQUALS MORE MONEY. KEEP IT SIMPLE.

NOTE: WHEN DRAFTING IN 3 VIEWS IT IS COMMON FOR DIFFERENT LINE TYPES TO END UP IN THE SAME LOCATION. THAT IS, IF YOU WERE TO DRAW THE LINES, THEY WOULD BE STACKED OR BEHIND EACH OTHER. VISIBLE LINES TAKE PRECEDENCE, THEN HIDDEN, THEN CENTER LINES.

INSTRUCTIONS:
ON A BLANK PIECE OF PAPER, REPRODUCE THE FOLLOWING ITEMS BY SKETCHING. NO SCALE IS REQUIRED.

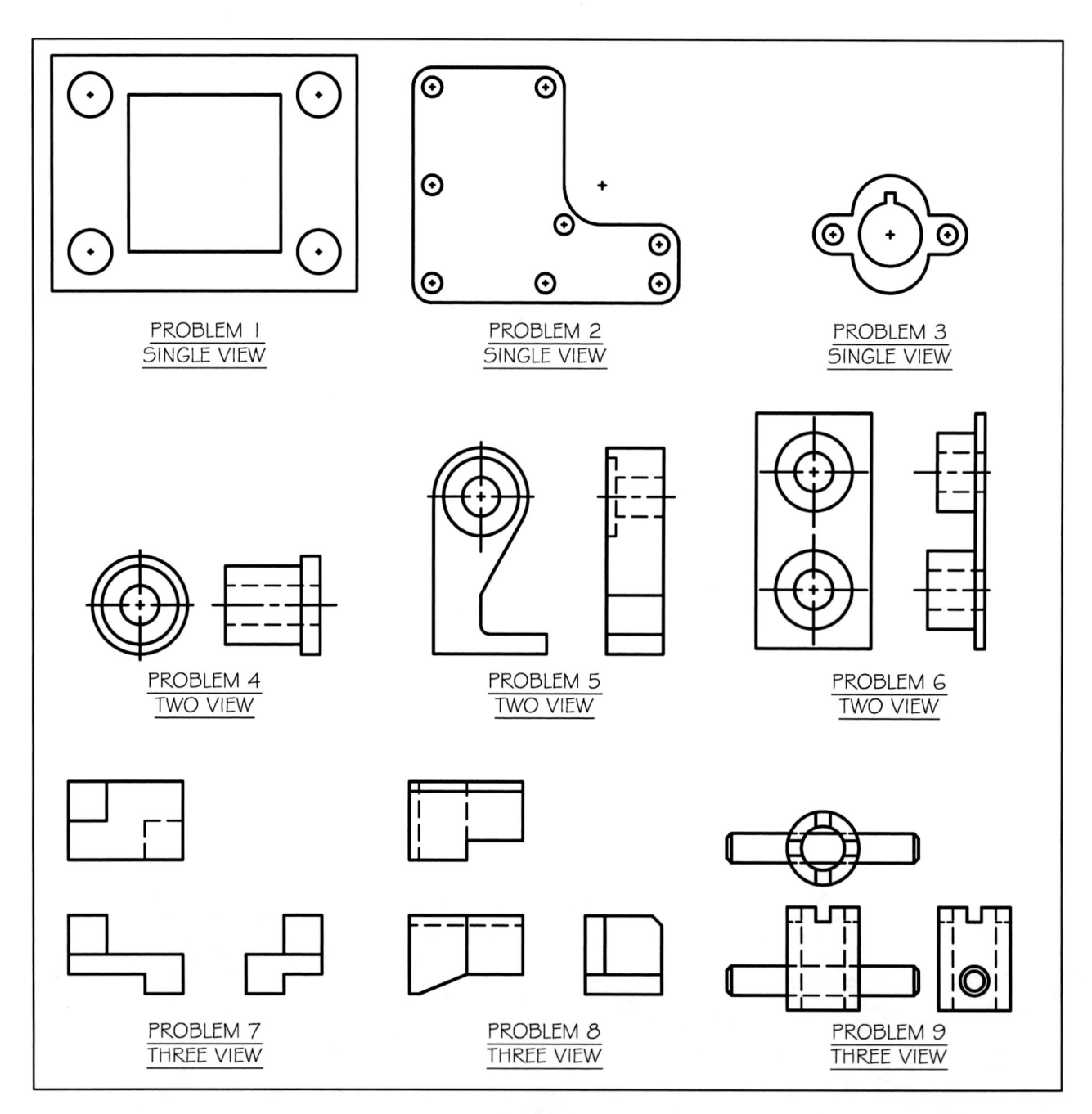

PROBLEM 1
SINGLE VIEW

PROBLEM 2
SINGLE VIEW

PROBLEM 3
SINGLE VIEW

PROBLEM 4
TWO VIEW

PROBLEM 5
TWO VIEW

PROBLEM 6
TWO VIEW

PROBLEM 7
THREE VIEW

PROBLEM 8
THREE VIEW

PROBLEM 9
THREE VIEW

LESSON 4.10
SKETCHING -- ISOMETRIC

NOTE:
ISOMETRIC SKETCHES ARE THE BEST WAY TO DESCRIBE A PART OR ASSEMBLY. ISOMETRIC SKETCHES & DRAWINGS ARE A QUICK WAY TO DESCRIBE COMPLICATED PARTS. AGAIN, IN A 3D MODELING SOFTWARE, THIS ISOMETRIC WOULD BE JUST AN AUXILIARY VIEW OF THE OBJECT. IT WOULD NOT HAVE TO BE CREATED, BECAUSE THE PART IS COMPLETE IN 3D. THERE WOULD JUST BE A WINDOW OR VIEW OF THE OBJECT SHOWING THE DESIRED VIEW OF THE PART IF REQUIRED.

NOTE:
WHEN DRAFTING IN ISOMETRIC, IT IS COMMON FOR DIFFERENT LINE TYPES TO END UP IN THE SAME LOCATION. THAT IS, IF YOU WERE TO DRAW THE LINES, THEY WOULD BE STACKED OR BEHIND EACH OTHER. VISIBLE LINES TAKE PRECEDENCE, THEN HIDDEN, THEN CENTER LINES.

INSTRUCTIONS:
ON A BLANK PIECE OF PAPER, REPRODUCE THE FOLLOWING ITEMS BY SKETCHING. NO SCALE IS REQUIRED.

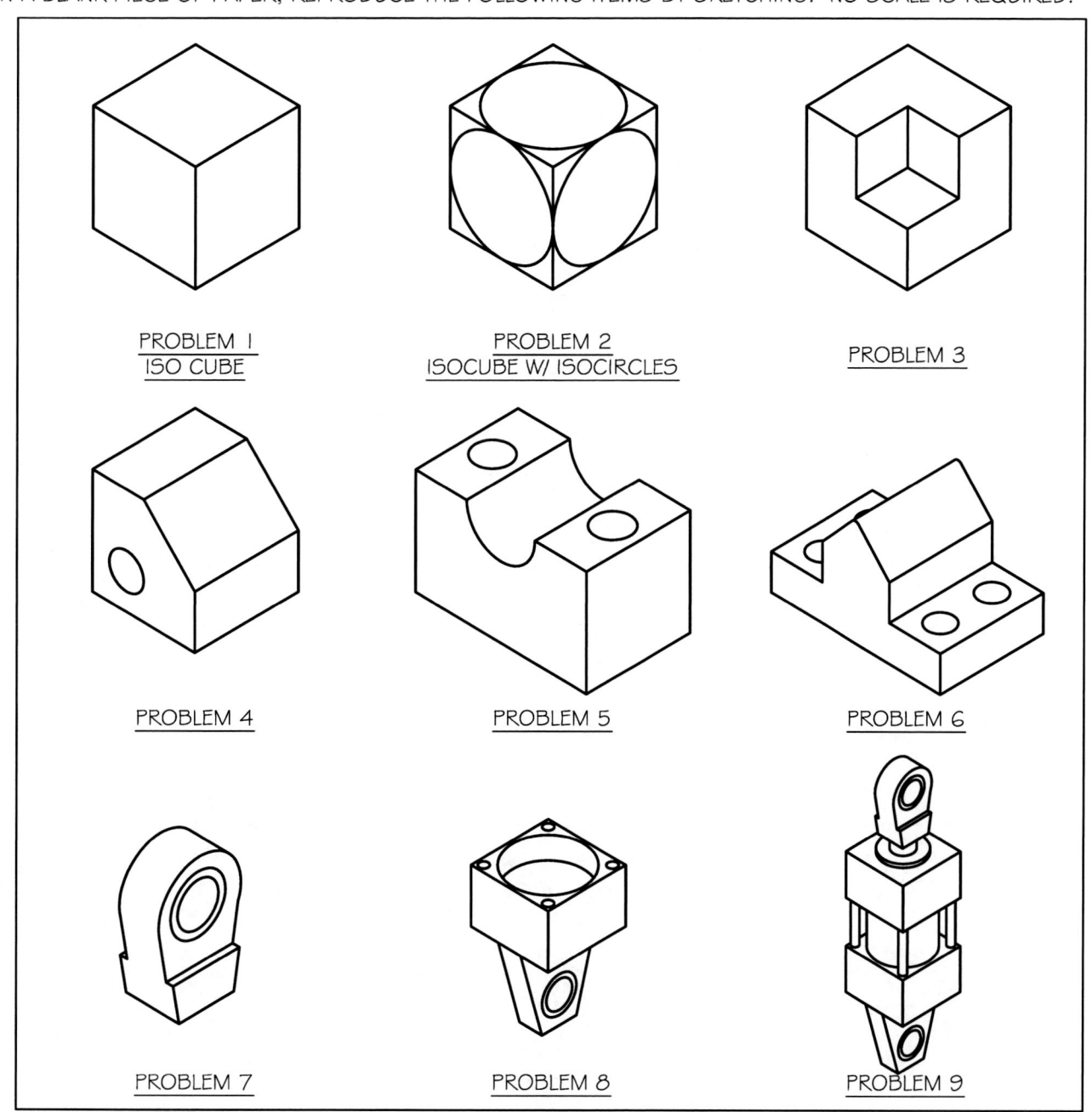

PROBLEM 1
ISO CUBE

PROBLEM 2
ISOCUBE W/ ISOCIRCLES

PROBLEM 3

PROBLEM 4

PROBLEM 5

PROBLEM 6

PROBLEM 7

PROBLEM 8

PROBLEM 9

LESSON 5.00
MULTIVIEW DRAWINGS

NOTE:
MULTIVIEW DRAWINGS DOMINATE THE ENGINEERING WORLD. COMPUTER MODELING IS THE LEADING EDGE OF TECHNOLOGY. THESE SOLID IMAGES ARE PASSED TO MACHINE TOOLS VIA CAM (COMPUTER AIDED MANUFACTURING) SOFTWARE & TRANSLATORS LIKE IGES & DXF. EVEN WITH ALL THIS SOPHISTICATION, THE SOLID MODEL IS STILL BROKEN DOWN INTO THE VIEWS OR FACES. THIS HELPS WITH VISUALIZATION & PART VERIFICATION; HOWEVER, BEING ABLE TO DIMENSION THE PART IS THE BEST REASON THE PARTS CAN BE MADE ON A MACHINE; HOWEVER, THE PARTS WILL STILL HAVE TO BE CHECKED BY HUMANS. A CAM PROGRAMMER WILL HAVE TO INSURE THE MACHINING CODE SENT TO THE MACHINE TOOL IS CORRECT. A TEST PIECE MADE OF WOOD OR ALUMINUM WILL BE SET UP TO TEST THE PROGRAM. THE DIMENSIONS WILL BE CHECKED. UNDERSTANDING WHAT IS BEING SHOWN IS CRITICAL.

INSTRUCTIONS:
CONSIDER EACH ISOMETRIC & PRODUCE A MULTIVIEW DRAWING OF EACH USING AS FEW VIEWS AS POSSIBLE. DO NOT DIMENSION. REPRODUCE THE FOLLOWING ITEMS BY SKETCHING, USING TOOLS, OR CAD. MAKE ORTHOGRAPHIC DRAWINGS USING ANY CONSISTENT SCALE (METRIC OR ENGLISH). THIS EXERCISE IS JUST FOR TRYING. THE FOLLOWING PAGES WILL SHOW YOU THE CORRECT APPROACH. AFTER COMPLETING THIS SECTION, COME BACK & SEE HOW YOU DID.

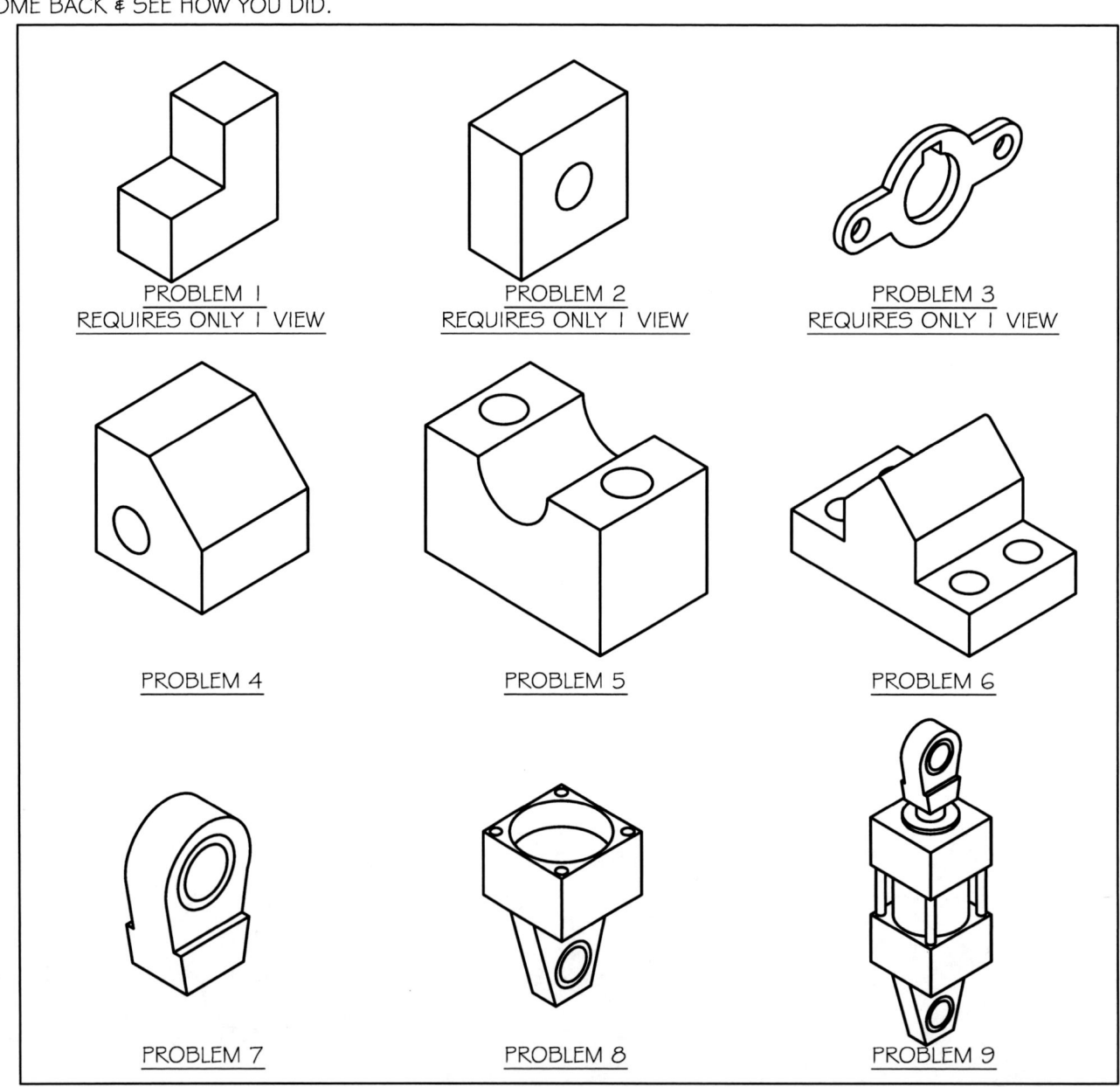

PROBLEM 1
REQUIRES ONLY 1 VIEW

PROBLEM 2
REQUIRES ONLY 1 VIEW

PROBLEM 3
REQUIRES ONLY 1 VIEW

PROBLEM 4

PROBLEM 5

PROBLEM 6

PROBLEM 7

PROBLEM 8

PROBLEM 9

LESSON 5.01
MULTIVIEW DRAWINGS

INSTRUCTIONS:
FILL IN THE MISSING LINES FOR ALL VIEWS. SEE SOLUTIONS SECTION OF BOOK FOR ANSWERS.

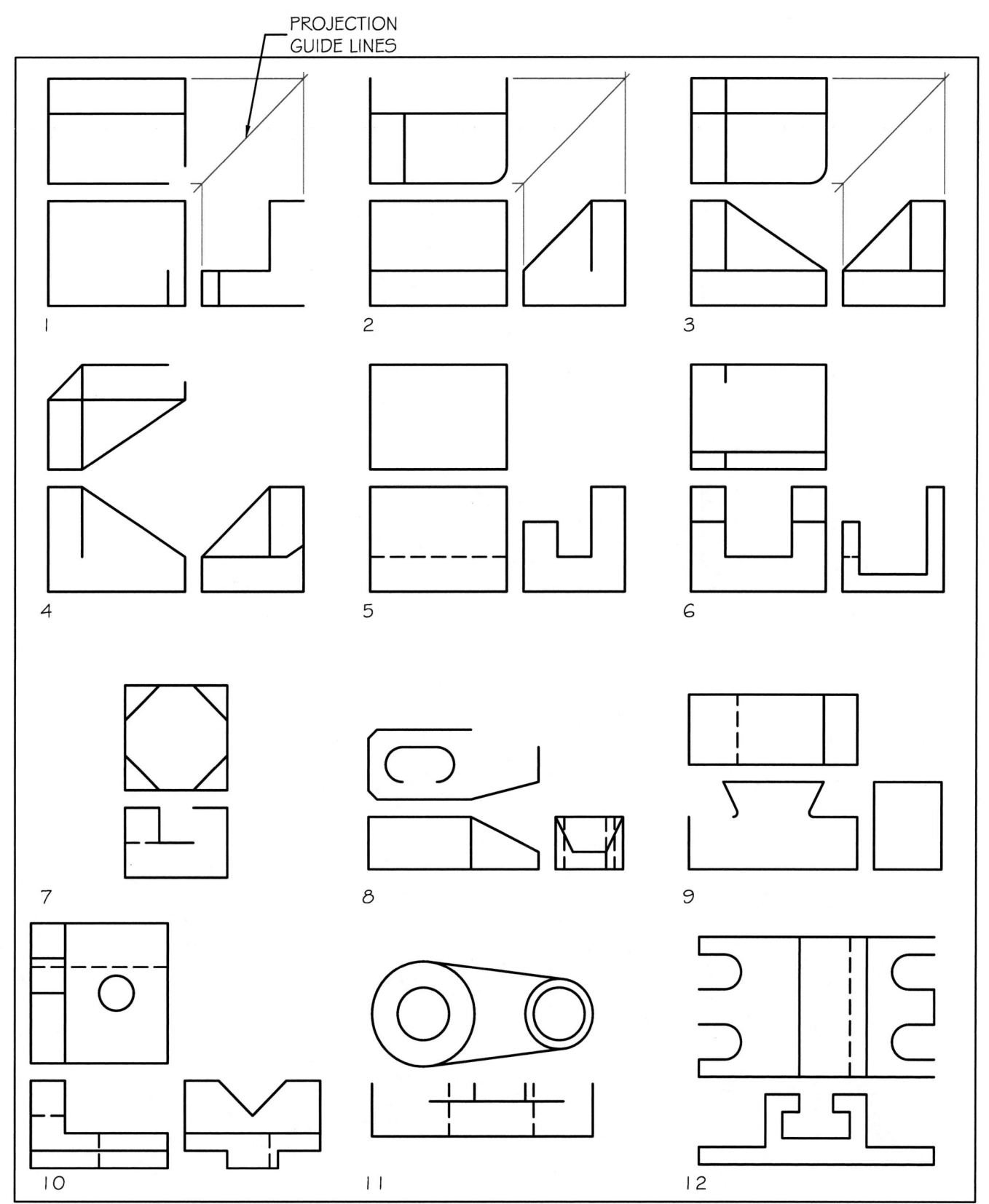

LESSON 5.02
MULTIVIEW DRAWINGS

NOTE:
OBSERVE THE PROJECTION & FOLDING LINES. THE PROJECTION LINES SHOW HOW ALL FEATURES ARE
PROJECTED AS THE PART IS UNFOLDED. THE FOLDING LINES SHOW HOW THE 6 NORMAL VIEWS ARE UNFOLDED.

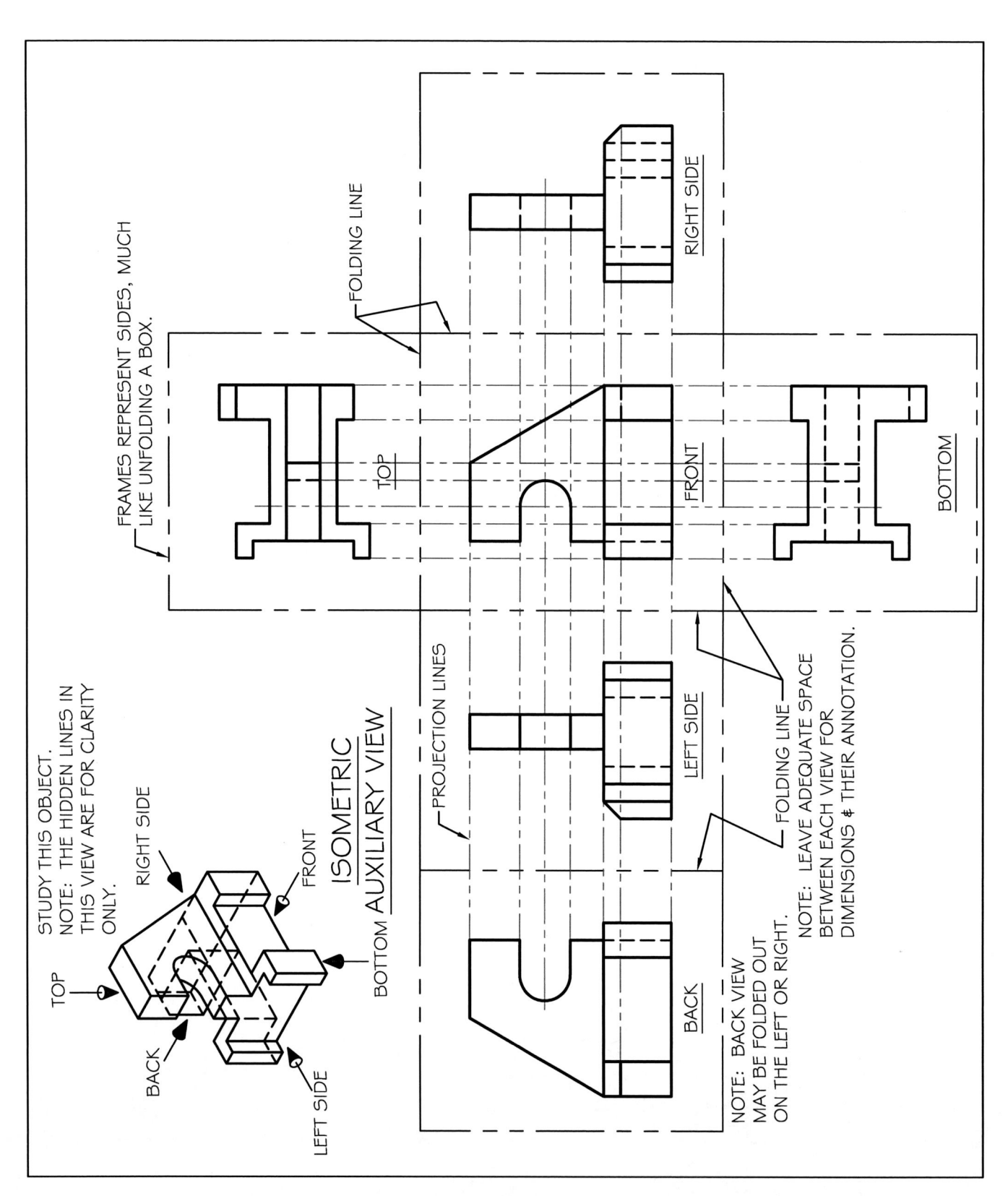

LESSON 5.03
MULTIVIEW DRAWINGS

NOTE:
REPRODUCE THIS PART BY THE METHOD OF YOUR CHOICE.

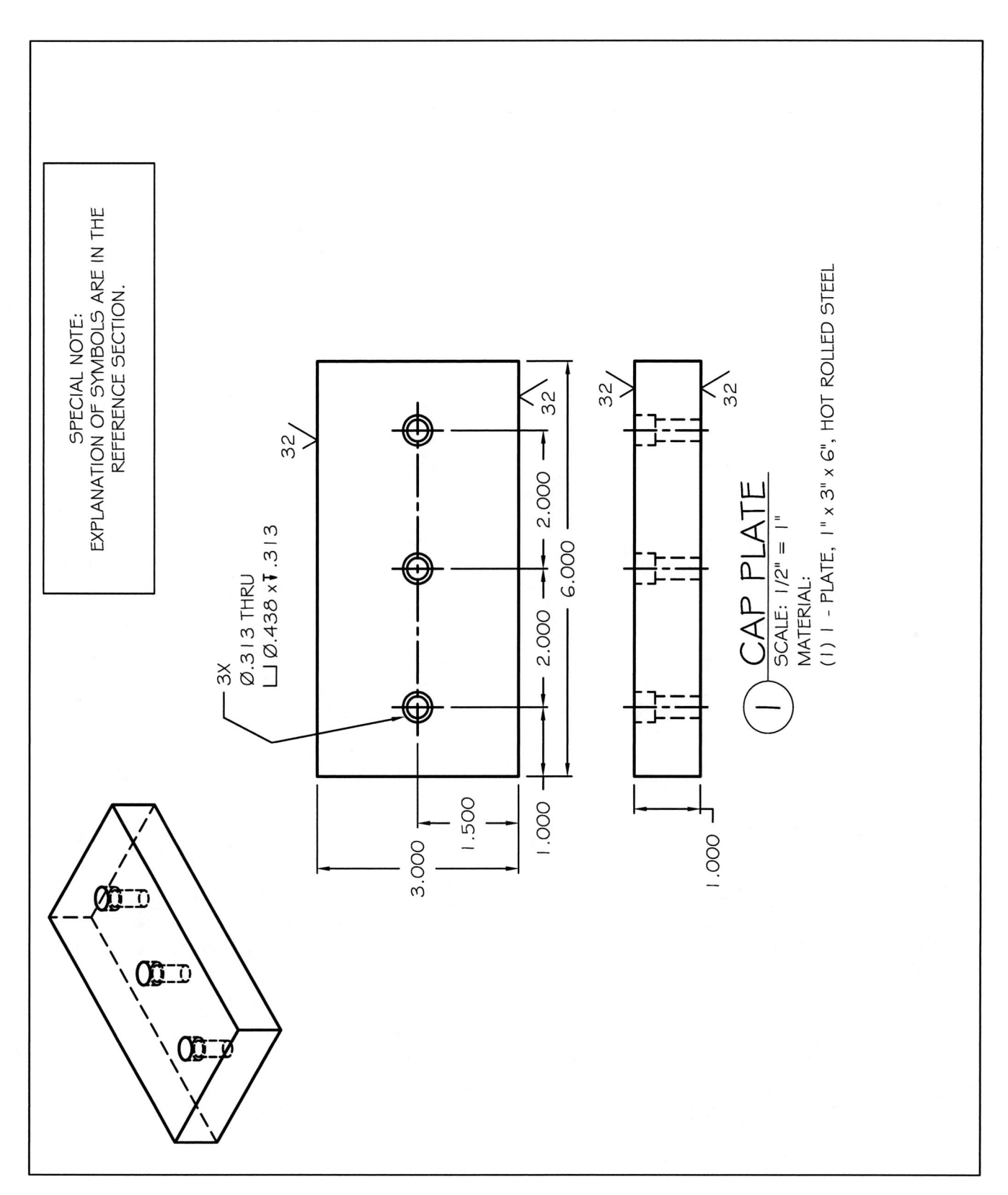

NOTE:
REPRODUCE THIS PART BY THE METHOD OF YOUR CHOICE.

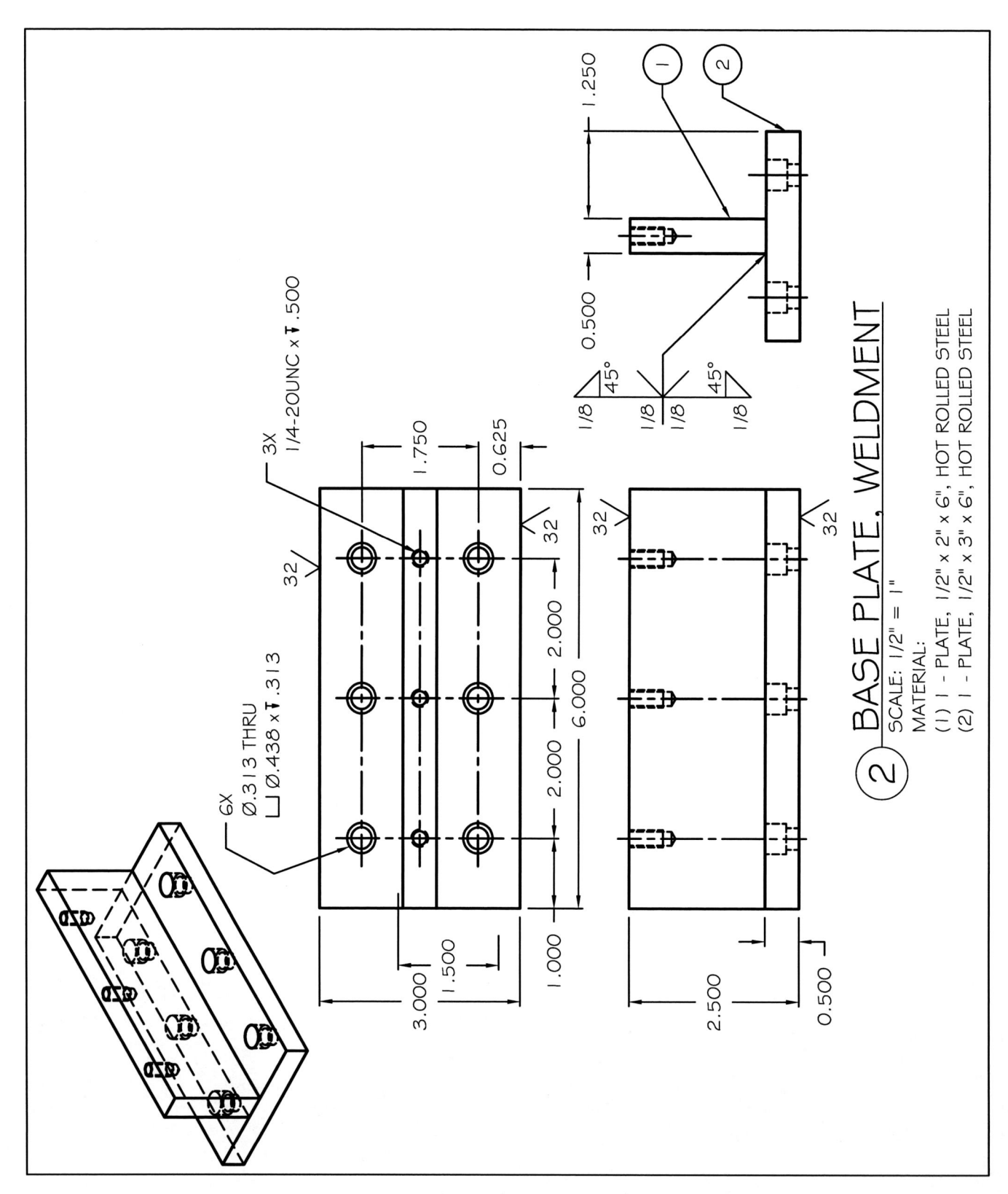

BASE PLATE, WELDMENT
SCALE: 1/2" = 1"
MATERIAL:
(1) 1 - PLATE, 1/2" x 2" x 6", HOT ROLLED STEEL
(2) 1 - PLATE, 1/2" x 3" x 6", HOT ROLLED STEEL

LESSON 5.05
MULTIVIEW DRAWINGS

NOTE:
REPRODUCE THIS PART BY THE METHOD OF YOUR CHOICE.

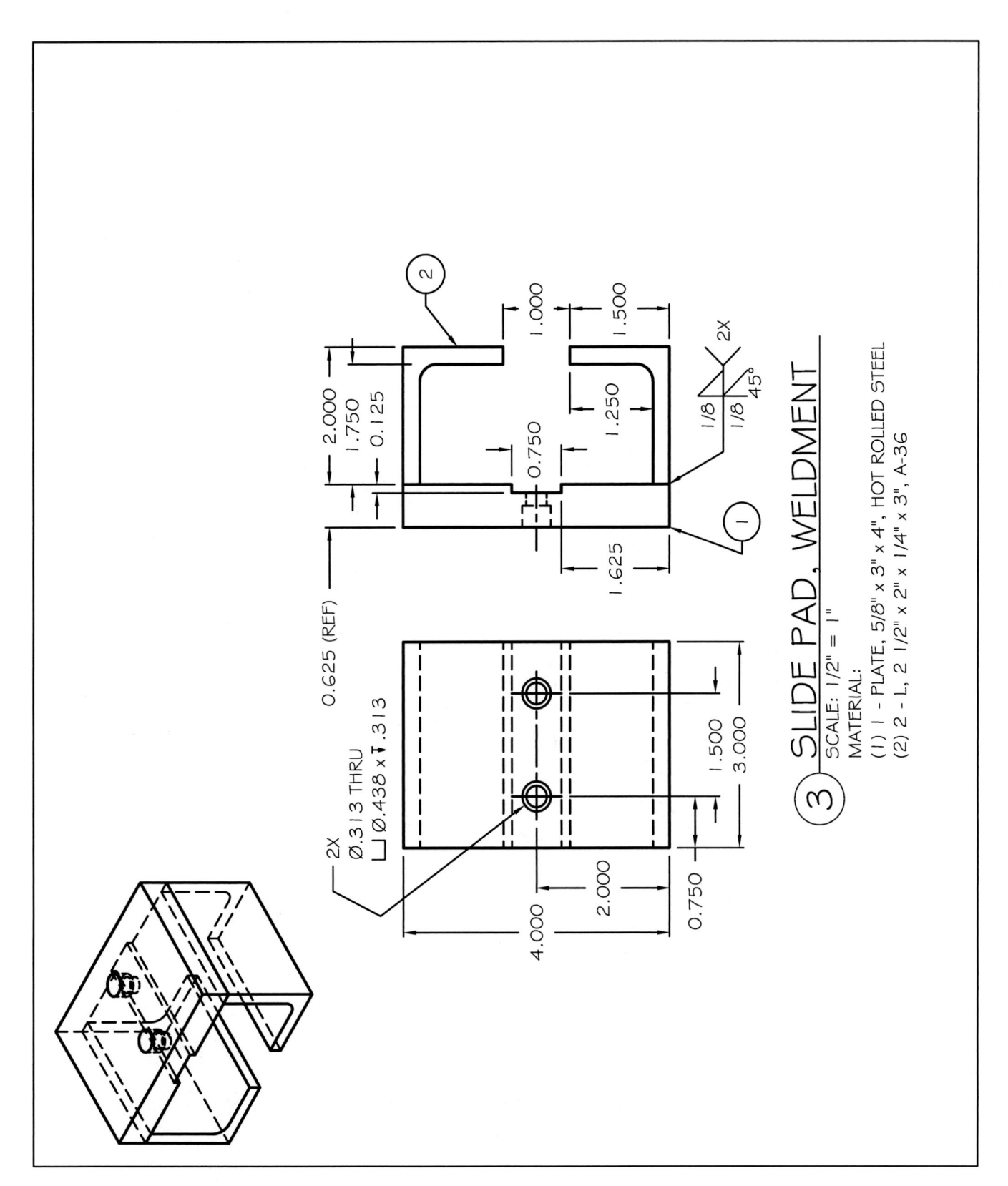

SLIDE PAD, WELDMENT

SCALE: 1/2" = 1"

MATERIAL:

(1) 1 - PLATE, 5/8" x 3" x 4", HOT ROLLED STEEL

(2) 2 - L, 2 1/2" x 2" x 1/4" x 3", A-36

2X Ø.313 THRU
⊔ Ø.438 x ▼.313

NOTE:
REPRODUCE THIS PART BY THE METHOD OF YOUR CHOICE.

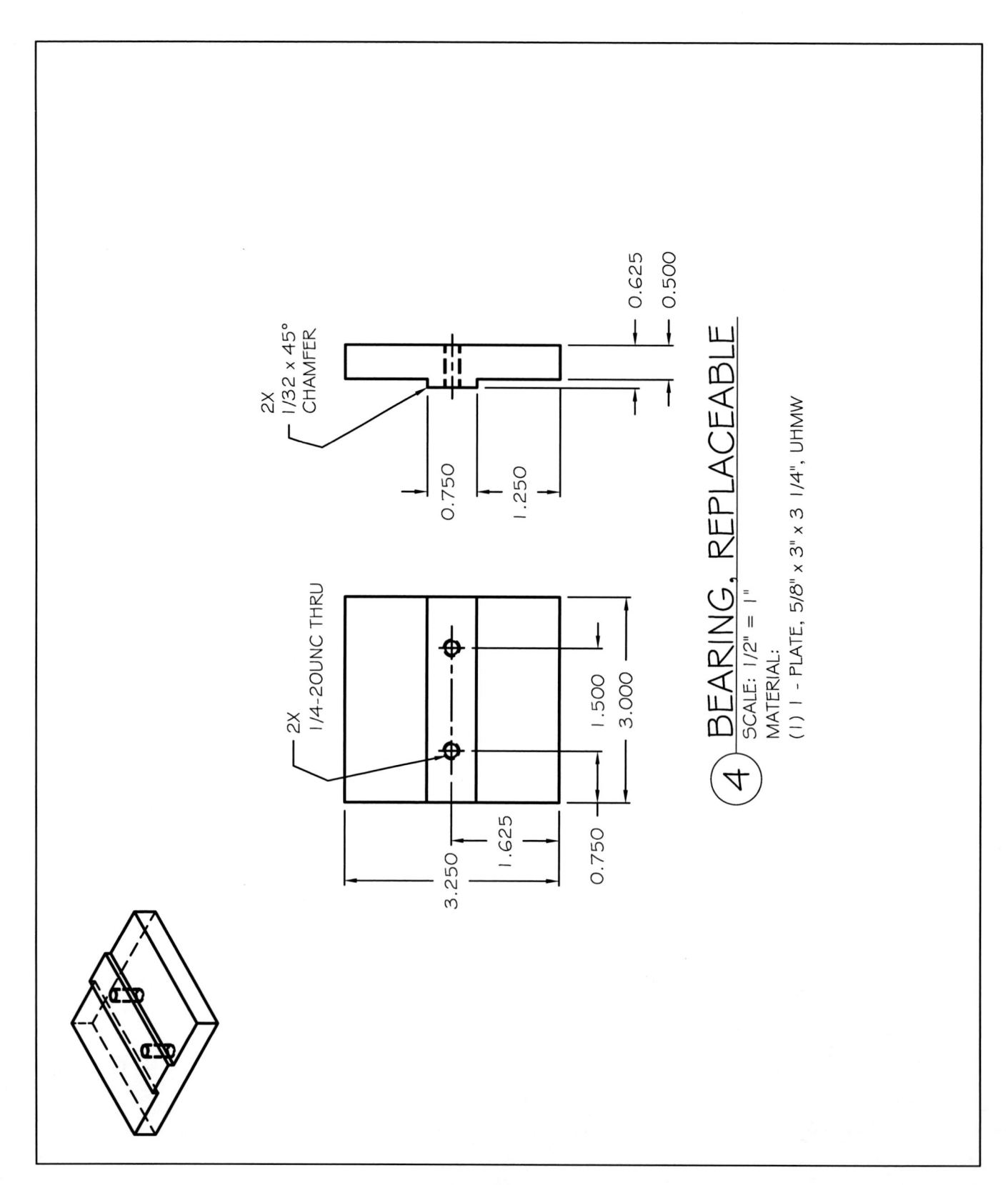

4 BEARING, REPLACEABLE

SCALE: 1/2" = 1"

MATERIAL:
(1) 1 - PLATE, 5/8" x 3" x 3 1/4", UHMW

LESSON 5.07
MULTIVIEW DRAWINGS

NOTE:
REPRODUCE THIS PART BY THE METHOD OF YOUR CHOICE.

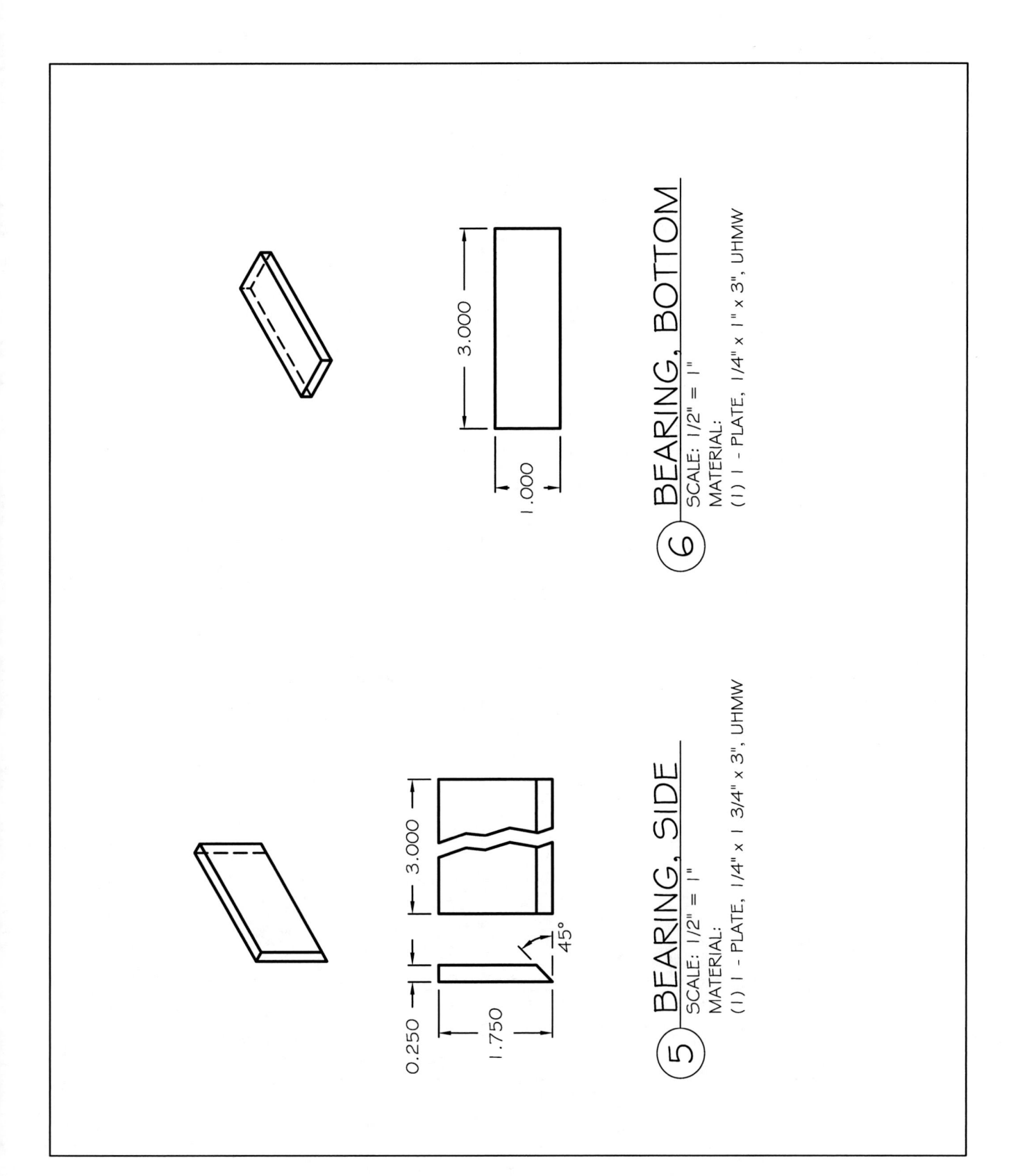

3.000

1.000

⑥ BEARING, BOTTOM
SCALE: 1/2" = 1"
MATERIAL:
(1) 1 - PLATE, 1/4" x 1" x 3", UHMW

3.000

0.250

1.750

45°

⑤ BEARING, SIDE
SCALE: 1/2" = 1"
MATERIAL:
(1) 1 - PLATE, 1/4" x 1 3/4" x 3", UHMW

LESSON 5.08
MULTIVIEW DRAWINGS

NOTE:
REPRODUCE THIS PART BY THE METHOD OF YOUR CHOICE. IT IS IMPORTANT TO NOTE THAT ASSEMBLY
DRAWINGS & THE ASSOCIATED BILL OF MATERIALS OR PARTS LIST CAN BE AS VARIED AS THE COMPANY YOU
MAY BE WORKING FOR. THE METHOD USED HERE IS LIKE A SHOP VERSION.

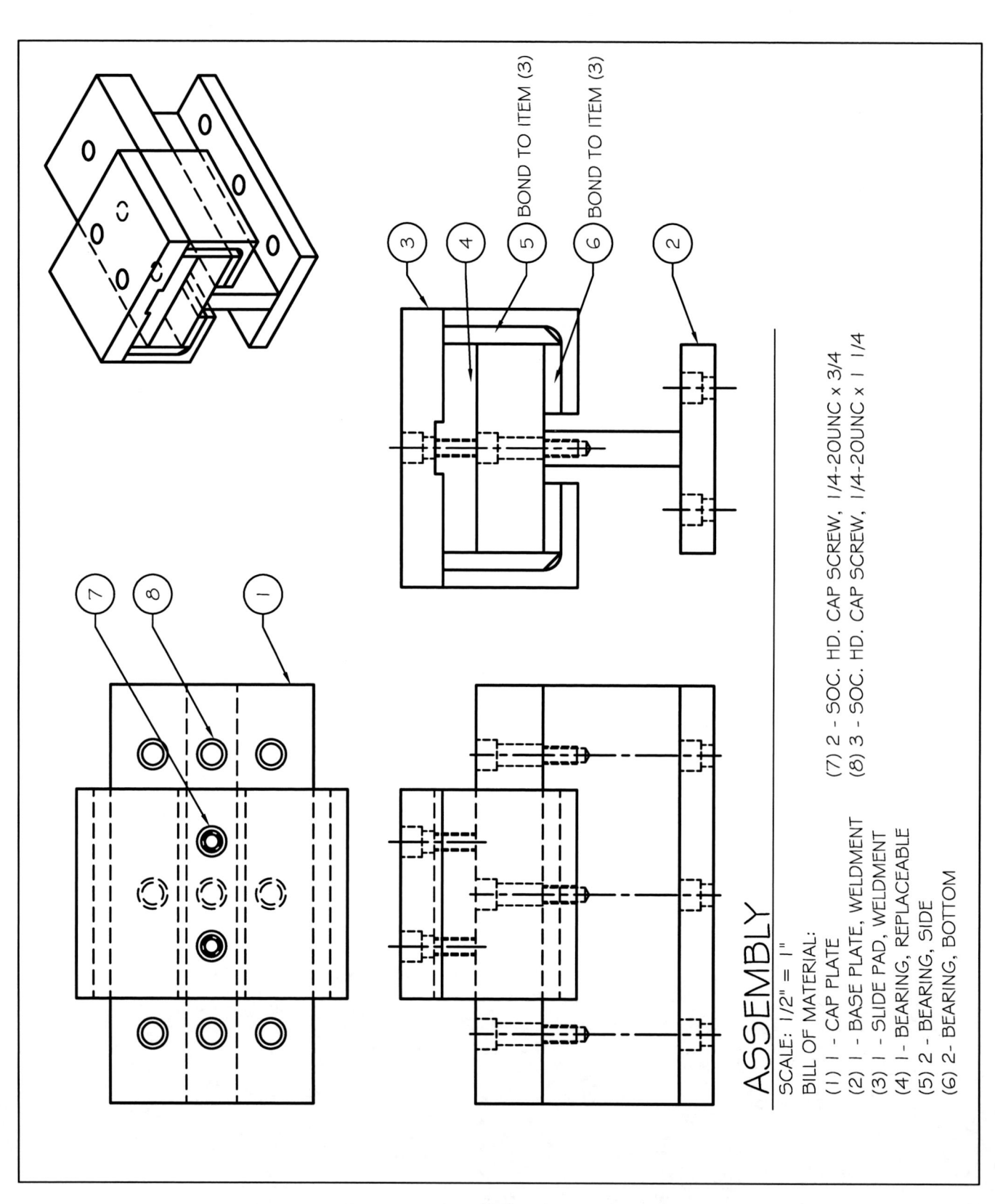

ASSEMBLY

SCALE: 1/2" = 1"
BILL OF MATERIAL:
(1) 1 - CAP PLATE
(2) 1 - BASE PLATE, WELDMENT
(3) 1 - SLIDE PAD, WELDMENT
(4) 1 - BEARING, REPLACEABLE
(5) 2 - BEARING, SIDE
(6) 2 - BEARING, BOTTOM
(7) 2 - SOC. HD. CAP SCREW, 1/4-20UNC x 3/4
(8) 3 - SOC. HD. CAP SCREW, 1/4-20UNC x 1 1/4

LESSON 5.09
MULTIVIEW DRAWINGS

NOTE:
THIS LESSON IS TO DEMONSTRATE NORMAL CONVENTIONS OF SIMPLIFIED DRAFTING.

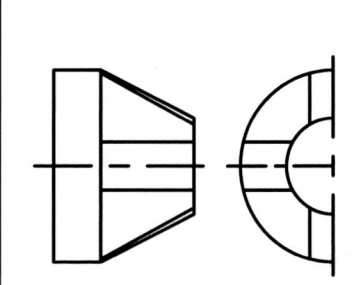

PARTIAL VIEW
THE PART IS SYMMETRICAL
& IT IS NOT REQUIRED TO
SHOW THE COMPLETE PART

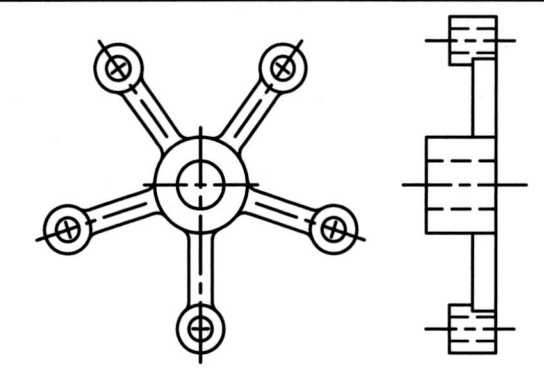

REVOLVED VIEW
THE PART HAS A FEATURE THAT COULD BE
CONFUSING IF DRAWN AS A PROJECTION. THE
SIDE VIEW IS DRAWN TO LOOK LIKE THE LEG
THAT GETS A NORMAL PROJECTION.

NOTE:
THERE ARE MANY CONVENTIONS THAT HELP WITH
DRAWING PRESENTATION & ANNOTATION (THAT IS
DENOTING THE DRAWING). ANNOTATION INCLUDES
DIMENSIONS, NOTES, WELDING SYMBOLS, ETC.
THESE METHODS WILL BE SHOWN IN THE FOLLOWING
PAGES.

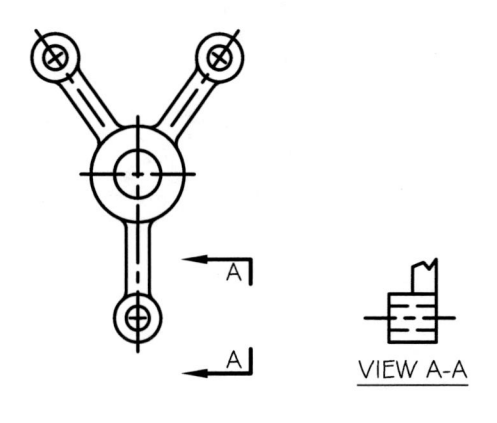

VIEW A-A

BROKEN VIEW
THIS VIEW ALLOWS THE PRESENTATION
OF ONLY THE INFORMATION REQUIRED.

LESSON 5.10
MULTIVIEW DRAWINGS

INSTRUCTIONS: 1.) REPRODUCE ALL THE ISOMETRICS BELOW TWICE THE SIZE OF THE ILLUSTRATIONS.
2.) CONSIDER EACH ISOMETRIC & PRODUCE AN ORTHOGRAPHIC MULTIVIEW DRAWING OF EACH SHOWING ALL
6 SIDES. PRODUCE THE DRAWINGS BY SKETCHING, USING TOOLS, OR CAD. MAKE ORTHOGRAPHIC DRAWINGS
FULL SIZE USING ENGLISH OR METRIC SCALE. SEE SOLUTIONS SECTION OF BOOK FOR ANSWERS.

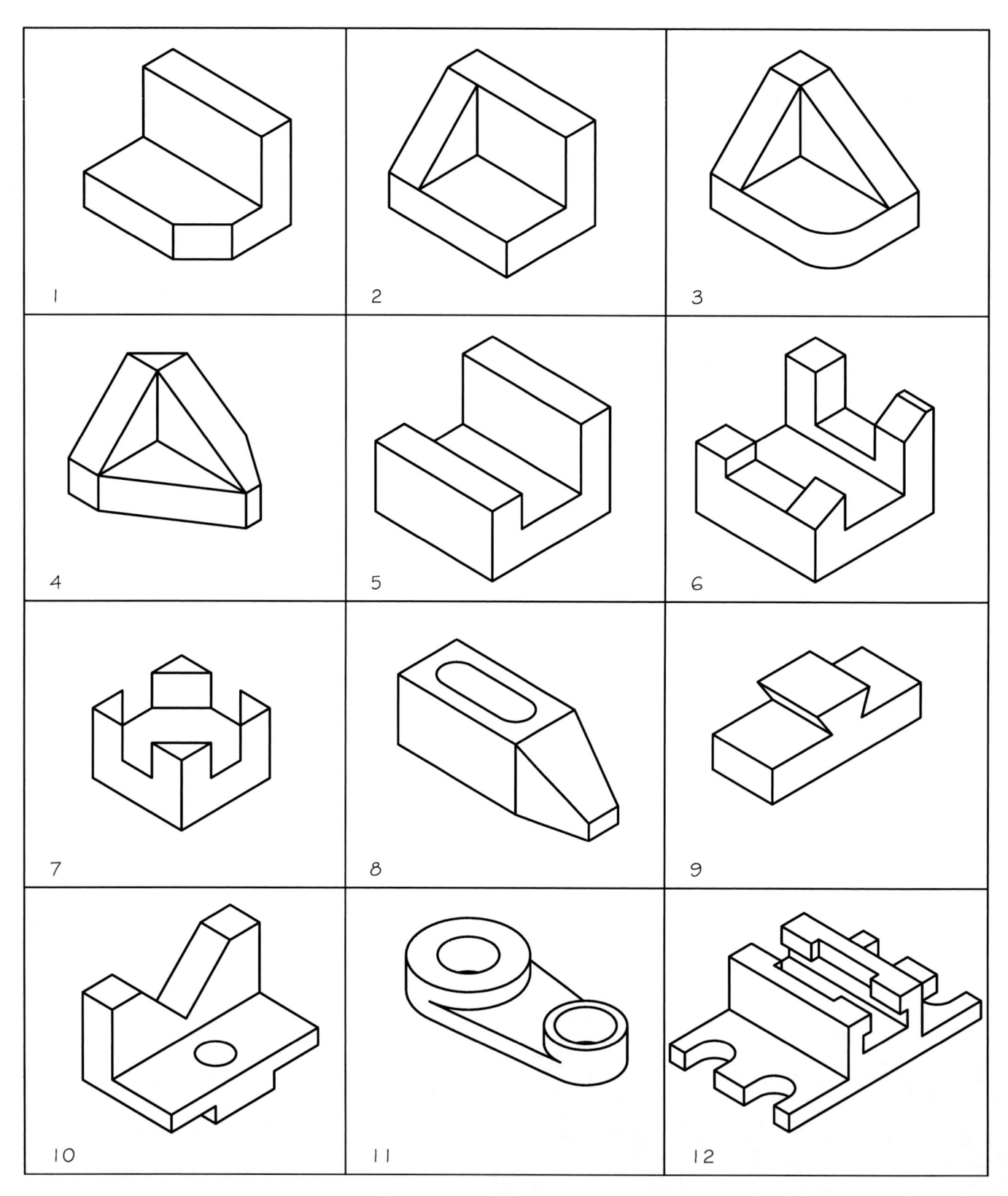

LESSON 6.00
BREAK-AWAY VIEWS & SECTIONS

NOTE:
BREAK-AWAY VIEWS & SECTIONS ARE VIEWS THAT SHOW THE INSIDE OF A PART TO ADD CLARITY OR FOR ADDING DIMENSIONS   THE BREAK-AWAY VIEW IS USED FOR SIMPLE CLARIFICATIONS. PARTIAL SECTIONS ARE PRIMARILY USED WHEN THE SECTION BEING CUT IS SYMMETRICAL. FULL SECTIONS ARE USED ONLY WHEN THE FIRST 2 OPTIONS DO NOT ADD THE NECESSARY CLARIFICATION. SECTIONS CAN BE CONFUSING & TIME CONSUMING. LOOK AT THE SAMPLES OF EACH TYPE OF BREAK-AWAY & SECTION BELOW.

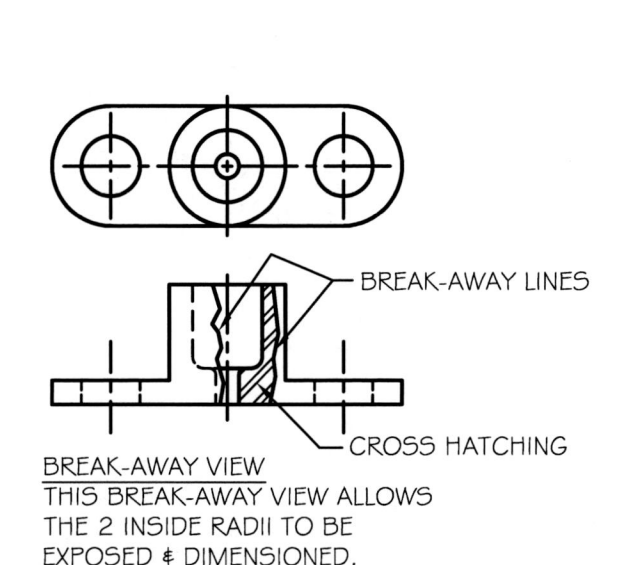

BREAK-AWAY LINES

CROSS HATCHING

BREAK-AWAY VIEW
THIS BREAK-AWAY VIEW ALLOWS THE 2 INSIDE RADII TO BE EXPOSED & DIMENSIONED.

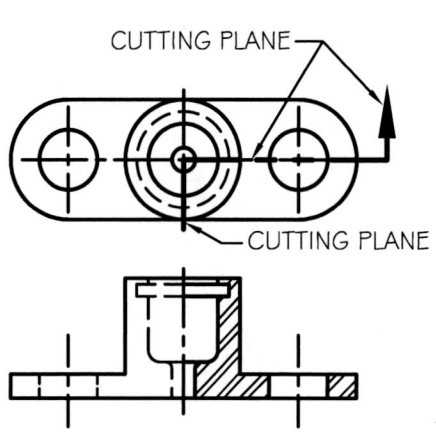

CUTTING PLANE

CUTTING PLANE

PARTIAL SECTION
THE PART IS SYMMETRICAL & WARRANTS A PARTIAL SECTION TO SHOW THE INTERNAL GROOVE AS WELL AS THE RADII.

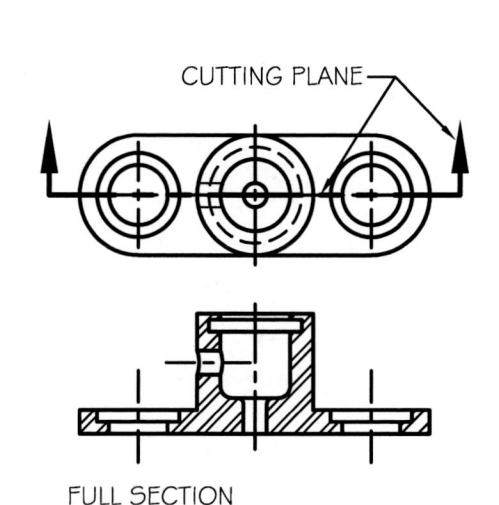

CUTTING PLANE

FULL SECTION
THE PART IS NOT SYMMETRICAL & WARRANTS A FULL SECTION TO SHOW THE HOLE, INTERNAL GROOVE & RADII.

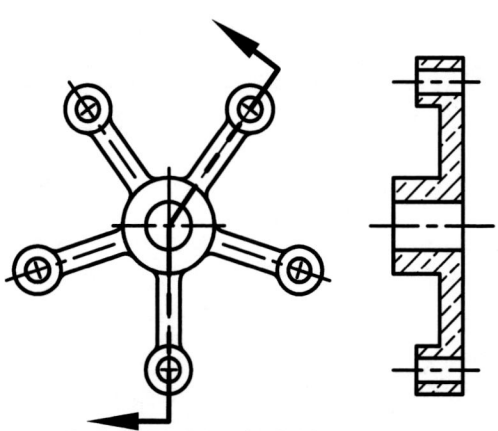

REVOLVED FULL SECTION
THE PART HAS A FEATURE THAT COULD BE CONFUSING IF DRAWN AS A PROJECTION. THE SECTION IS DRAWN TO LOOK LIKE THE LEG THAT GETS A NORMAL PROJECTION.

LESSON 6.01
BREAKAWAY VIEWS & SECTIONS

NOTE:
REMOVED SECTIONS OR SECTION OF MATERIAL AT A SPECIFIC CUTTING PLANE IN A PART THAT TRANSITIONS FROM ONE SHAPE TO ANOTHER. OFFSET SECTIONS CAN SHOW FEATURES THAT OCCUR ON DIFFERENT PLANES USING THE SAME CUTTING PLANE.

BREAKING LONG OBJECTS FOR CLARITY & SIMPLIFICATION CAN BE SHOWN USING STANDARD BREAK SYMBOLS & LINES.

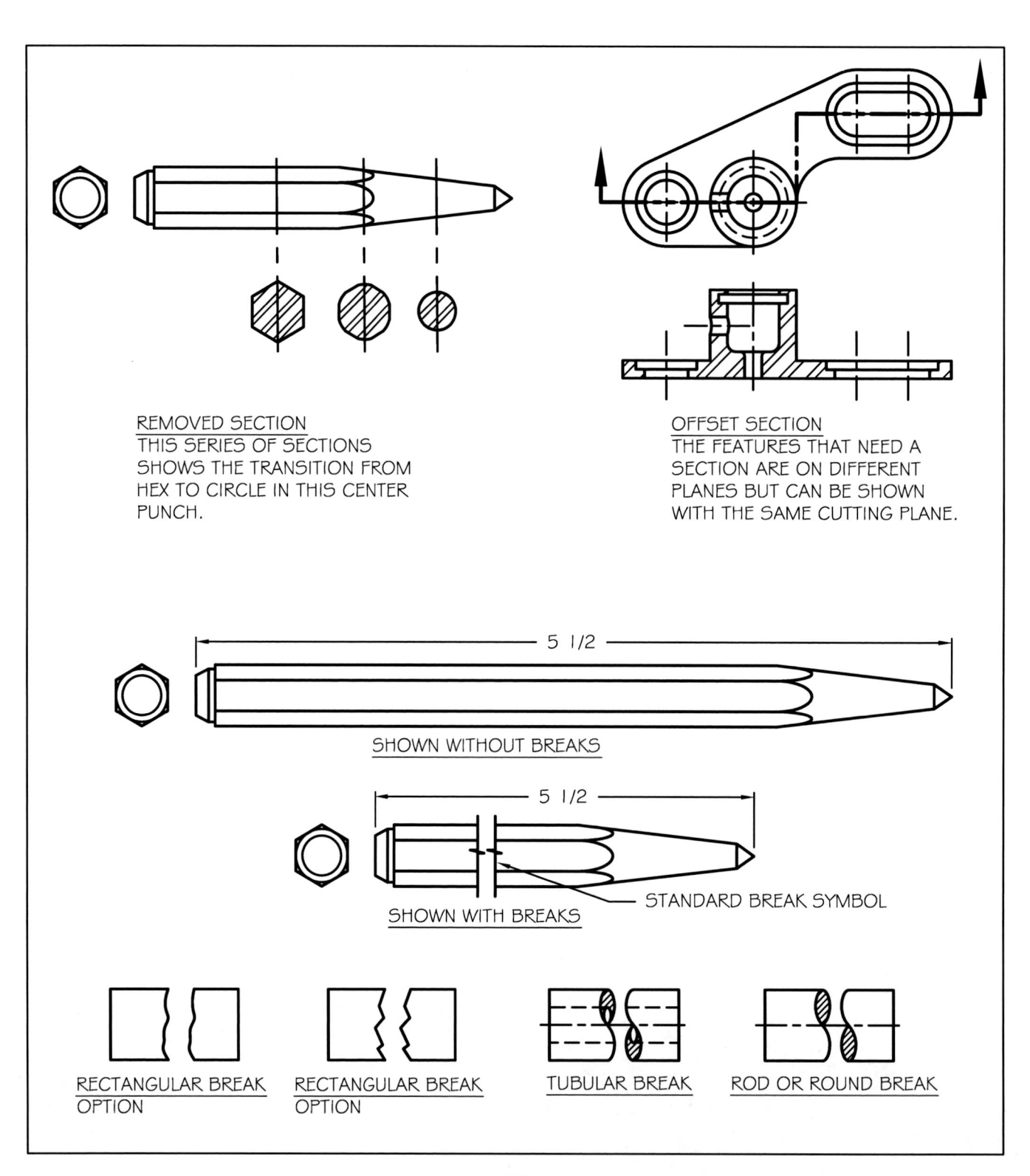

REMOVED SECTION
THIS SERIES OF SECTIONS SHOWS THE TRANSITION FROM HEX TO CIRCLE IN THIS CENTER PUNCH.

OFFSET SECTION
THE FEATURES THAT NEED A SECTION ARE ON DIFFERENT PLANES BUT CAN BE SHOWN WITH THE SAME CUTTING PLANE.

SHOWN WITHOUT BREAKS

SHOWN WITH BREAKS — STANDARD BREAK SYMBOL

RECTANGULAR BREAK OPTION

RECTANGULAR BREAK OPTION

TUBULAR BREAK

ROD OR ROUND BREAK

LESSON 6.02
BREAK-AWAY VIEWS & SECTIONS

NOTE:
WHEN SECTIONS OR BREAK-AWAY VIEWS ARE SHOWN, THE MATERIAL OF THE PART BEING CUT IS TO BE SHOWN. THERE ARE STANDARD CROSS HATCH PATTERNS FOR ALMOST EVERY AVAILABLE MATERIAL. NOTE THAT IF 2 PARTS ARE TOUCHING OR ARE SURFACE TO SURFACE, THE ANGLE OR TYPE OF PATTERN IS CHANGED. THIS IS USED IN SHOWING SECTIONS OF ASSEMBLIES. SEE THE PATTERNS BELOW.

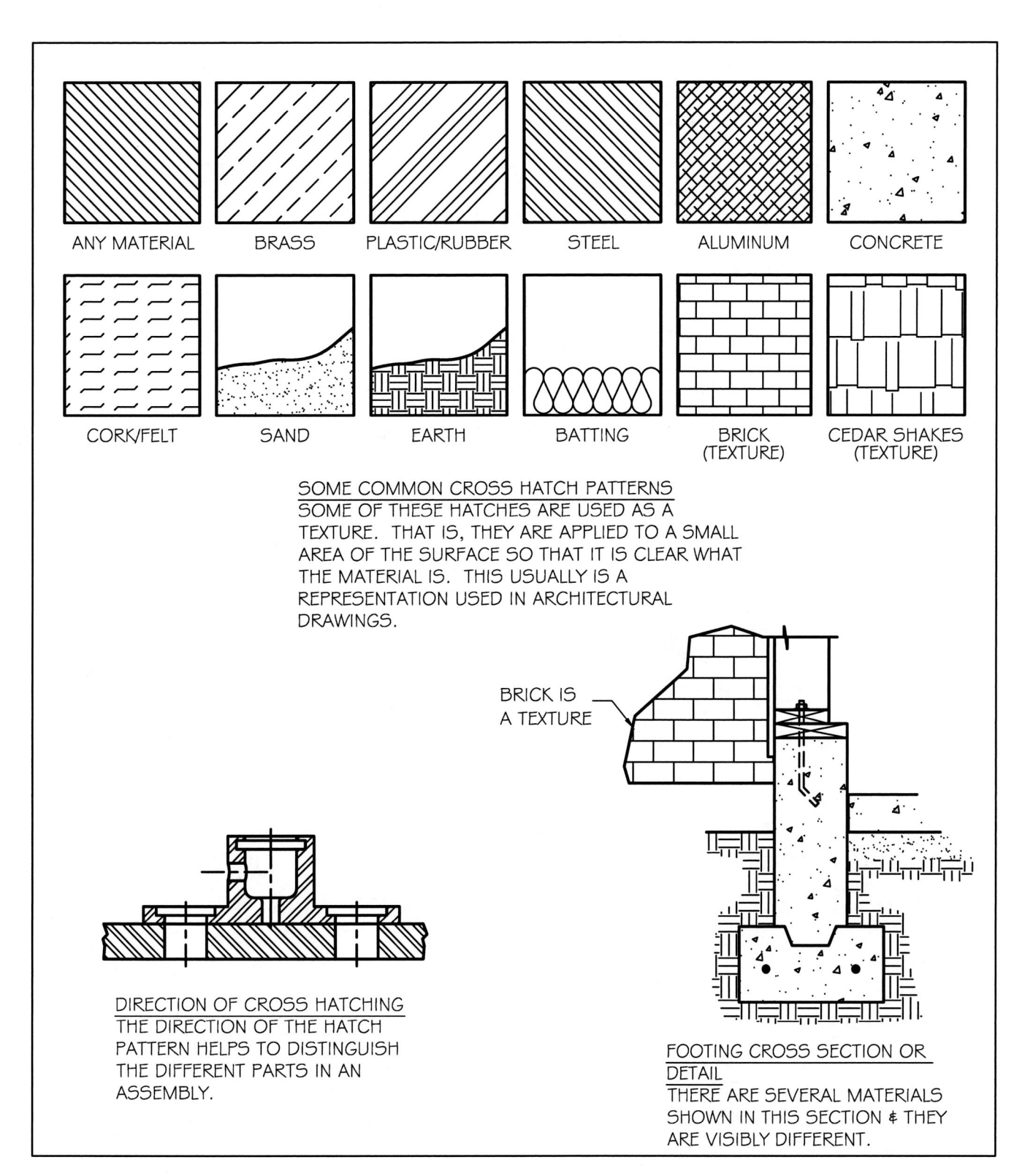

SOME COMMON CROSS HATCH PATTERNS
SOME OF THESE HATCHES ARE USED AS A TEXTURE. THAT IS, THEY ARE APPLIED TO A SMALL AREA OF THE SURFACE SO THAT IT IS CLEAR WHAT THE MATERIAL IS. THIS USUALLY IS A REPRESENTATION USED IN ARCHITECTURAL DRAWINGS.

DIRECTION OF CROSS HATCHING
THE DIRECTION OF THE HATCH PATTERN HELPS TO DISTINGUISH THE DIFFERENT PARTS IN AN ASSEMBLY.

FOOTING CROSS SECTION OR DETAIL
THERE ARE SEVERAL MATERIALS SHOWN IN THIS SECTION & THEY ARE VISIBLY DIFFERENT.

LESSON 6.03
BREAKAWAY VIEWS & SECTIONS

INSTRUCTIONS:
FILL IN THE MISSING LINES & CROSS HATCHING FOR ALL SECTIONS. CHOOSE THE STYLE OF CROSS HATCH FROM THE PATTERNS SHOWN IN THE PREVIOUS SHEETS. SEE SOLUTIONS SECTION OF BOOK FOR SOLUTIONS.

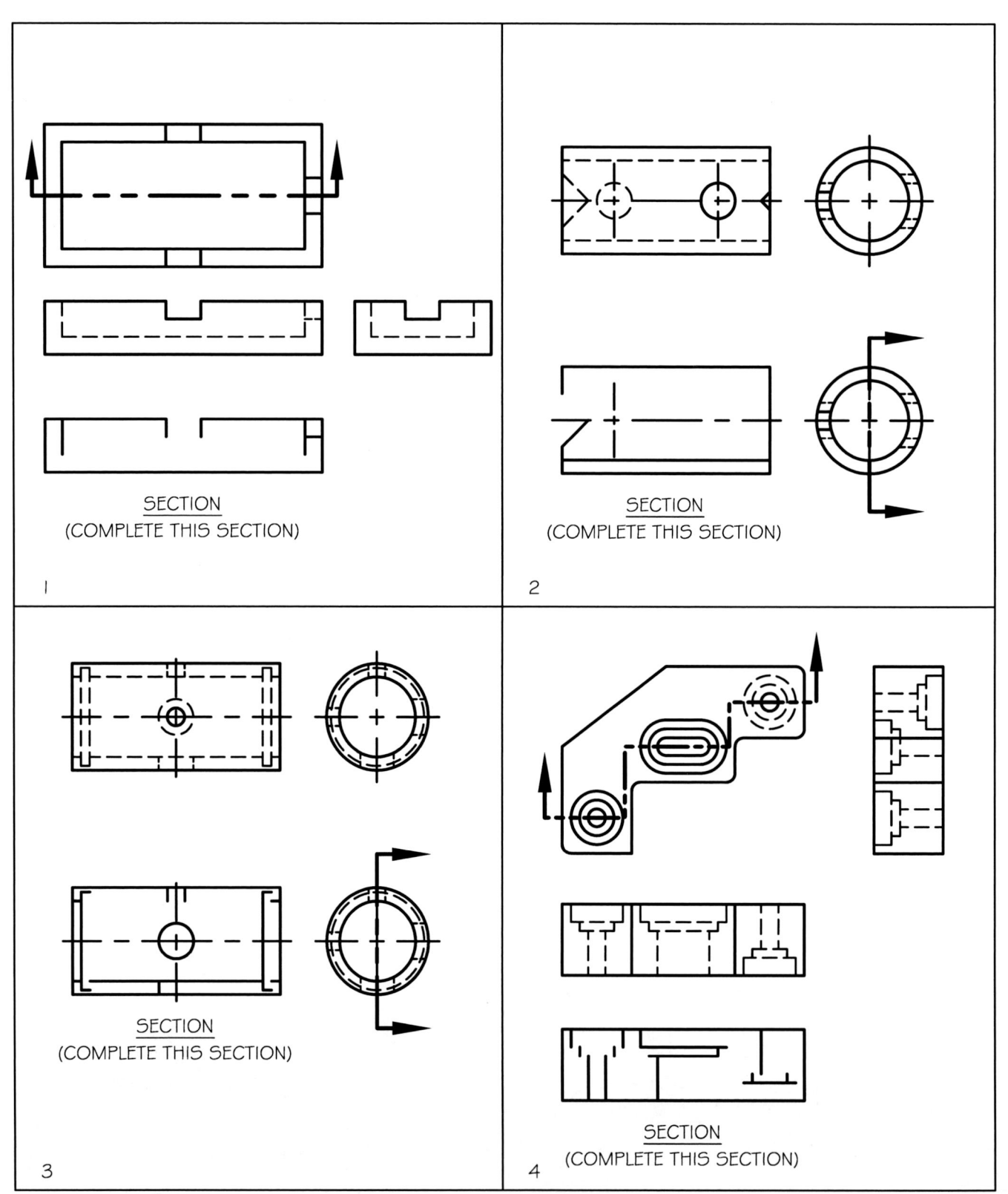

LESSON 7.00
DIMENSIONING & ANNOTATION

NOTE:
DIMENSIONING IS CRITICAL. DIMENSIONS DEFINE. DIMENSIONS OVERRULE THE SCALING OF DRAWINGS. NEAT & UNDERSTANDABLE DIMENSIONS CAN MAKE THE DIFFERENCE OF A PART THAT FITS & ONE THAT DOES NOT. THERE HAS BEEN A DEBATE ABOUT WHICH MEASURING SCALE IS SUPERIOR; IT IS CLEAR THAT BOTH OFFER BENEFITS & DRAWBACKS SO THE DEBATE WILL NOT CONTINUE HERE. WE WILL DEAL WITH BOTH ENGLISH & METRIC SCALES. NEITHER IS MORE ACCURATE. ONE CAN BE EASIER TO WORK WITH IN SOME WAYS. IT BOILS DOWN TO WHAT IS REQUIRED OR DESIRED BY THE CUSTOMER. THE KEY IS TO UNDERSTAND THAT BOTH SYSTEMS ARE ALIVE & WELL IN MOST OF THE WORLD. THE WORLD USES METRIC, EXCEPT WHEN THE COUNTRIES USE AMERICAN MACHINERY & EQUIPMENT. AMERICA IS THE ONLY COUNTRY THAT STILL USES THE ENGLISH SYSTEM FOR ITS NATIONAL MEASURING SYSTEM. FOR THOSE OF US THAT DEAL IN BOTH SYSTEMS THERE ARE CONVERSION TABLES. THESE TABLES ALLOW UNITS OF MEASURE LIKE MILLIMETERS TO BE EFFORTLESSLY CONVERTED TO INCHES, METERS TO FEET, KILOMETERS TO MILES, ETC.

ANNOTATION IS THE WORDS & SYMBOLS THAT HELP THE PICTURE THAT HAS BEEN CREATED MAKE EVEN MORE SENSE TO THE PERSON MAKING OR CHECKING THE PART. THIS CAN BE TO CLARIFY HOW A PART IS MANUFACTURED, WELDED, THE SURFACE FINISH, THE PAINT OR COATINGS, ETC.

FOR THE PURPOSE OF THIS BOOK, THE DIMENSIONS SHOWN WILL REFLECT ENGLISH OR ENGLISH & METRIC. THE METRIC MEASUREMENT WILL BE IN MILLIMETERS & WILL APPEAR IN SQUARE BRACKETS [mm] UNLESS OTHERWISE SPECIFIED.

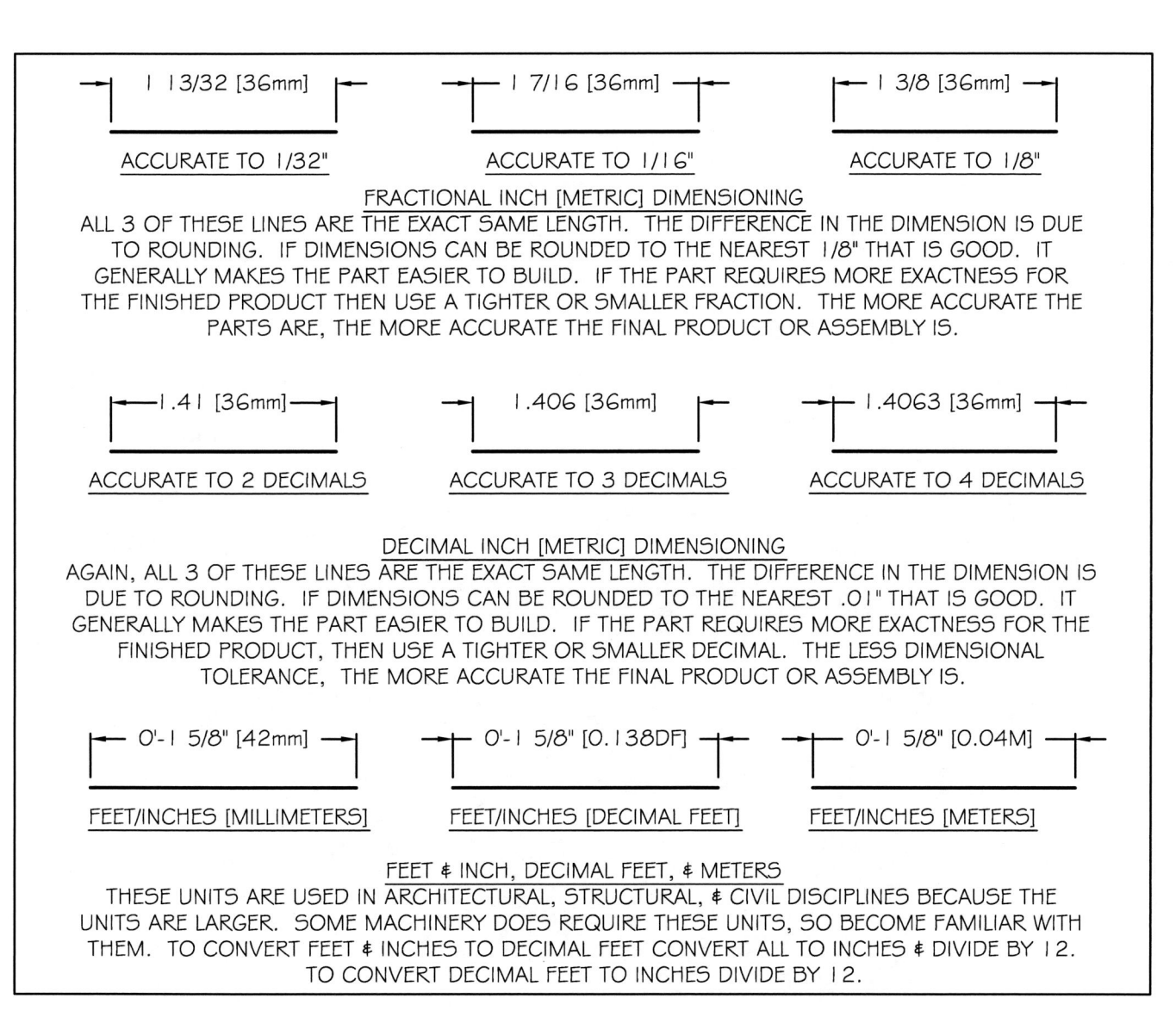

1 13/32 [36mm]	1 7/16 [36mm]	1 3/8 [36mm]
ACCURATE TO 1/32"	ACCURATE TO 1/16"	ACCURATE TO 1/8"

FRACTIONAL INCH [METRIC] DIMENSIONING
ALL 3 OF THESE LINES ARE THE EXACT SAME LENGTH. THE DIFFERENCE IN THE DIMENSION IS DUE TO ROUNDING. IF DIMENSIONS CAN BE ROUNDED TO THE NEAREST 1/8" THAT IS GOOD. IT GENERALLY MAKES THE PART EASIER TO BUILD. IF THE PART REQUIRES MORE EXACTNESS FOR THE FINISHED PRODUCT THEN USE A TIGHTER OR SMALLER FRACTION. THE MORE ACCURATE THE PARTS ARE, THE MORE ACCURATE THE FINAL PRODUCT OR ASSEMBLY IS.

1.41 [36mm]	1.406 [36mm]	1.4063 [36mm]
ACCURATE TO 2 DECIMALS	ACCURATE TO 3 DECIMALS	ACCURATE TO 4 DECIMALS

DECIMAL INCH [METRIC] DIMENSIONING
AGAIN, ALL 3 OF THESE LINES ARE THE EXACT SAME LENGTH. THE DIFFERENCE IN THE DIMENSION IS DUE TO ROUNDING. IF DIMENSIONS CAN BE ROUNDED TO THE NEAREST .01" THAT IS GOOD. IT GENERALLY MAKES THE PART EASIER TO BUILD. IF THE PART REQUIRES MORE EXACTNESS FOR THE FINISHED PRODUCT, THEN USE A TIGHTER OR SMALLER DECIMAL. THE LESS DIMENSIONAL TOLERANCE, THE MORE ACCURATE THE FINAL PRODUCT OR ASSEMBLY IS.

0'-1 5/8" [42mm]	0'-1 5/8" [0.138DF]	0'-1 5/8" [0.04M]
FEET/INCHES [MILLIMETERS]	FEET/INCHES [DECIMAL FEET]	FEET/INCHES [METERS]

FEET & INCH, DECIMAL FEET, & METERS
THESE UNITS ARE USED IN ARCHITECTURAL, STRUCTURAL, & CIVIL DISCIPLINES BECAUSE THE UNITS ARE LARGER. SOME MACHINERY DOES REQUIRE THESE UNITS, SO BECOME FAMILIAR WITH THEM. TO CONVERT FEET & INCHES TO DECIMAL FEET CONVERT ALL TO INCHES & DIVIDE BY 12. TO CONVERT DECIMAL FEET TO INCHES DIVIDE BY 12.

LESSON 7.01
DIMENSIONING & ANNOTATION

NOTE:
DIMENSIONS ON A DRAWING REFLECTS THE DESIRED DIMENSION, NOT NECESSARILY THE SIZE OF THE OBJECT. THERE ARE MANY CASES WHEN THE PART OR ASSEMBLY SIMPLY WILL NOT FIT ON A PAGE WITHOUT SCALING DOWN THE DRAWING, OR A PART CAN BE SO SMALL & INVOLVED THAT THE PART MAY HAVE TO BE DRAWN LARGER THAN FULL SIZE SO THAT IT CAN BE ANNOTATED. CAD MAKES THIS ALL SO EASY. IT IS STILL IMPORTANT TO UNDERSTAND DRAWINGS. IT IS IMPORTANT THAT THE SCALE BE NOTED ON THE DRAWING IN THE TITLE BLOCK OR BY EACH PART OR DETAIL. SOME OF THE DIMENSIONING STANDARDS THAT WERE SET YEARS BEFORE CAD HAVE FALLEN BY THE WAYSIDE. THE COMPUTER FORCES SOME COMPROMISES; HOWEVER, IT IS BEST TO ATTEMPT TO FOLLOW THE ORIGINAL DRAFTING STANDARDS FOR DIMENSIONING. THE DRAWINGS IN THIS BOOK WILL MAKE EVERY ATTEMPT TO SHOW DIMENSIONS PER STANDARDS.

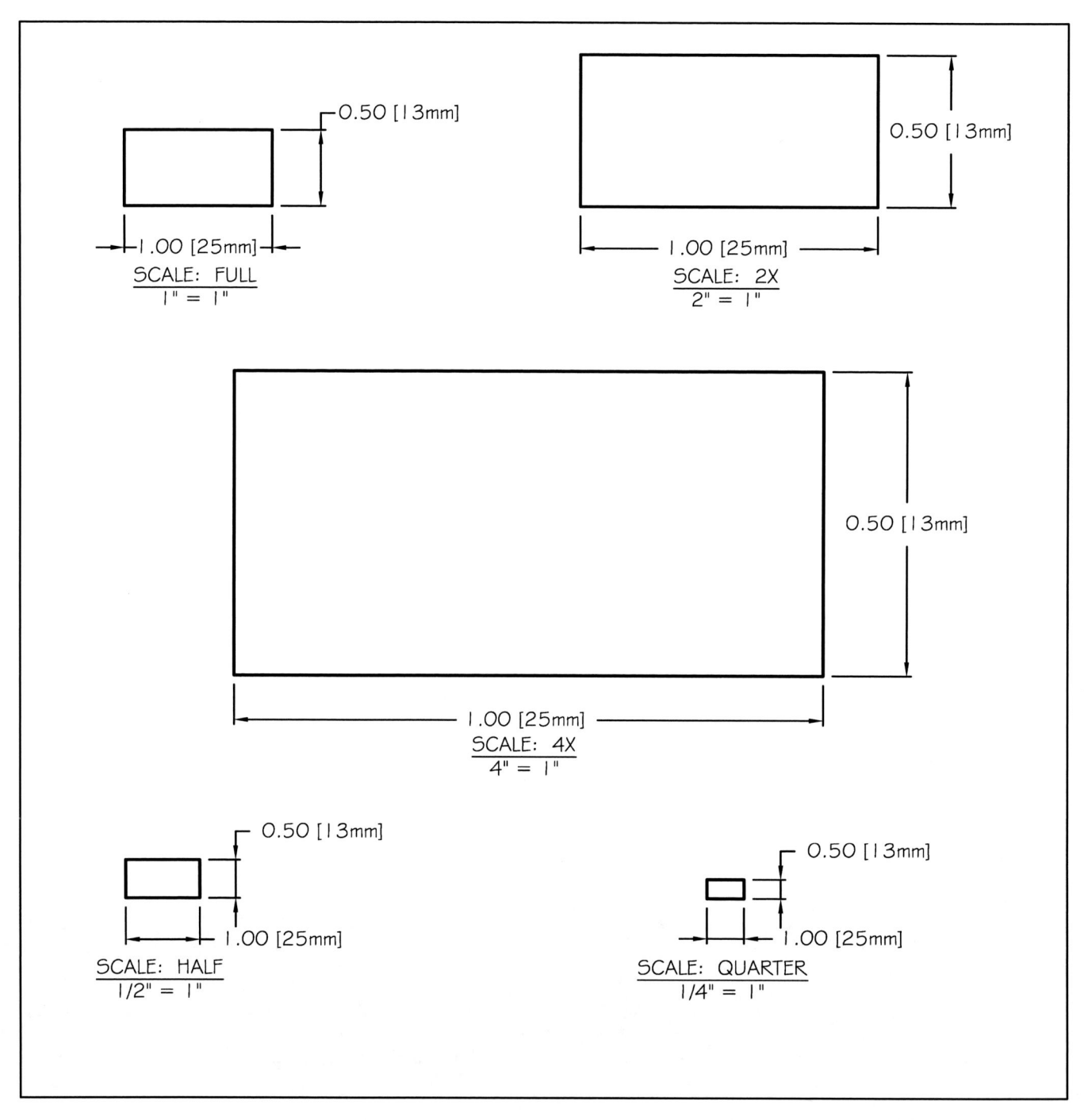

LESSON 7.02
DIMENSIONING & ANNOTATION

NOTE:
IN MECHANICAL OR MACHINE DRAWINGS, DIMENSION LINES ARE TERMINATED WITH ARROW HEADS POINTING TO THE EXTENTS OF THE DIMENSION OR FEATURE. OTHER DIMENSION TERMINATIONS ARE ACCEPTABLE GIVEN THE SPACE & DISCIPLINE. IN ARCHITECTURAL DRAWINGS, TICK MARKS ON THE DIMENSION LINES DEFINE THE EXTENTS.

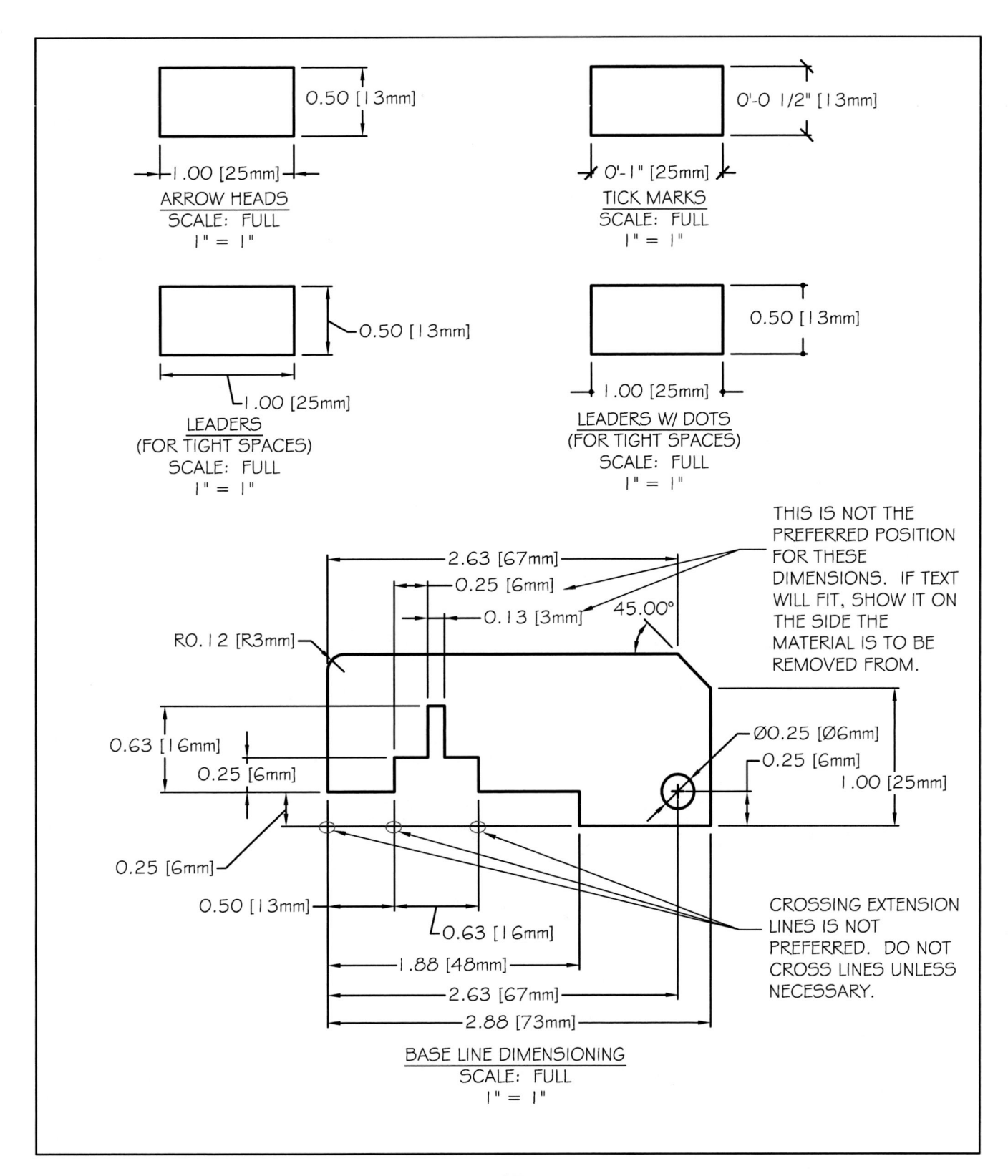

LESSON 7.03
DIMENSIONING & ANNOTATION

NOTE:
THERE ARE 4 BASIC TYPES OF DIMENSIONING THAT ARE USED: BASELINE, CHAIN, GEOMETRIC, & ORDINATE. SEE THE FOLLOWING SAMPLES OF EACH TYPE. EACH HAVE THEIR BENEFITS, EACH HAS ITS PLACE.

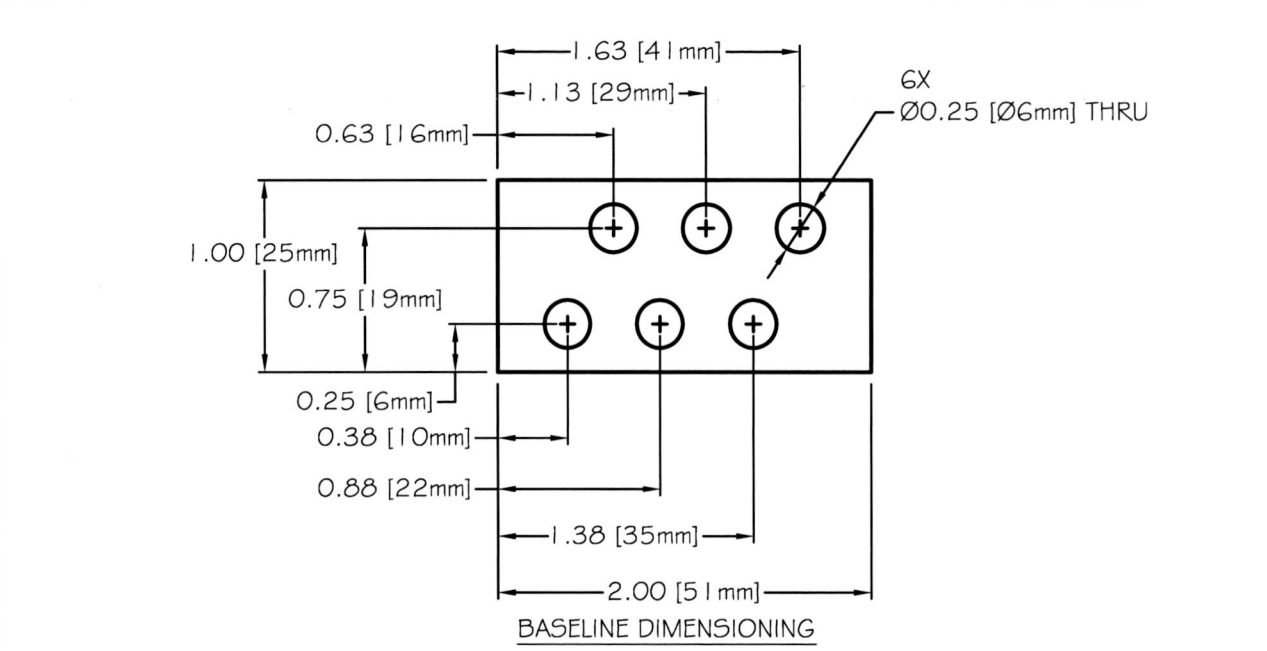

BASELINE DIMENSIONING

THIS STYLE OF DIMENSIONING USES A BASE POINT. ALL OF THE DIMENSIONS START FROM THIS POINT & EVERY FEATURE IS DIMENSIONED FROM THAT POINT.
BENEFIT: EASY TO SET UP PART FOR MACHINING & CHECKING.
DRAW BACK: DIFFICULT TO CONTROL DIMENSIONS & TOLERANCE BUILD UP BETWEEN FEATURES.

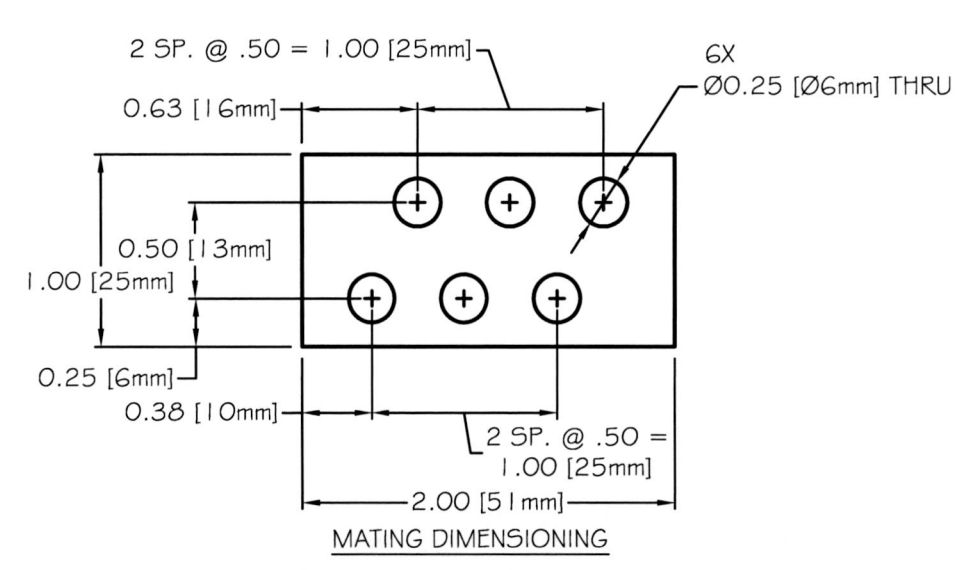

MATING DIMENSIONING

THIS STYLE OF DIMENSIONING USES A LOCATING DIMENSION TO START. THEN FEATURES THAT MATE TO OTHER PARTS ARE DIMENSIONED AS A PATTERN.
BENEFIT: EASY TO CONTROL DIMENSIONS & TOLERANCE BUILD UP BETWEEN FEATURES.
DRAW BACK: CAN TAKE LONGER TO DO.

LESSON 7.04
DIMENSIONING & ANNOTATION

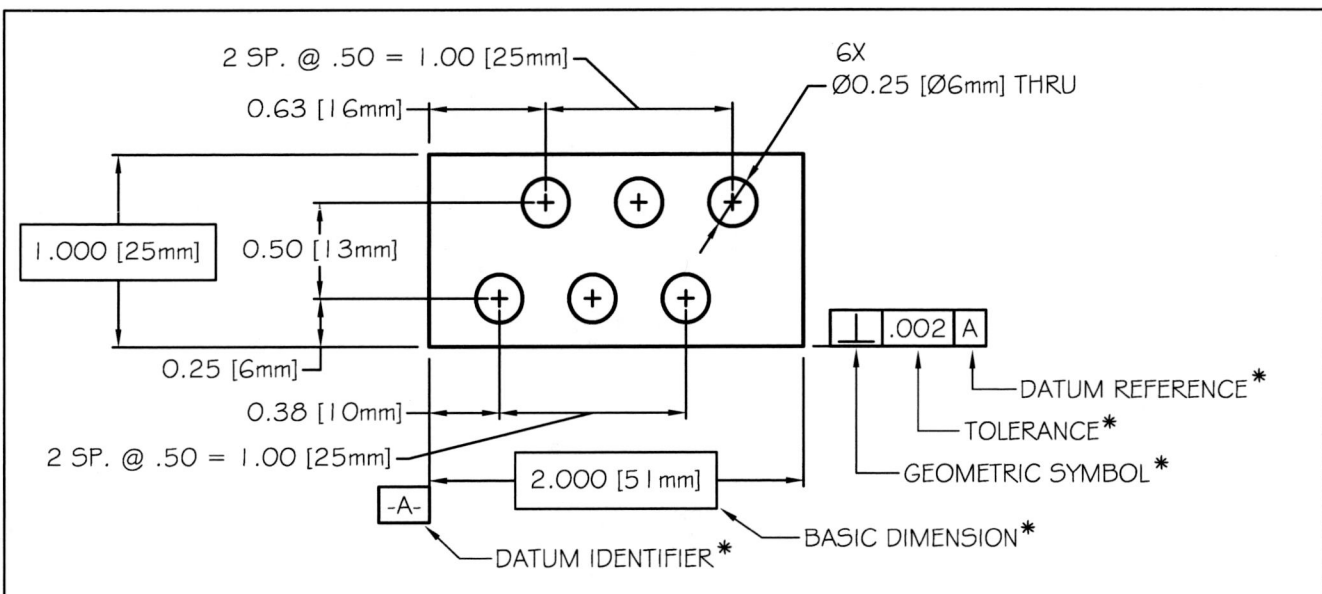

GEOMETRIC DIMENSIONING & TOLERANCING

THIS STYLE OF DIMENSIONING IS USED MOSTLY IN MANUFACTURING & MACHINING ENVIRONMENTS. IT IS BASED ON THEORETICALLY PERFECT FORMS OF VARIOUS SHAPES. THE BASIC DIMENSION IS IN THE BOX & IT INDICATES THAT THIS DIMENSION MUST BE EXACT. THIS DIMENSION REPRESENTS THE THEORETICALLY "PERFECT" DIMENSION & ASSUMES THERE IS ZERO TOLERANCE BETWEEN THE FEATURES THAT HAVE A BASIC DIMENSION. THIS SUBJECT IS COMPLEX; THERE ARE MANY BOOKS & CLASSES JUST ON THIS SUBJECT. THIS INFORMATION IS JUST A BRIEF INTRODUCTION. SEE THE REFERENCE SECTION OF THIS BOOK.

BENEFIT: CLEARLY DEFINES FOR THE MACHINIST & QUALITY ASSURANCE CHECKER WHAT THE IMPORTANT RELATIONSHIPS ARE.

DRAW BACK: CAN BECOME COMPLEX. NOT EVERYONE IN EVERY ENGINEERING GROUP OR MACHINE SHOP UNDERSTANDS THIS TYPE OF DIMENSIONING.

GEOMETRIC DIMENSIONING & TOLERANCING SYMBOLS

LOCATION		ORIENTATION		FORM		PROFILE	
⊕	TRUE POSITION	∠	ANGULARITY	—	STRAIGHTNESS	⌒	PROFILE OF A LINE
◎	CONCENTRICITY	⊥	PERPENDICULARY	⟋	FLATNESS	⌓	PROFILE OF A SURFACE
		∥	PARALLELISM	○	ROUNDNESS		RUNOUT
DATUM				⌭	CYLINDRICITY	↗	RUNOUT
-A-	DATUM	BASIC					
		1.00	BASIC DIMENSION			↗↗	TOTAL RUNOUT

* DATUM IDENTIFIER: THIS IS A REFERENCE PLANE, FACE, OR SURFACE.
  BASIC DIMENSION: THEORETICALLY PERFECT DIMENSION.
  GEOMETRIC SYMBOL: THIS SYMBOL INDICATES A PERPENDICULAR CONDITION.
  TOLERANCE: THIS IS THE AMOUNT THAT THE DIMENSION CAN VARY & STILL FIT PROPERLY.
  DATUM REFERENCE: THIS LETTER INDICATES WHICH SURFACE OR FEATURE IT IS RELATED WITH OR APPLIED TO.

LESSON 7.05
DIMENSIONING & ANNOTATION

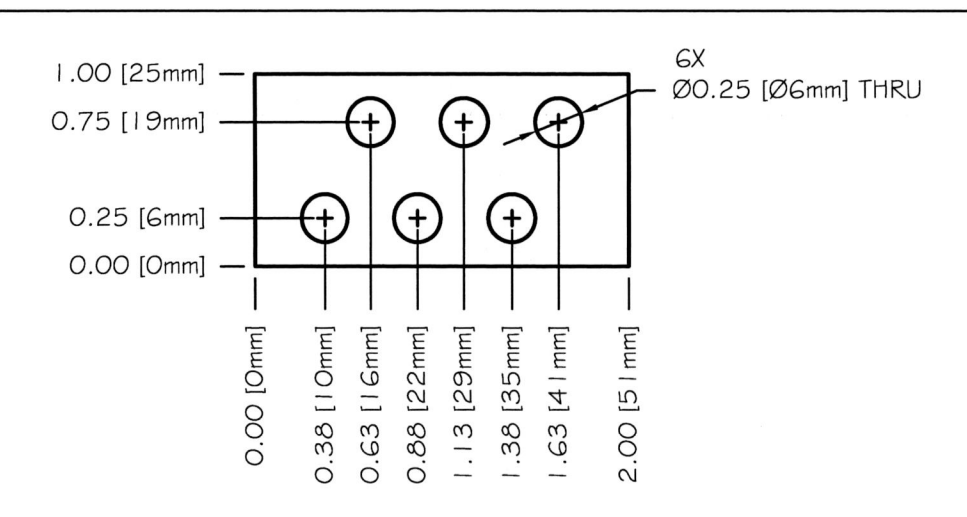

ORDINATE DIMENSIONING

THIS STYLE OF DIMENSIONING USES A BASE POINT. ALL OF THE DIMENSIONS START FROM THIS POINT & EVERY FEATURE IS DIMENSIONED FROM THAT POINT. USED PRIMARILY IN PANEL LAYOUTS & OTHER PERFORATED PARTS.

BENEFIT: EASY TO SET UP PART FOR PUNCHING & CHECKING.

DRAW BACK: DIFFICULT TO CONTROL DIMENSIONS & TOLERANCE BUILD UP BETWEEN FEATURES.

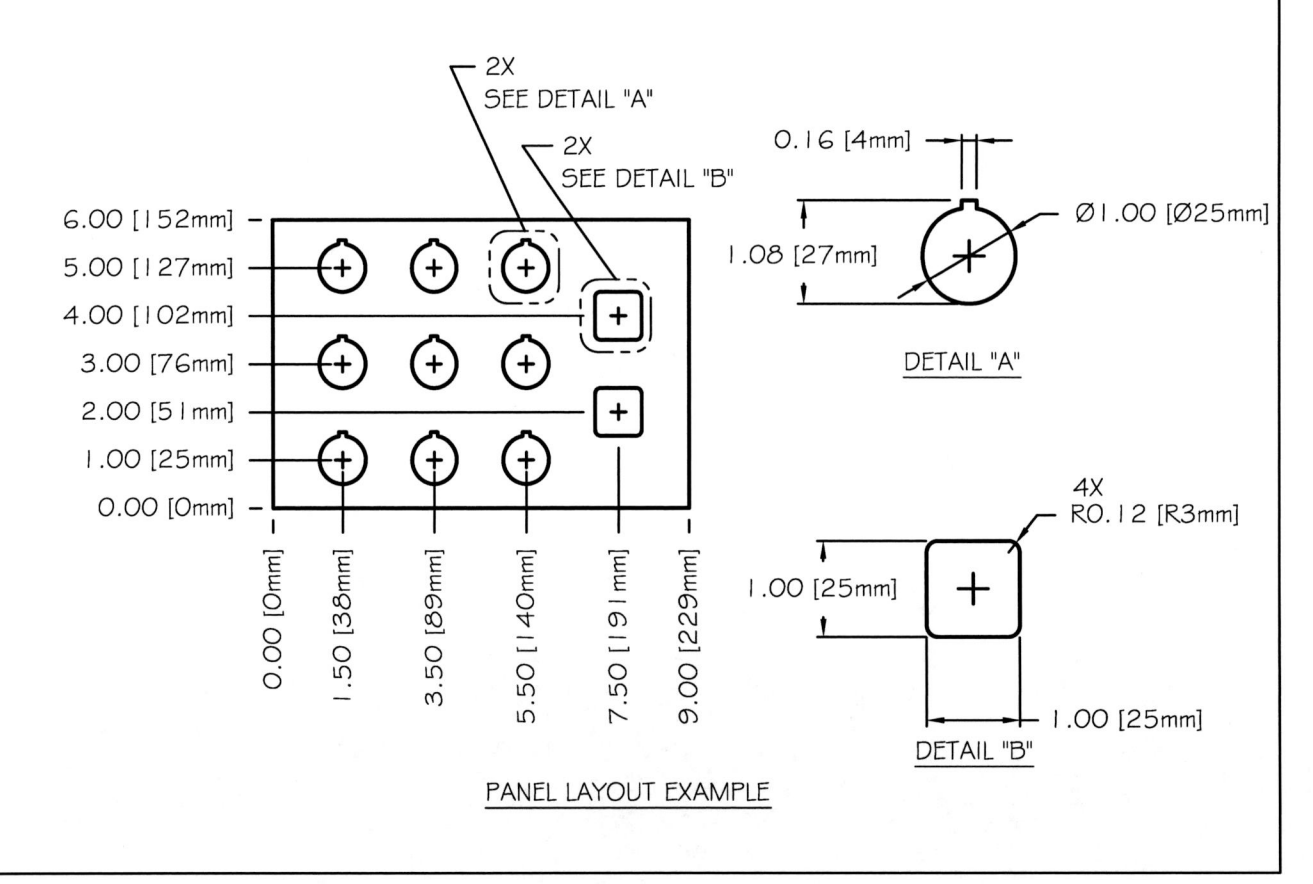

LESSON 7.06
DIMENSIONING & ANNOTATION

NOTE:
DIMENSIONING TOLERANCE CAN BE A SIMPLE MATTER. PART OF THE COMPLEXITY COMES FROM THE UNKNOWN. THAT IS, IT IS IMPORTANT TO UNDERSTAND SOME OF THE MECHANICS OF WHAT YOU ARE DESIGNING. THERE ARE DIFFERENT LEVELS OF TOLERANCE FOR EVERY TYPE OF WORK. A MACHINED PART WILL BE HELD TO A MUCH TIGHTER OR SMALLER TOLERANCE ALLOWANCE THAN A HOUSE. BOTH HAVE STANDARD WORKING TOLERANCES THAT ARE ACCEPTABLE TO THE FINAL PRODUCT.

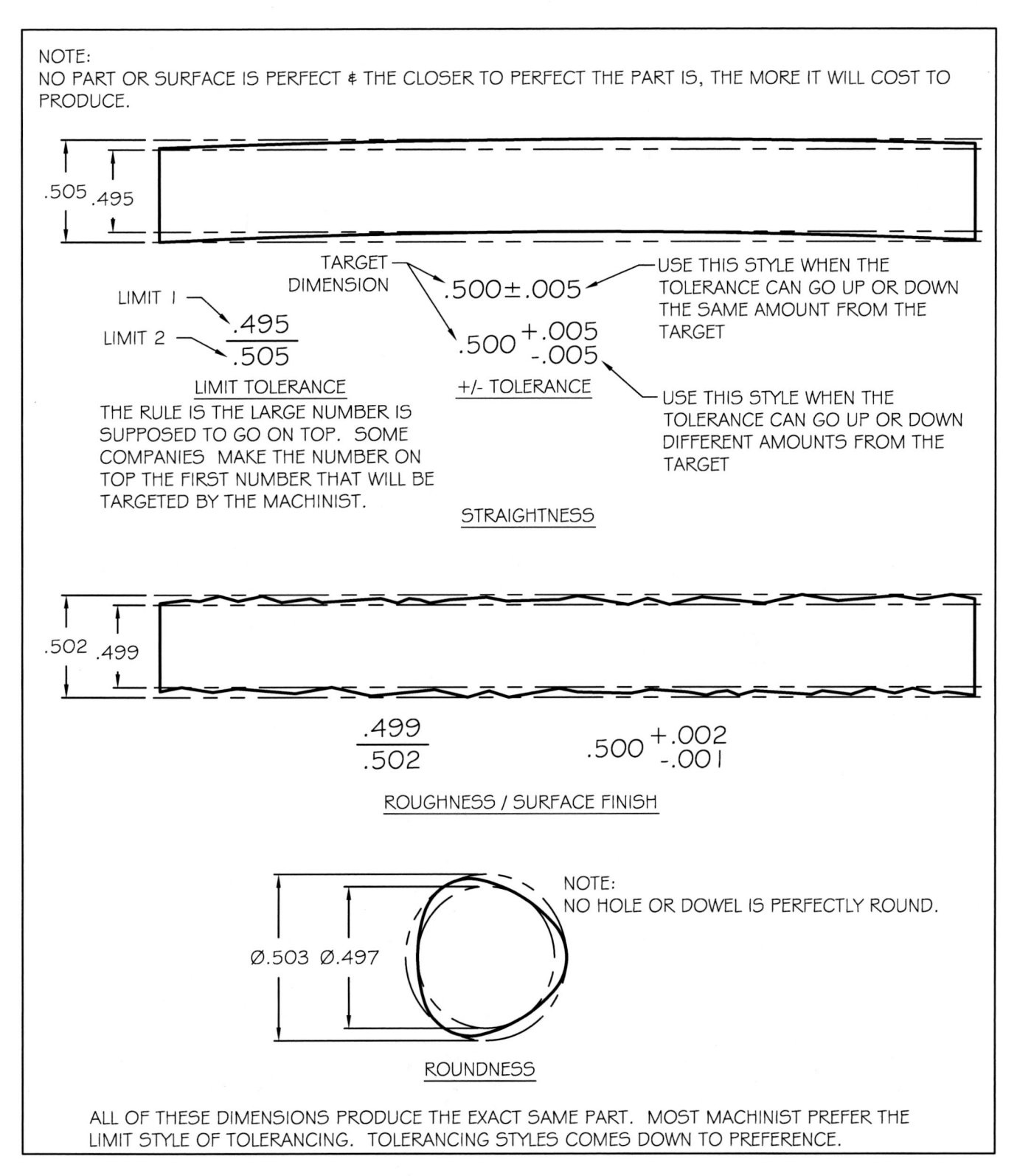

NOTE:
NO PART OR SURFACE IS PERFECT & THE CLOSER TO PERFECT THE PART IS, THE MORE IT WILL COST TO PRODUCE.

.505 .495

LIMIT 1 — .495
LIMIT 2 — .505

TARGET DIMENSION → .500±.005 ← USE THIS STYLE WHEN THE TOLERANCE CAN GO UP OR DOWN THE SAME AMOUNT FROM THE TARGET

.500 +.005 / -.005

LIMIT TOLERANCE
THE RULE IS THE LARGE NUMBER IS SUPPOSED TO GO ON TOP. SOME COMPANIES MAKE THE NUMBER ON TOP THE FIRST NUMBER THAT WILL BE TARGETED BY THE MACHINIST.

+/- TOLERANCE

USE THIS STYLE WHEN THE TOLERANCE CAN GO UP OR DOWN DIFFERENT AMOUNTS FROM THE TARGET

STRAIGHTNESS

.502 .499

.499 / .502

.500 +.002 / -.001

ROUGHNESS / SURFACE FINISH

Ø.503 Ø.497

NOTE:
NO HOLE OR DOWEL IS PERFECTLY ROUND.

ROUNDNESS

ALL OF THESE DIMENSIONS PRODUCE THE EXACT SAME PART. MOST MACHINIST PREFER THE LIMIT STYLE OF TOLERANCING. TOLERANCING STYLES COMES DOWN TO PREFERENCE.

LESSON 7.07
DIMENSIONING & ANNOTATION

NOTE:
DIMENSIONING BETWEEN FEATURES WITH A WORKABLE TOLERANCE IS IMPORTANT TO ALL MANUFACTURED PARTS. BEING ABLE TO TAKE A FENDER OFF OF ONE 1993 FORD ESCORT & HAVE IT FIT ON TO ANY OTHER 1993 FORD ESCORT IS IMPORTANT. THE BODY & HOLES SHOULD ALL MATCH WITHOUT DIFFICULTY. THIS IS THE BEAUTY OF MASS PRODUCTION & PROPER TOLERANCING OF PARTS.

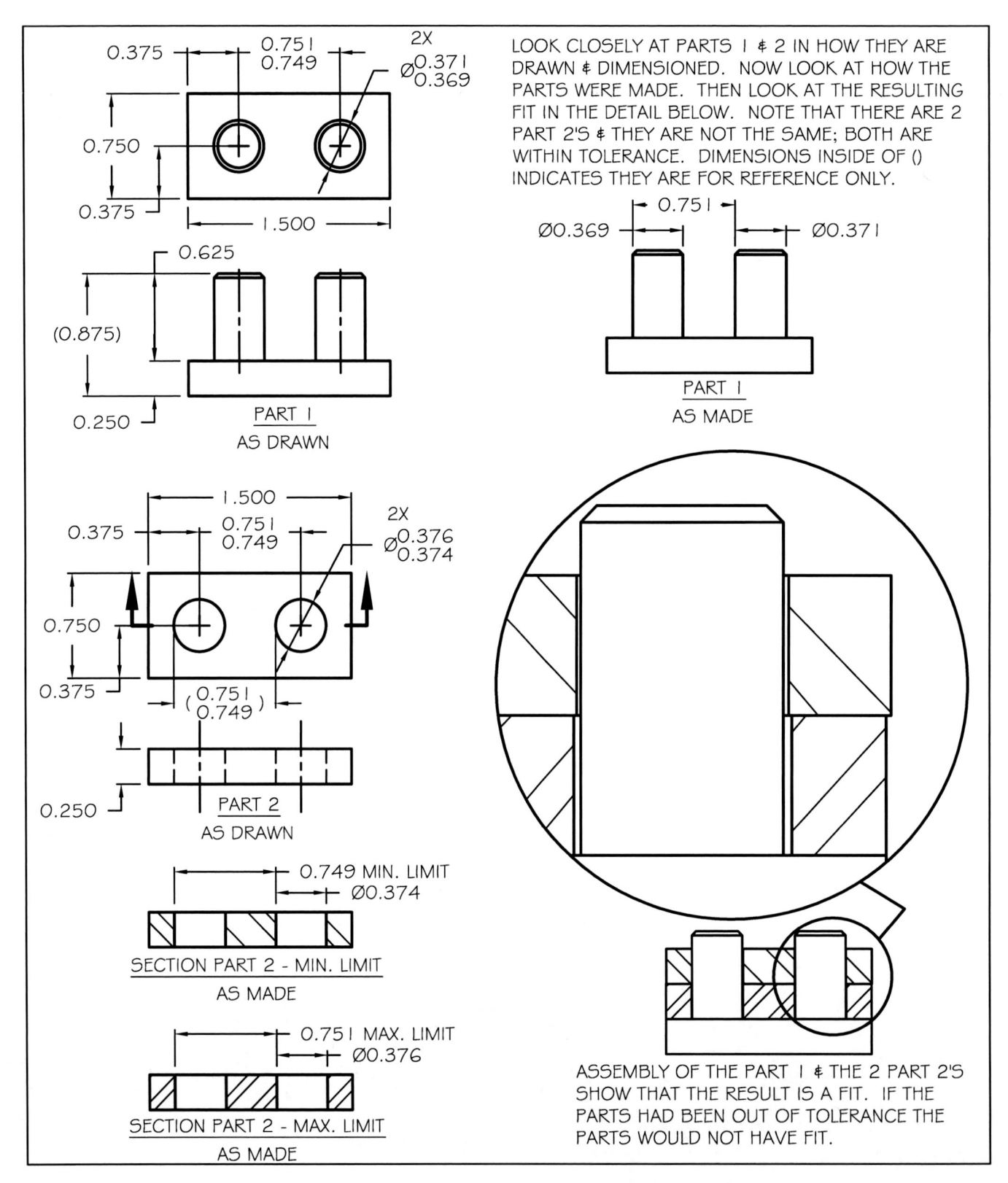

LOOK CLOSELY AT PARTS 1 & 2 IN HOW THEY ARE DRAWN & DIMENSIONED. NOW LOOK AT HOW THE PARTS WERE MADE. THEN LOOK AT THE RESULTING FIT IN THE DETAIL BELOW. NOTE THAT THERE ARE 2 PART 2'S & THEY ARE NOT THE SAME; BOTH ARE WITHIN TOLERANCE. DIMENSIONS INSIDE OF () INDICATES THEY ARE FOR REFERENCE ONLY.

PART 1
AS DRAWN

PART 1
AS MADE

PART 2
AS DRAWN

SECTION PART 2 - MIN. LIMIT
AS MADE

SECTION PART 2 - MAX. LIMIT
AS MADE

ASSEMBLY OF THE PART 1 & THE 2 PART 2'S SHOW THAT THE RESULT IS A FIT. IF THE PARTS HAD BEEN OUT OF TOLERANCE THE PARTS WOULD NOT HAVE FIT.

LESSON 7.08
DIMENSIONING & ANNOTATION

INSTRUCTIONS:
REPRODUCE THE FOLLOWING DRAWINGS & DIMENSION FULLY. DRAW THEM AT THE SCALE INDICATED BY EACH DRAWING. USE 2 PLACE DECIMAL INCHES. SEE FRACTIONAL INCH TO DECIMAL INCH CHART IN THE REFERENCE SECTION. SEE SOLUTIONS SECTION OF THE BOOK FOR ANSWERS.

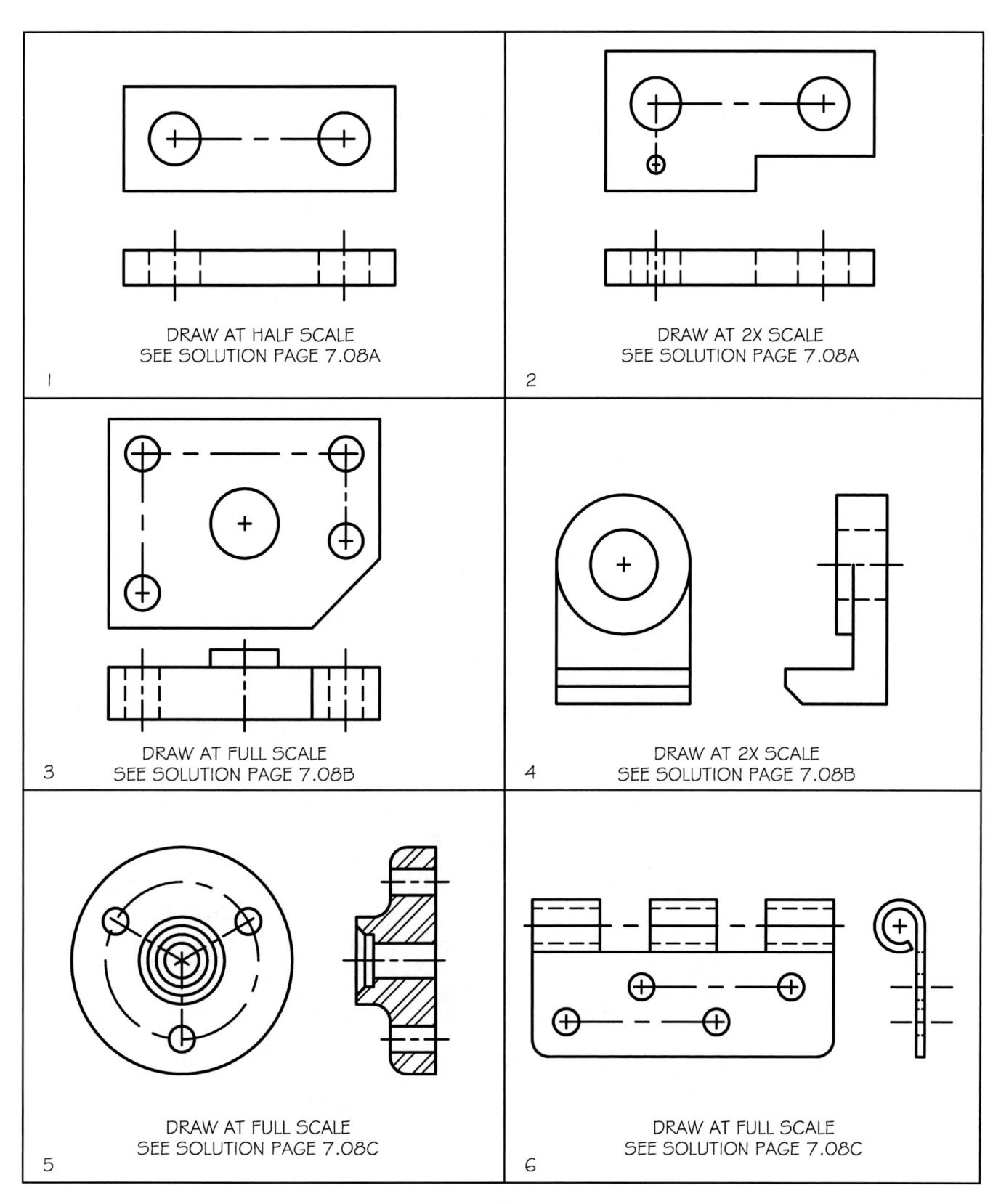

1

DRAW AT HALF SCALE
SEE SOLUTION PAGE 7.08A

2

DRAW AT 2X SCALE
SEE SOLUTION PAGE 7.08A

3

DRAW AT FULL SCALE
SEE SOLUTION PAGE 7.08B

4

DRAW AT 2X SCALE
SEE SOLUTION PAGE 7.08B

5

DRAW AT FULL SCALE
SEE SOLUTION PAGE 7.08C

6

DRAW AT FULL SCALE
SEE SOLUTION PAGE 7.08C

LESSON 7.09
DIMENSIONING & ANNOTATION

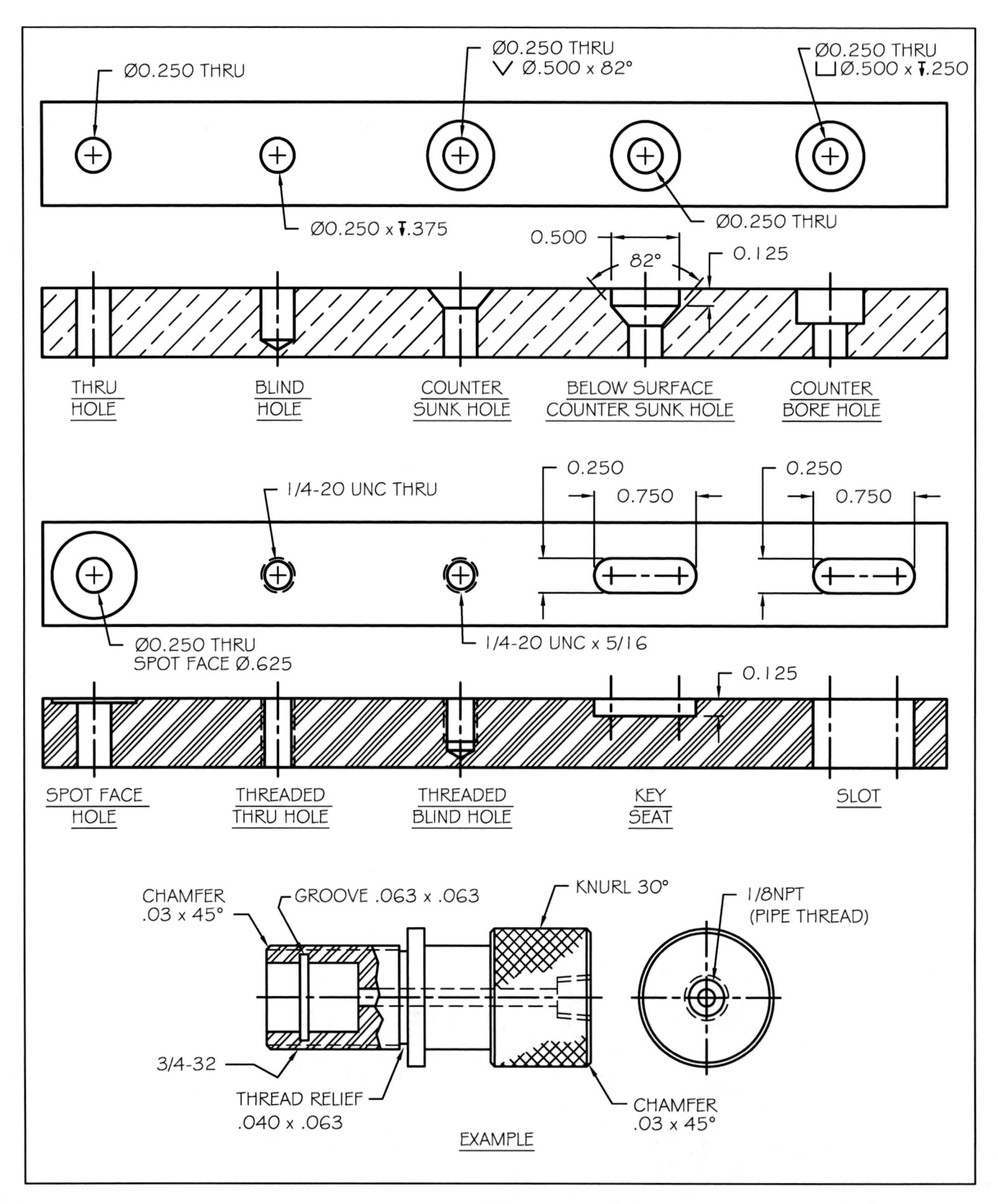

74

LESSON 7.10
DIMENSIONING & ANNOTATION

NOTE:
BELOW ARE SOME SPECIALIZED DIMENSIONING SITUATIONS. DIMENSIONING & SECTIONING SHOWN FOR EACH ITEM.

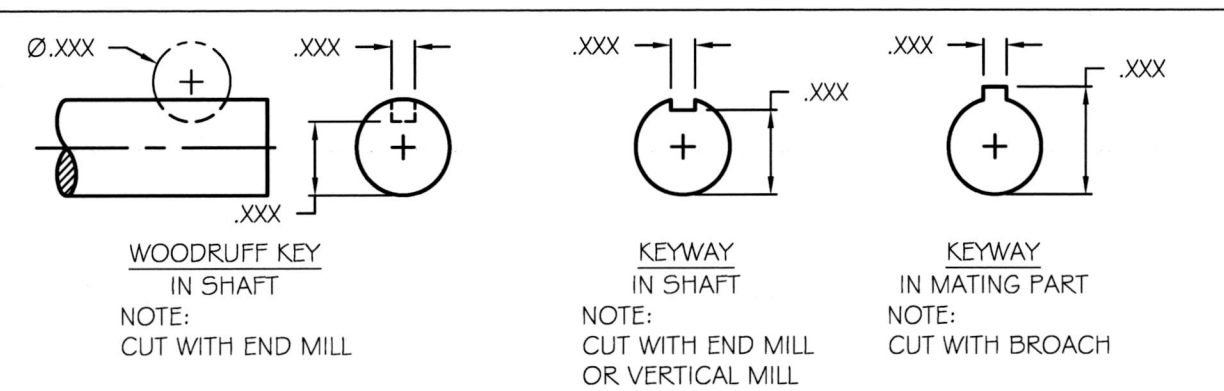

WOODRUFF KEY
IN SHAFT
NOTE:
CUT WITH END MILL

KEYWAY
IN SHAFT
NOTE:
CUT WITH END MILL
OR VERTICAL MILL

KEYWAY
IN MATING PART
NOTE:
CUT WITH BROACH

KEYS & KEYWAYS
THE BEST WAY TO ACQUIRE THE PROPER DIMENSIONS FOR A KEYWAY IS TO GET IT OUT OF A MACHINIST HANDBOOK OR GUIDE. SEE THE REFERENCE SECTION FOR A LIST OF BOOKS. THE STANDARD KEY TYPES ARE WOODRUFF, STRAIGHT SQUARE, STRAIGHT RECTANGLE, & TAPER.

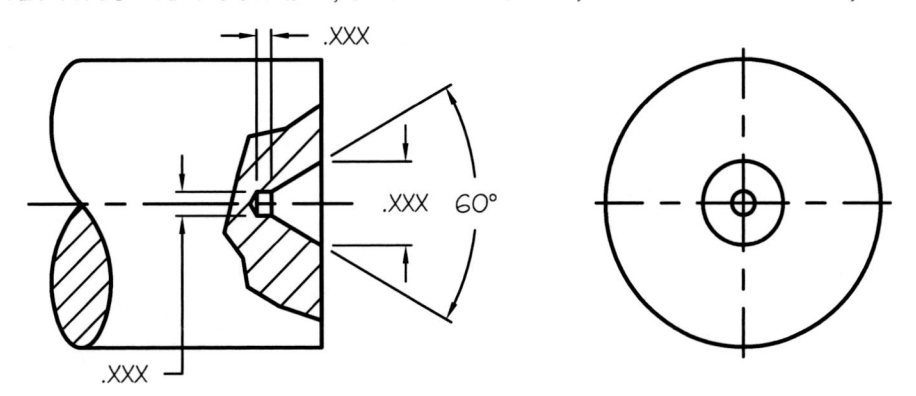

MACHINE OR LATHE CENTER
THE SIZE OF THE ITEM DETERMINES THE DIMENSIONS USED. THE BEST WAY TO ACQUIRE THE PROPER DIMENSIONS FOR A MACHINE CENTER IS TO REFER TO A MACHINIST HANDBOOK OR GUIDE. SEE THE REFERENCE SECTION FOR A LIST OF BOOKS.

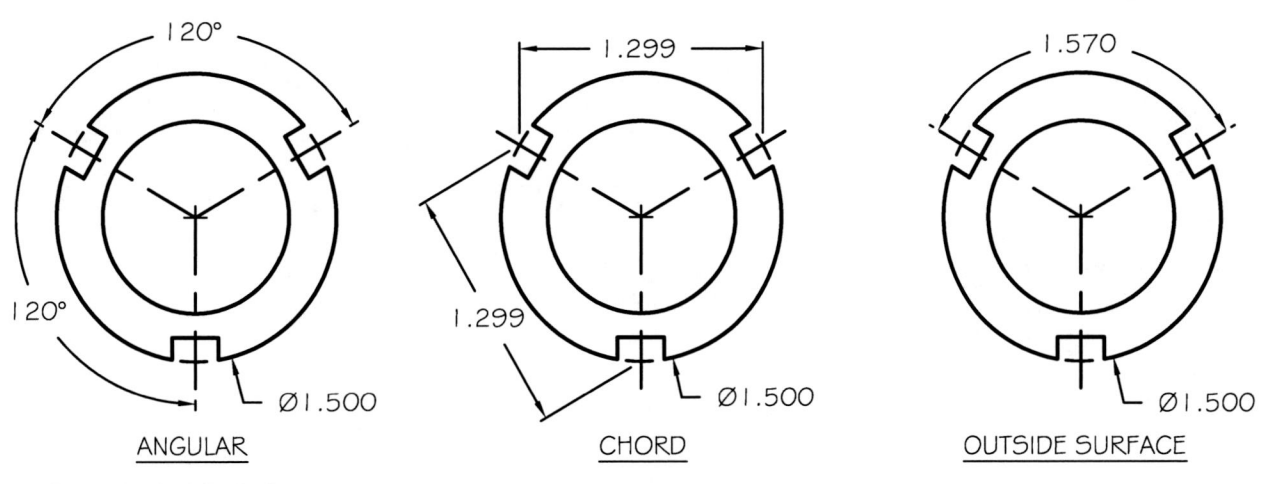

ANGULAR

CHORD

OUTSIDE SURFACE

CURVED SURFACES
ANY OF THESE METHODS ARE ACCEPTABLE FOR LOCATING FEATURES ON A CURVED SURFACE.

LESSON 7.11
DIMENSIONING & ANNOTATION

NOTE:
BELOW ARE SOME SPECIALIZED ANNOTATIONS.

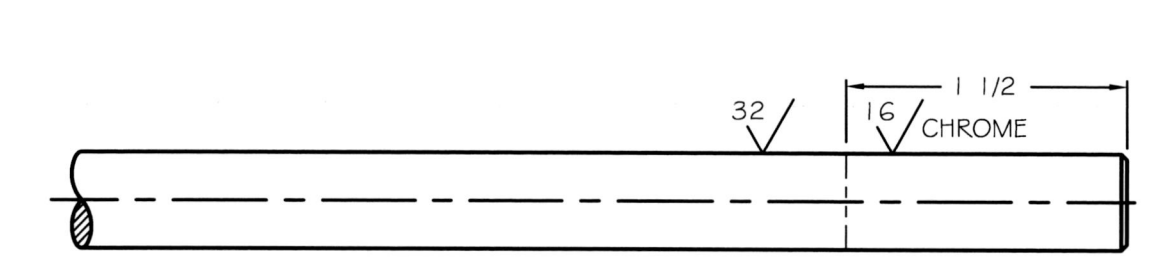

SURFACE FINISH   SPECIAL OPERATION

SURFACE FINISHES & SPECIAL SURFACE OPERATIONS
SURFACE FINISHES RELATE TO THE SURFACE OF AN ITEM OR A SPECIFIC FEATURE OF A PART.
SURFACE WAVINESS & ROUGHNESS IS MEASURED IN MICROINCHES; A MICROINCH IS ONE-MILLIONTH
OF AN INCH. THE NUMBER INDICATES HOW MANY MICROINCHES THE SURFACE CAN VARY EITHER IN
WAVINESS OR ROUGHNESS. THE SYSTEM OF SYMBOLS HAS BEEN DEVELOPED BY THE AMERICAN
SOCIETY OF MECHANICAL ENGINEERS (ASME). THE SYMBOLS ARE IN ANSI Y14.36. SEE THE
REFERENCE SECTION FOR MORE INFORMATION.

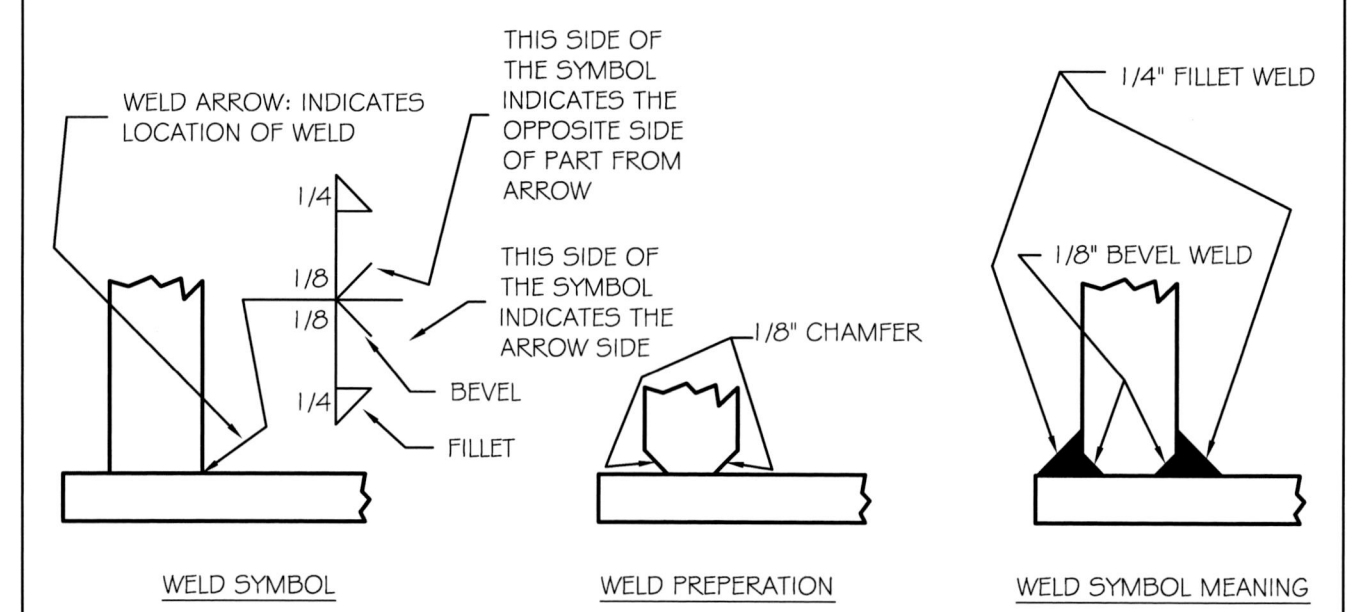

WELD SYMBOL   WELD PREPERATION   WELD SYMBOL MEANING

WELDING SYMBOLS
WELDING IS AN IMPORTANT PART OF ENGINEERING & MANUFACTURING. THE SYSTEM OF SYMBOLS
HAS BEEN DEVELOPED BY THE AMERICAN WELDING SOCIETY (AWS). SEE THE REFERENCE SECTION
FOR MORE INFORMATION.

LESSON 8.00
ALLOWANCE, TOLERANCE & FIT

NOTE:
THIS LESSON IS AN INTRODUCTION TO SOME TOLERANCING TERMS & CONCEPTS. FACTORS THAT AFFECT FITS ARE TYPE OF USE, TEMPERATURE, SIZE OF PART, AMOUNT OF ENGAGEMENT, MATERIALS, STRESS, & OTHER FACTORS. FOR A COMPLETE & THOROUGH UNDERSTANDING, OTHER BOOKS WILL NEED TO BE REFERENCED. THE STANDARD REFERENCE GUIDE IS MACHINERY'S HANDBOOK BY INDUSTRIAL PRESS INC. & ANSI STANDARDS. SEE REFERENCE SECTION FOR MORE INFORMATION.

DEFINITIONS:
FIT: THE AMOUNT OF SPACE BETWEEN 2 OR MORE PARTS. THERE ARE SEVERAL TYPES & CLASSES. SEE BELOW.

NOMINAL SIZE: THIS IS USED FOR IDENTIFICATION ONLY. EXAMPLE: 2" PIPE IS NOT EXACTLY 2" IN DIAMETER.

ALLOWANCE: THE SPACE LEFT BETWEEN PARTS AT MAXIMUM MATERIAL CONDITION (MMC). SOME EXAMPLES OF MMC ARE: A SHAFT WOULD BE MADE TO THE LARGEST ACCEPTABLE DIMENSION. A HOLE WOULD BE MADE TO THE SMALLEST ACCEPTABLE DIMENSION.

TOLERANCE: THE AMOUNT A FINISHED PART MAY VARY. EXAMPLE: 1.000±.010 STATES THAT THE FINISHED PART SHOULD BE 1.000; HOWEVER, IF IT IS MADE AT 1.010 OR 0.990, IT WILL STILL WORK.

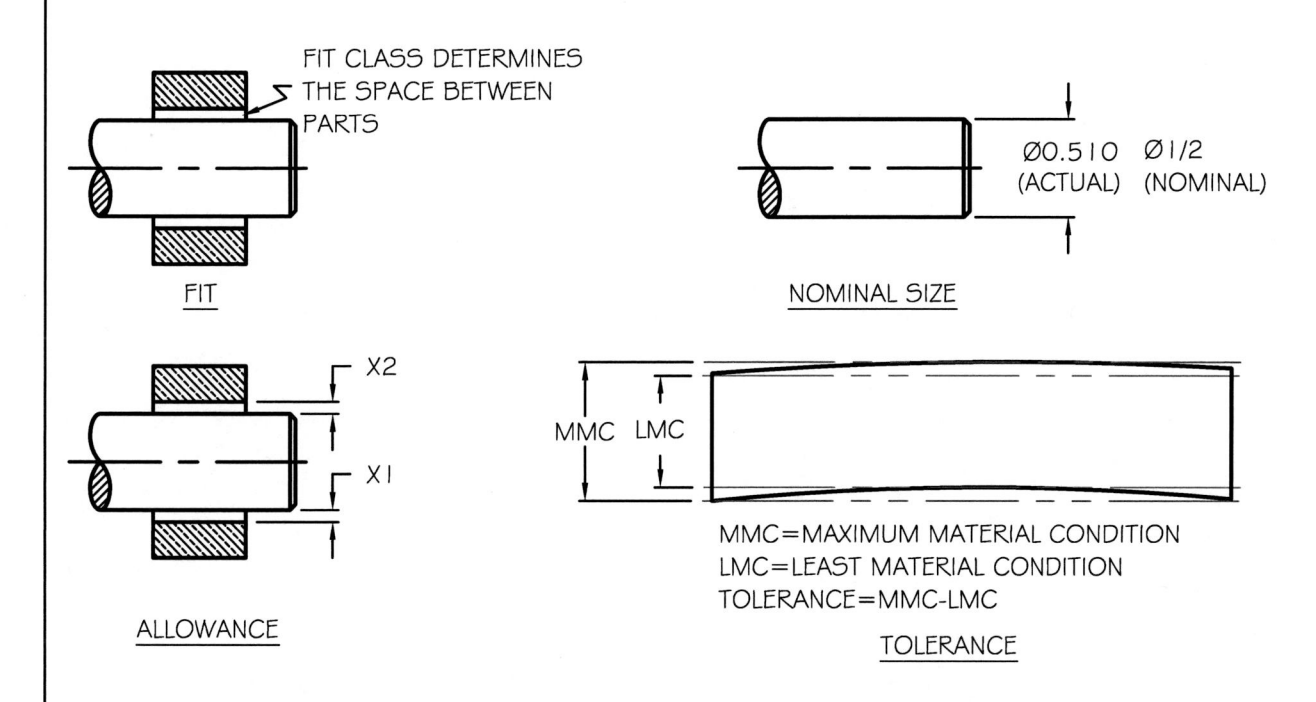

FIT CLASS DETERMINES THE SPACE BETWEEN PARTS

FIT

Ø0.510 (ACTUAL)   Ø1/2 (NOMINAL)

NOMINAL SIZE

X2

X1

ALLOWANCE

MMC LMC

MMC=MAXIMUM MATERIAL CONDITION
LMC=LEAST MATERIAL CONDITION
TOLERANCE=MMC-LMC

TOLERANCE

ANSI STANDARD FITS OR CLASSES: THE LARGER NUMBER INDICATES MORE ALLOWANCE.
RC1 THRU RC9: RUNNING OR CLEARANCE FIT. USED FOR SLIDING OR ROTATING PARTS.

LC1 THRU LC11: LOCATIONAL CLEARANCE FIT. USED FOR PARTS THAT ARE PRIMARILY STATIONARY BUT MAY BE DISASSEMBLED.

LT1 THRU LT6: TRANSITION CLEARANCE OR INTERFERENCE FIT. AN INTERMEDIATE CLASS BETWEEN LC & LN INCLUDE BOTH CLEARANCE & INTERFERENCE.

LN1 THRU LN3: LOCATIONAL INTERFERENCE FIT. USE WHEN LOCATION IS THE PRIMARY CONSIDERATION.

FN1 THRU FN5: FORCE FITS. USED FOR PERMANENT ASSEMBLIES. ASSEMBLIES MAY REQUIRE DRIVING, PRESSING, SHRINKAGE, OR EXPANSION.

LESSON 9.00
SURFACE TEXTURE

NOTE:
SURFACE TEXTURE DESCRIBES THE ACTUAL SURFACE FINISH. TEXTURES CAN BE CALLED OUT BY A SYSTEM OF SYMBOLS AS NOTED IN ANSI Y14.36. THIS LESSON IS A BASIC OVERVIEW. THE TYPES & COMBINATIONS SEEMS ENDLESS. SEE THE REFERENCE SECTION FOR MORE INFORMATION.

SURFACE TEXTURE IS MEASURED IN MICROINCHES (μin) OR MICROMETERS (μm). A MICROINCH IS ONE MILLIONTH OF AN INCH. ONE MICROMETER IS ONE MILLIONTH OF A METER. 1 μin = .0254μm.

TEXTURE IS ROUGHNESS, WAVINESS, & LAY.

ROUGHNESS IS THE FINE PITCHES OF PEAKS & VALLEYS THAT MAKE A SURFACE.

WAVINESS IS THE LARGER SPACED PEAKS & VALLEYS THAT MAKE A SURFACE.

LAY IS THE DIRECTION OR CONTOUR OF THE PEAKS & VALLEYS THAT MAKE UP A SURFACE.

THESE FEATURE CHARACTERISTICS ARE A DIRECT RESULT OF THE OPERATIONS OR TOOLS THAT PRODUCED THE PART. TORCH CUTTING, SAWING, MILLING, GRINDING, & POLISHING ALL PRODUCE SPECIFIC TOOL PATTERNS. THE SPEED OF THE CUTTING TOOL, THE FEED SPEED, THE MATERIAL, & OTHER VARIABLES WILL DETERMINE THE RESULTING SURFACE TEXTURE.

BASIC SURFACE TEXTURE SYMBOL. PRODUCED BY ANY METHOD.

MATERIAL REMOVAL BY MACHINING IS REQUIRED.

MATERIAL REMOVAL BY MACHINING IS REQUIRED. THE AMOUNT OF MATERIAL TO BE REMOVED IS SPECIFIED.

NO MATERIAL REMOVAL ALLOWED. SURFACE MUST BE PRODUCED BY OTHER METHODS SUCH AS CASTING.

COMPOSITE SYMBOL.

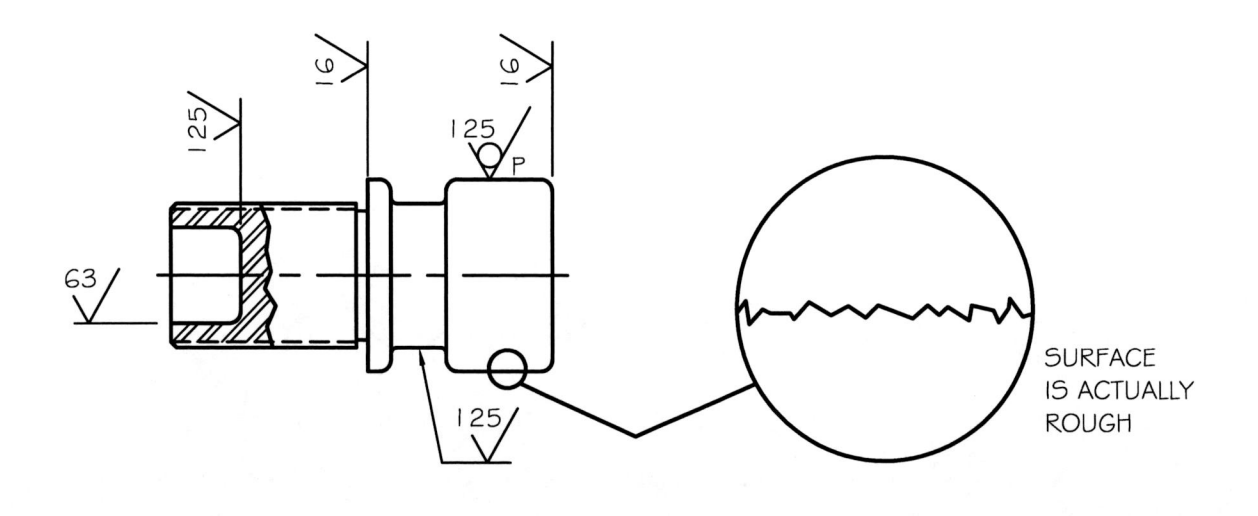

SURFACE IS ACTUALLY ROUGH

LESSON 10.00
THREADS & FASTENERS

NOTE:
THREADS WERE DISCOVERED LONG AGO. THE EGYPTIANS USED A TYPE OF SCREW TO PUMP WATER FROM THE NILE RIVER TO THE CROP FIELDS. THERE ARE SEVERAL TYPES OF THREADS, EACH HAS ITS STRONG POINTS FOR USE. EARLY THREADS WERE MADE BY HAND & WERE NOT STANDARD. TODAY METRIC & ENGLISH THREAD HAVE BOTH BEEN STANDARDIZED. CUSTOM THREADS CAN STILL BE DEVELOPED AS NON-STANDARD. THREADS ARE HELIX, SPIRAL, OR RAMP. THINK OF THREADS AS VERY EFFICIENT SIMPLE MACHINES.

THREADS CAN BE CREATED BY CUTTING, ROLLING, TAPPING, CASTING, & VARIOUS TYPES OF MOLDING. THREADS HAVE DIFFERENT CLASSES. THESE CLASSES VARY FROM LOOSE THREADS TO INTERFERENCE THREADS THAT ARE FOR PERMANENT ASSEMBLIES. FOR MORE INFORMATION ON SPECIFIC THREAD CLASSES, PLEASE REFER TO MACHINERY'S HANDBOOK; IT COVERS THIS SUBJECT THOROUGHLY.

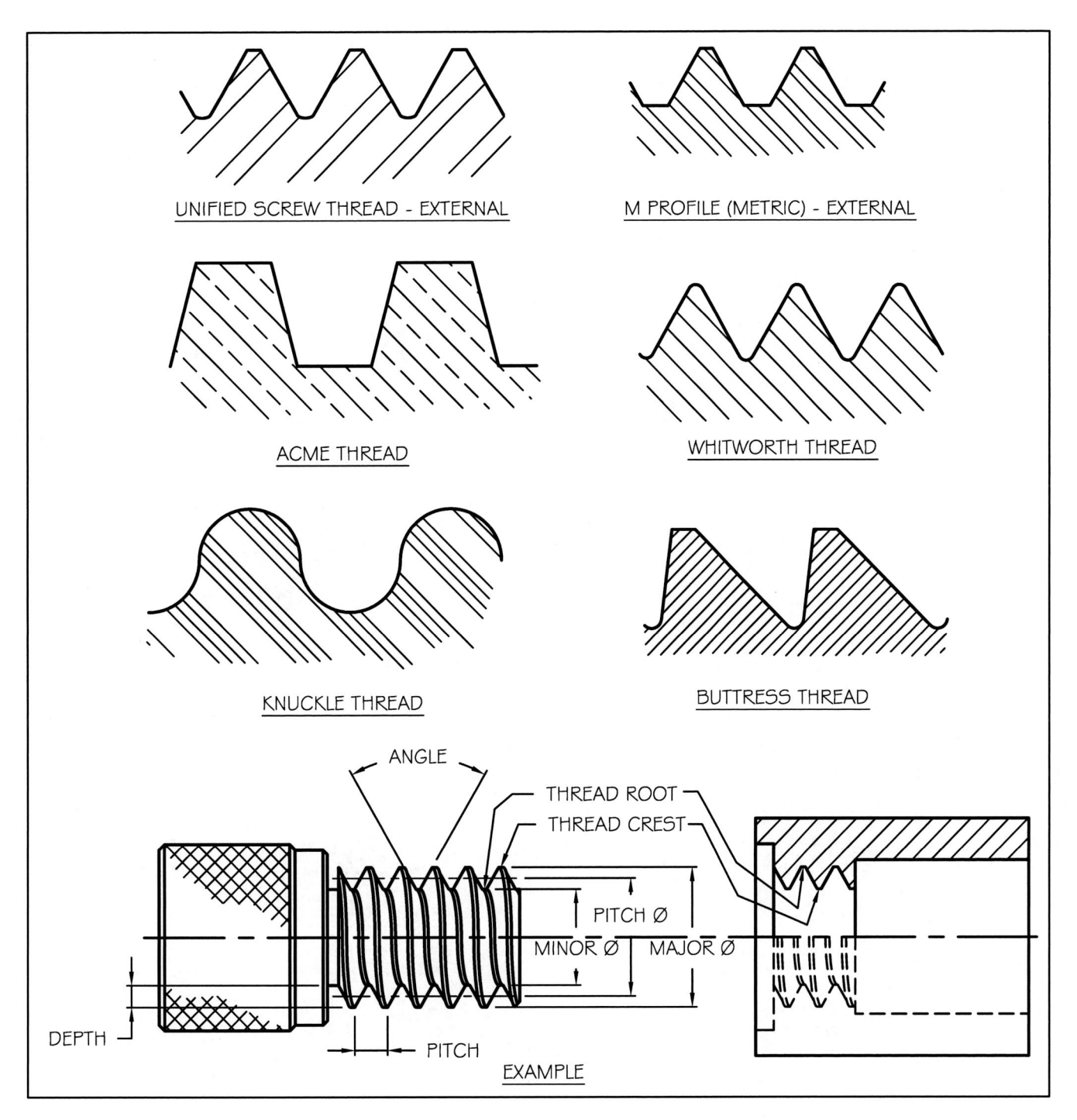

UNIFIED SCREW THREAD - EXTERNAL

M PROFILE (METRIC) - EXTERNAL

ACME THREAD

WHITWORTH THREAD

KNUCKLE THREAD

BUTTRESS THREAD

EXAMPLE

LESSON 10.01
THREADS & FASTENERS

NOTE:
INTRODUCTION TO THREADS. RIGHT & LEFT HAND THREADS. AMERICAN NATIONAL STANDARD (ANSI B1.7) UNIFIED SCREW THREADS & M PROFILE METRIC THREADS.

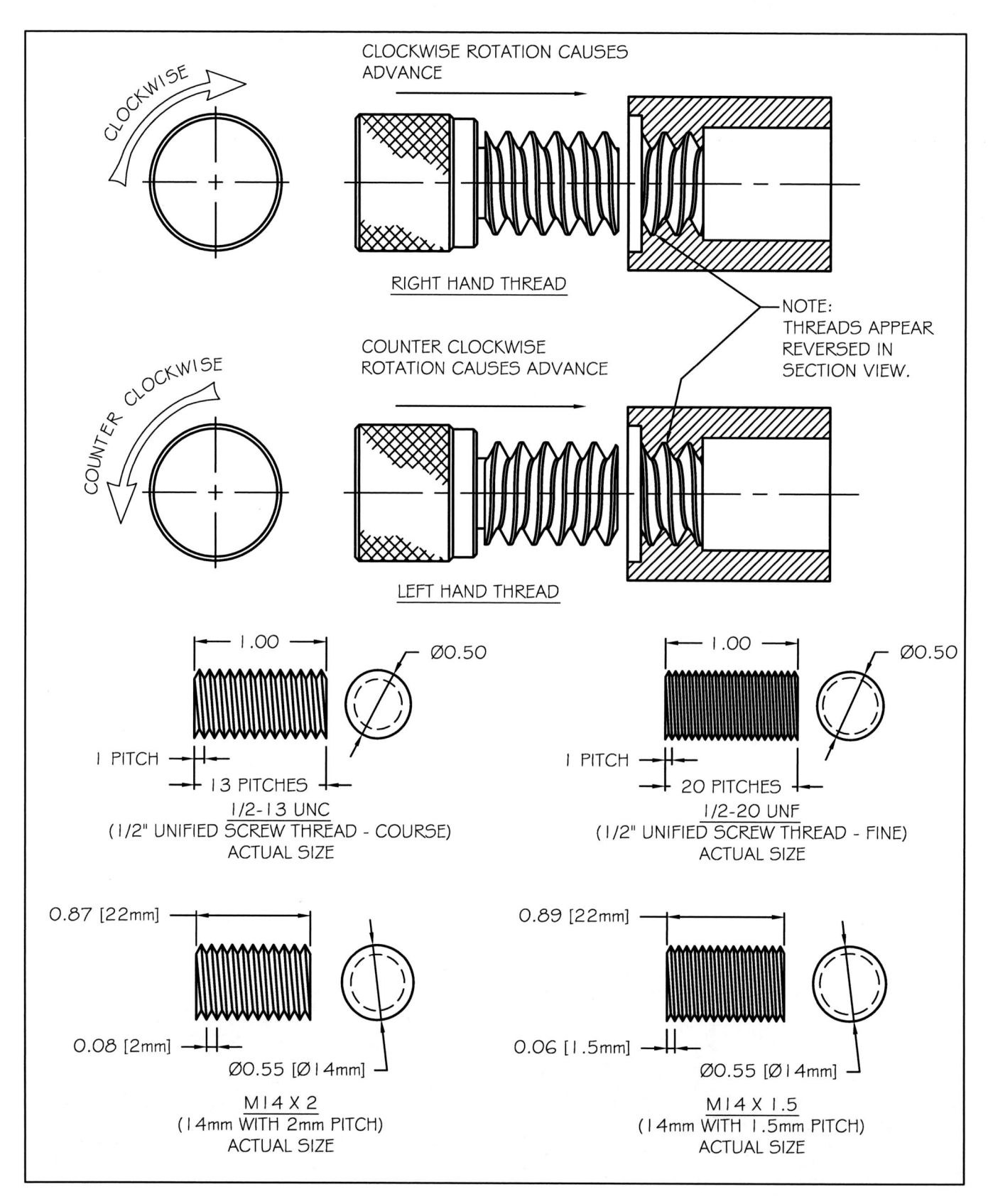

CLOCKWISE

CLOCKWISE ROTATION CAUSES ADVANCE

RIGHT HAND THREAD

NOTE:
THREADS APPEAR REVERSED IN SECTION VIEW.

COUNTER CLOCKWISE

COUNTER CLOCKWISE ROTATION CAUSES ADVANCE

LEFT HAND THREAD

1.00
Ø0.50
1 PITCH
13 PITCHES
1/2-13 UNC
(1/2" UNIFIED SCREW THREAD - COURSE)
ACTUAL SIZE

1.00
Ø0.50
1 PITCH
20 PITCHES
1/2-20 UNF
(1/2" UNIFIED SCREW THREAD - FINE)
ACTUAL SIZE

0.87 [22mm]
0.08 [2mm]
Ø0.55 [Ø14mm]
M14 X 2
(14mm WITH 2mm PITCH)
ACTUAL SIZE

0.89 [22mm]
0.06 [1.5mm]
Ø0.55 [Ø14mm]
M14 X 1.5
(14mm WITH 1.5mm PITCH)
ACTUAL SIZE

LESSON 10.02
THREADS & FASTENERS

NOTE:
DRAWING THREADS & THREAD REPRESENTATION. THREADS ARE A HELIX THAT IS FORMED AT A CONSTANT ANGLE. THIS HELIX IS A SPIRAL RAMP. BELOW ARE SOME STANDARD METHODS FOR SHOWING THREADS.

RIGHT HAND THREAD

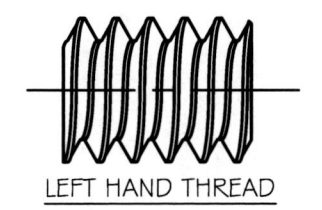

LEFT HAND THREAD

THESE 2 EXTERNAL THREADS ARE DRAWN IN A SLIGHTLY EXAGGERATED MANNER TO DEMONSTRATE THAT THE SURFACES OF THE THREAD CREST & ROOT ARE NOT STRAIGHT LINES. THEY ARE SLIGHTLY CURVED. A TRUE PROJECTION OF THIS FORM TAKES TOO MUCH TIME TO ACTUALLY DRAW & AFFORDS NO BENEFIT. WITH THE ADVENT OF STANDARD THREADS, DRAWING SIMPLIFIED THREADS WITH THE PROPER CALL OUT CAN SAVE CONSIDERABLE TIME. THIS CHAPTER COVERS SOME FULL DETAIL, SIMPLIFIED, & SCHEMATIC METHODS TO SHOW THREADS.

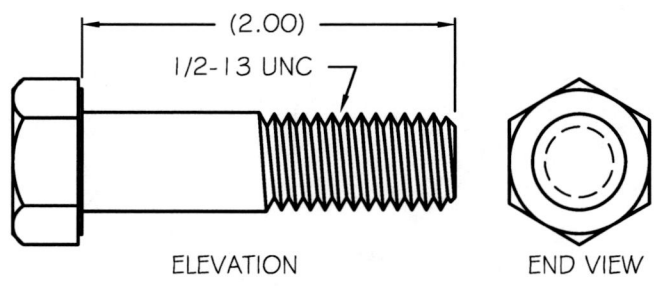

ELEVATION   END VIEW
1/2-13 UNC x 2 HEX HEAD CAP SCREW
SHOWN WITH FULL THREADS

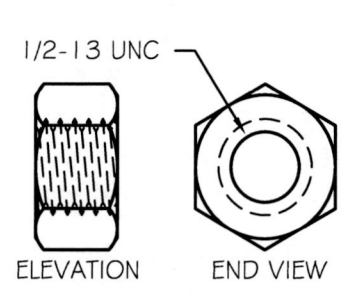

ELEVATION   END VIEW
1/2-13 UNC HEX NUT
SHOWN WITH FULL THREADS
ROOT & CREST LINES NOT REQUIRED

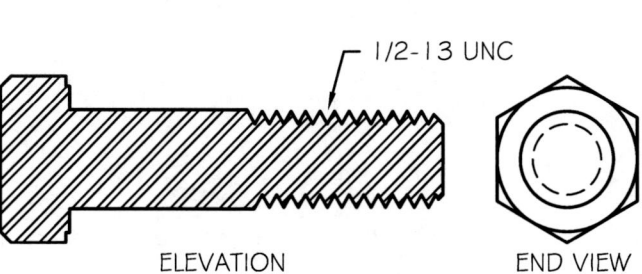

ELEVATION   END VIEW
1/2-13 UNC x 2 HEX HEAD CAP SCREW
SHOWN WITH FULL THREADS
IN SECTION VIEW

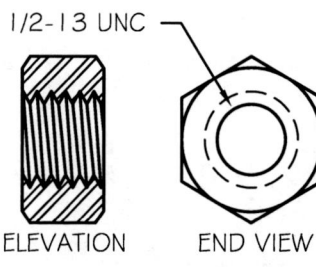

ELEVATION   END VIEW
1/2-13 UNC HEX NUT
SHOWN WITH FULL THREADS
IN SECTION VIEW

LESSON 10.03
THREADS & FASTENERS

SIMPLIFIED & SCHEMATIC THREAD REPRESENTATION.

INSTRUCTIONS:
REPRODUCE THE FOLLOWING ITEMS. DRAW EACH ITEM FULL SCALE COMPLETE WITH ANNOTATION.

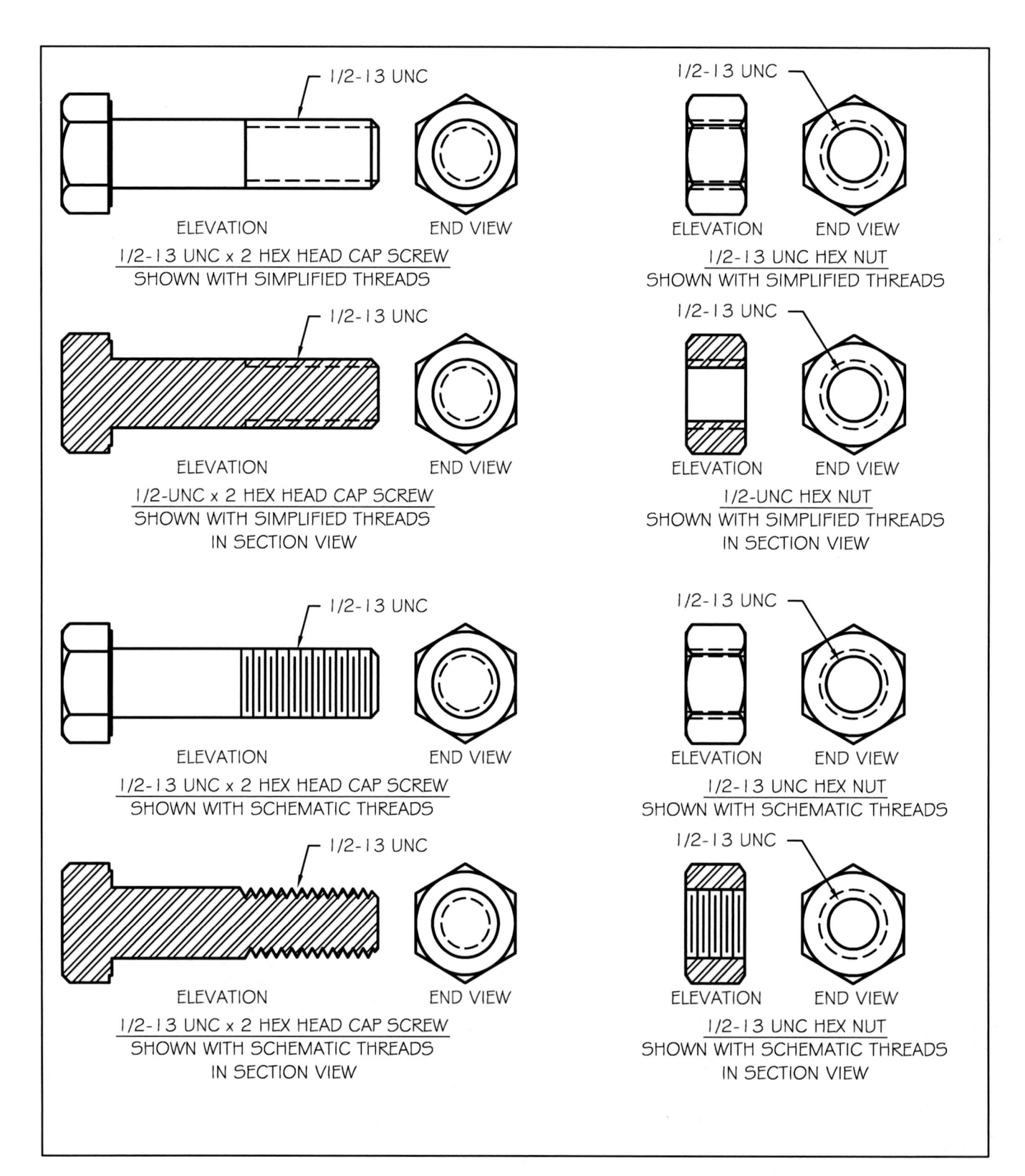

1/2-13 UNC

ELEVATION END VIEW

1/2-13 UNC x 2 HEX HEAD CAP SCREW
SHOWN WITH SIMPLIFIED THREADS

1/2-13 UNC

ELEVATION END VIEW

1/2-13 UNC HEX NUT
SHOWN WITH SIMPLIFIED THREADS

1/2-13 UNC

ELEVATION END VIEW

1/2-UNC x 2 HEX HEAD CAP SCREW
SHOWN WITH SIMPLIFIED THREADS
IN SECTION VIEW

1/2-13 UNC

ELEVATION END VIEW

1/2-UNC HEX NUT
SHOWN WITH SIMPLIFIED THREADS
IN SECTION VIEW

1/2-13 UNC

ELEVATION END VIEW

1/2-13 UNC x 2 HEX HEAD CAP SCREW
SHOWN WITH SCHEMATIC THREADS

1/2-13 UNC

ELEVATION END VIEW

1/2-13 UNC HEX NUT
SHOWN WITH SCHEMATIC THREADS

1/2-13 UNC

ELEVATION END VIEW

1/2-13 UNC x 2 HEX HEAD CAP SCREW
SHOWN WITH SCHEMATIC THREADS
IN SECTION VIEW

1/2-13 UNC

ELEVATION END VIEW

1/2-13 UNC HEX NUT
SHOWN WITH SCHEMATIC THREADS
IN SECTION VIEW

LESSON 10.04
THREADS & FASTENERS

NOTE:
THREADS ARE ONLY THEORETICALLY SHARP, IN REALITY THE CRESTS & VALLEYS ARE FLAT OR ROUNDED.
REPRESENTATIONS OF THREAD ARE PRIMARILY SHOWN AS SHARP.

INSTRUCTIONS:
REPRODUCE THE FOLLOWING ITEMS. DRAW EACH ITEM FULL SCALE COMPLETE WITH ANNOTATION.

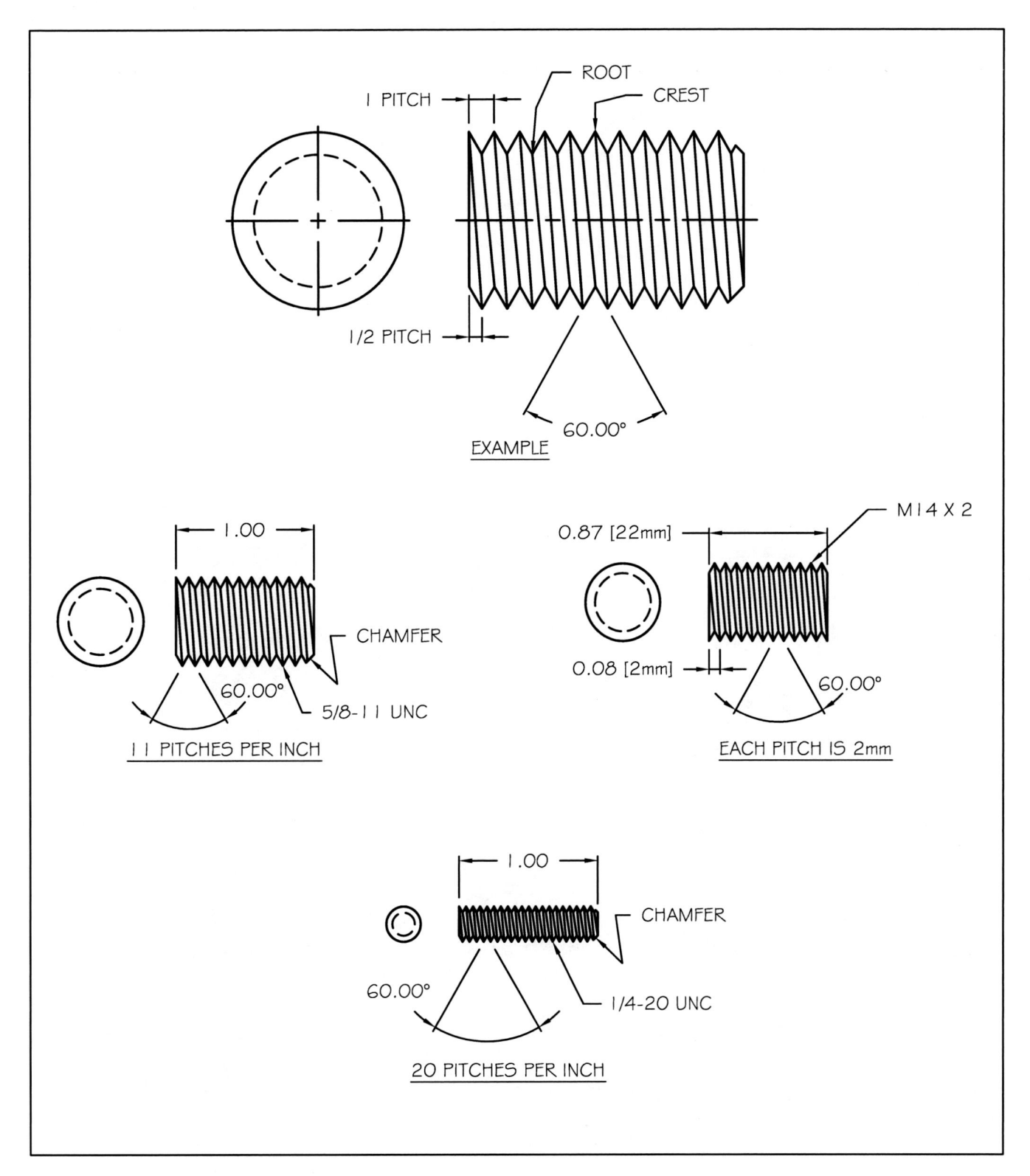

LESSON 10.05
THREADS & FASTENERS

NOTE:
THREADS ARE ONLY THEORETICALLY SHARP, IN REALITY THE CRESTS & VALLEYS ARE FLAT OR ROUNDED.
REPRESENTATIONS OF THREAD ARE PRIMARILY SHOWN AS SHARP.

INSTRUCTIONS:
REPRODUCE THE FOLLOWING ITEMS. DRAW EACH ITEM FULL SCALE COMPLETE WITH ANNOTATION.

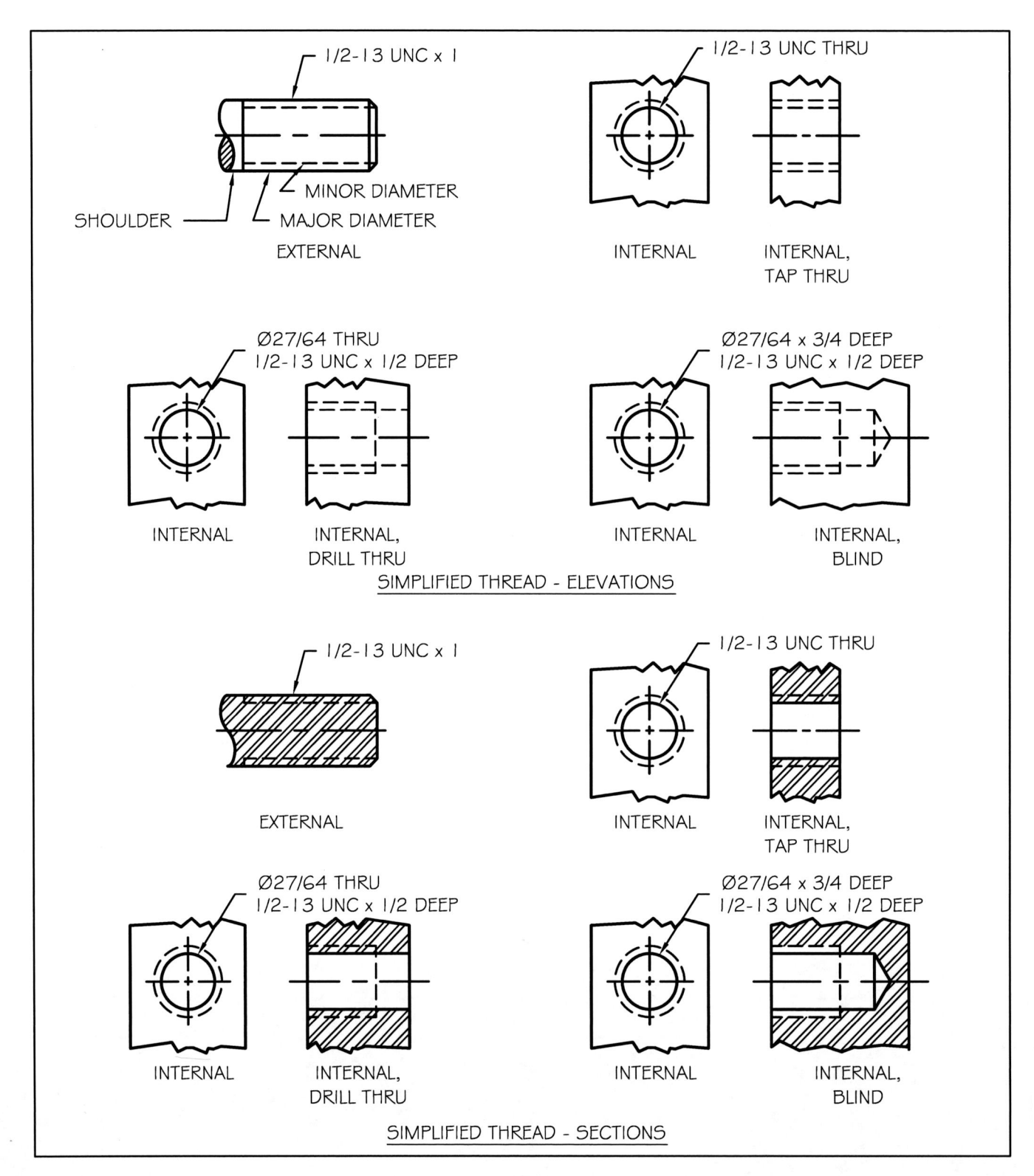

LESSON 10.06
THREADS & FASTENERS

INSTRUCTIONS:
REPRODUCE THE FOLLOWING ITEMS. DRAW EACH ITEM FULL SCALE COMPLETE WITH ANNOTATION.

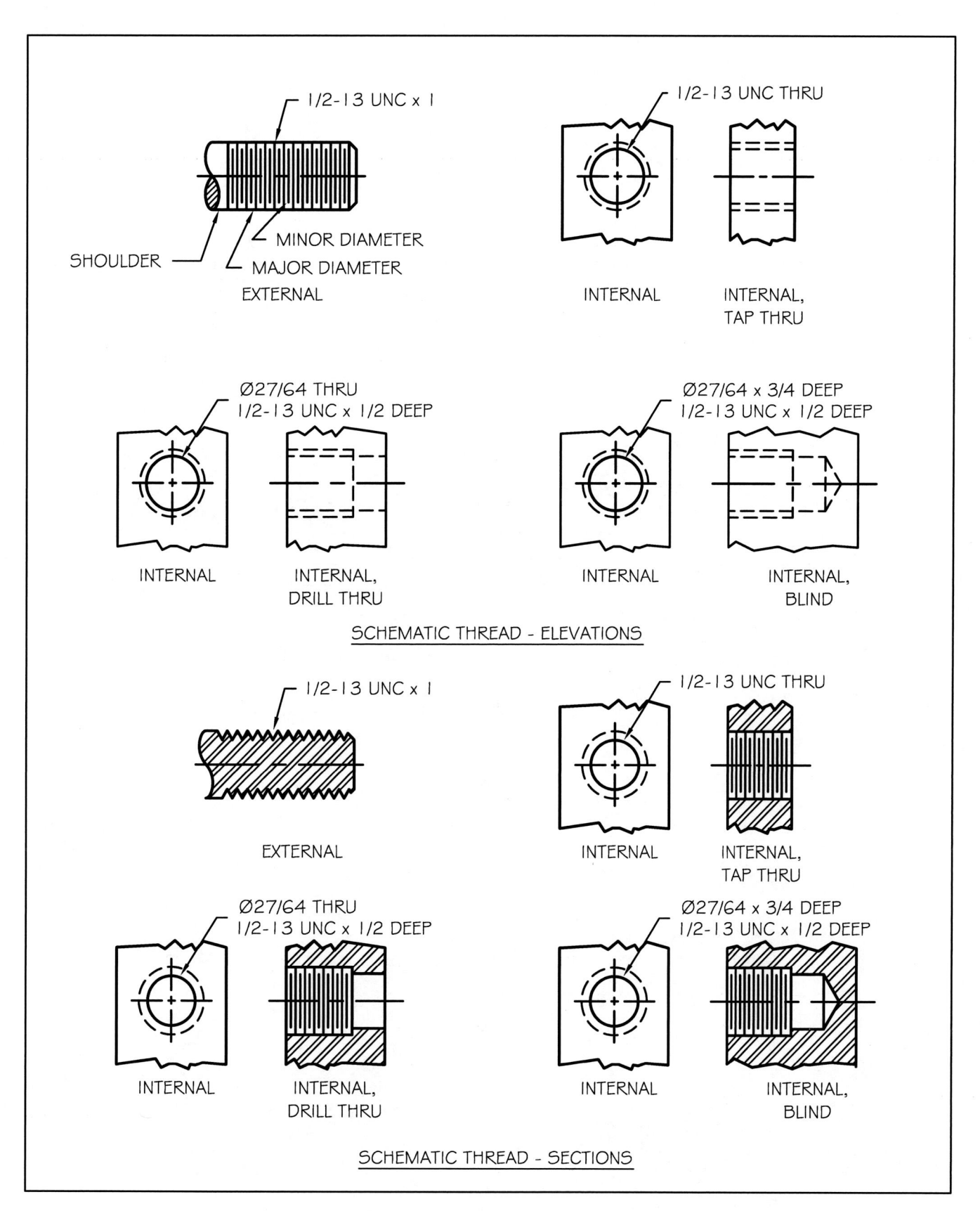

SCHEMATIC THREAD - ELEVATIONS

SCHEMATIC THREAD - SECTIONS

LESSON 10.07
THREADS & FASTENERS

NOTE:
THERE ARE LITERALLY HUNDREDS OF DIFFERENT TYPES OF FASTENERS. MOST FALL INTO JUST A FEW CATEGORIES: SCREW, BOLT, NUT, RIVET, PIN, RETAINING RINGS, HOOKS, EYES, ADHESIVE. THE PROFILES BELOW WILL HELP IN IDENTIFYING FASTENERS.

INSTRUCTIONS:
REPRODUCE ALL OF THE FOLLOWING ITEMS.

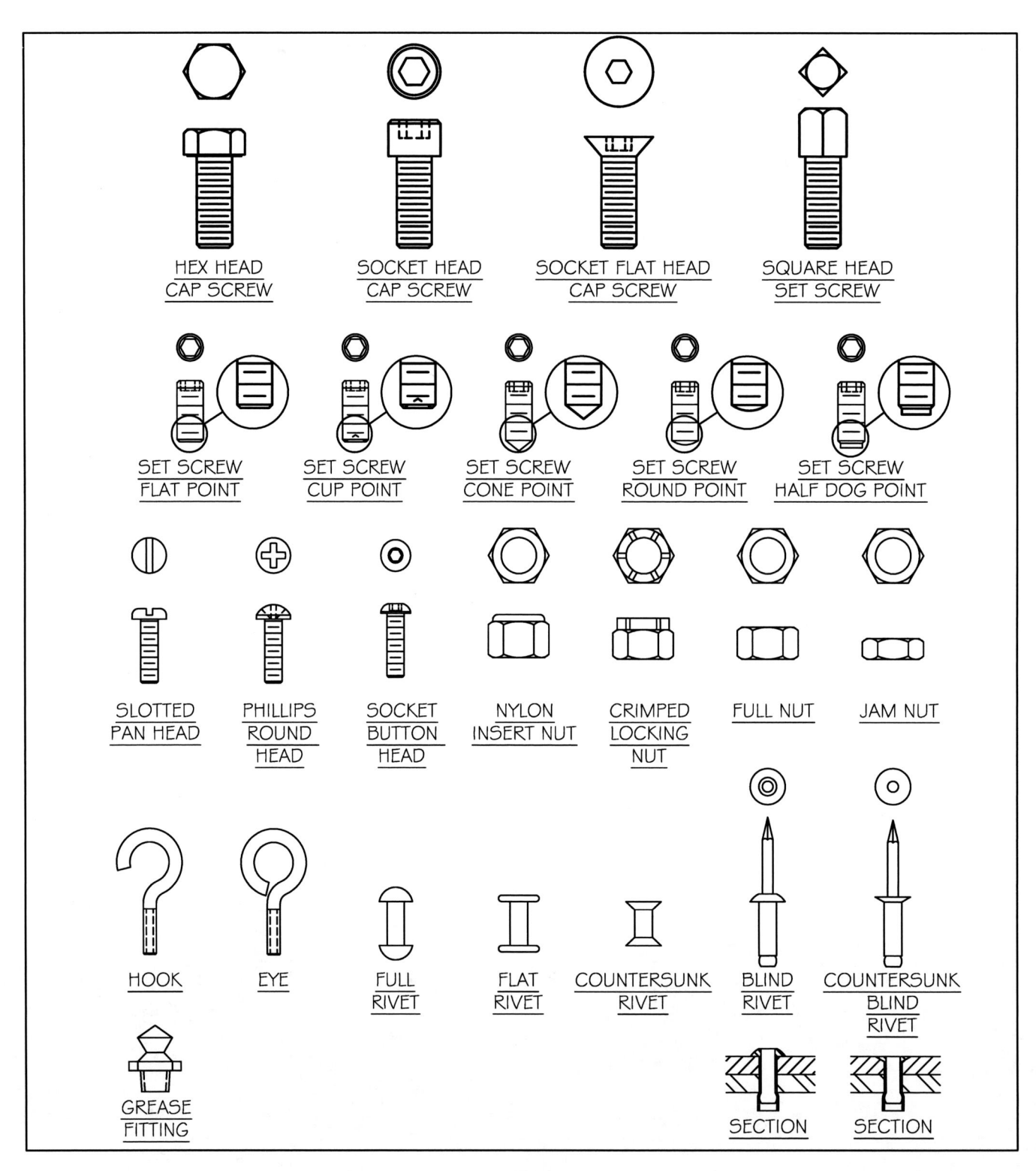

LESSON 11.00
WELDING, SYMBOLS, & JOINTS

NOTE:
WELDING IS A CRITICAL PART OF METAL & PLASTIC FABRICATIONS. WELDING IS DESCRIBED ON A DRAWING WITH A SYSTEM OF SYMBOLS THAT DESCRIBE THE SIZE, TYPE, & LOCATION OF EACH DESIRED WELD. THIS IS ANOTHER COMPLEX SUBJECT THAT IS COVERED IN BOOKS WRITTEN BY WELDING & METALLURGICAL EXPERTS. TO FULLY UNDERSTAND THE SUBJECT OF WELDING MUCH STUDY & WORK IS REQUIRED. THIS LESSON IS ONLY TO INFORM OF SOME OF THE SYMBOLS USED. THE SYMBOLS SHOWN ARE BASED ON ANSI & AWS STANDARDS.

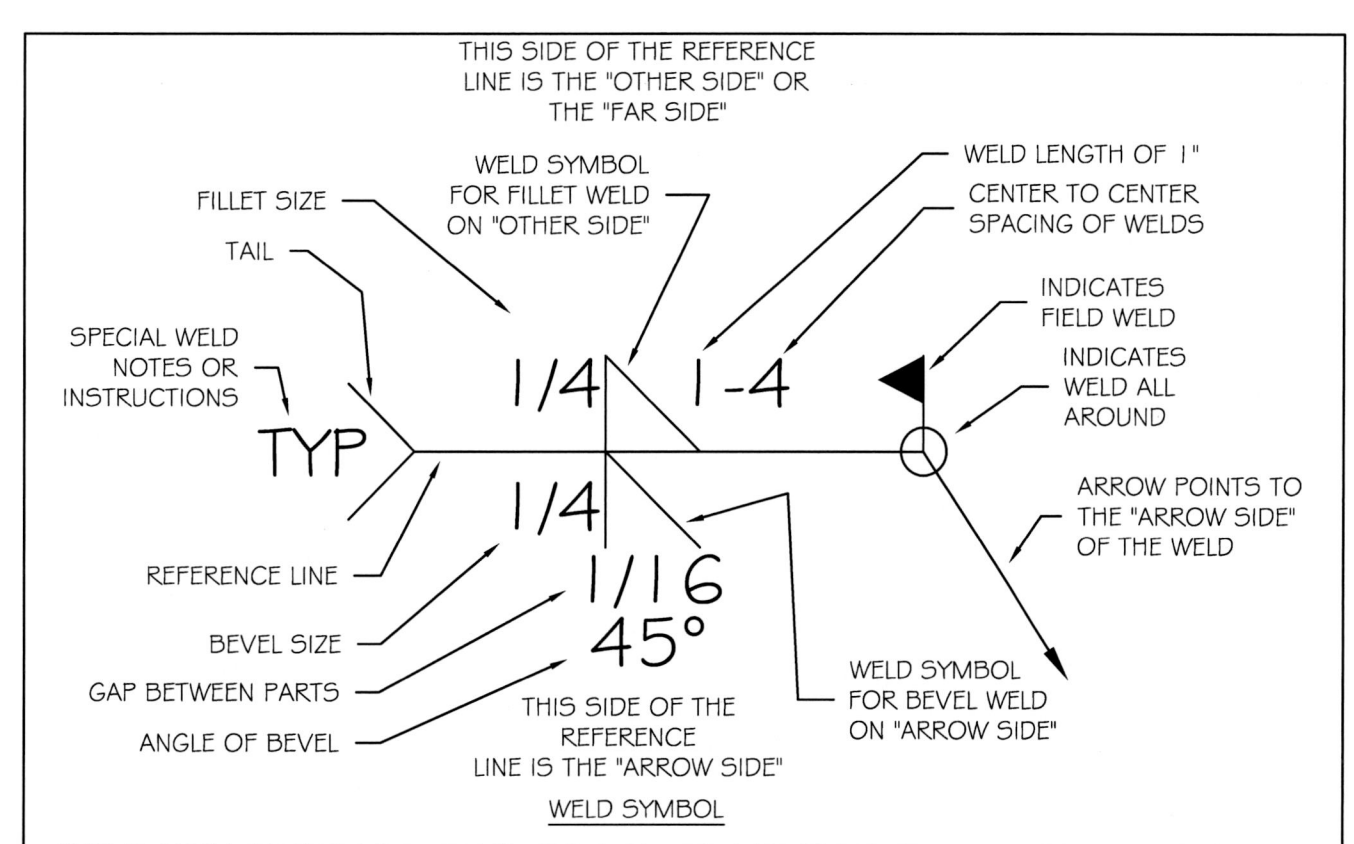

WELD SYMBOL

THIS IS JUST A SAMPLE WELD. THE SYMBOLS CAN BE MIXED TOGETHER IN MANY COMBINATIONS TO ACHIEVE THE CORRECT WELD. THERE ARE MANY SPECIAL WELD PROCEDURES THAT CAN ALSO BE INCLUDED WITH WELDING SYMBOLS. SOMETIMES THE PARTS BEING WELDED WILL HAVE TO BE PUT INTO A LARGE OVEN TO BE PREHEATED PRIOR TO WELDING. AFTER WELDING, THE PARTS MAY HAVE TO BE COOLED DOWN AT A SPECIFIC RATE OR A SPECIFIC TIME PERIOD. THERE ARE WELDING ENGINEERS THAT CAN FIGURE OUT THE EXACT WELD & SPECIFICATION FOR EVERY TYPE OF POSSIBLE WELD. SOME WELDS REQUIRE ELABORATE MACHINING PRIOR TO WELDING.

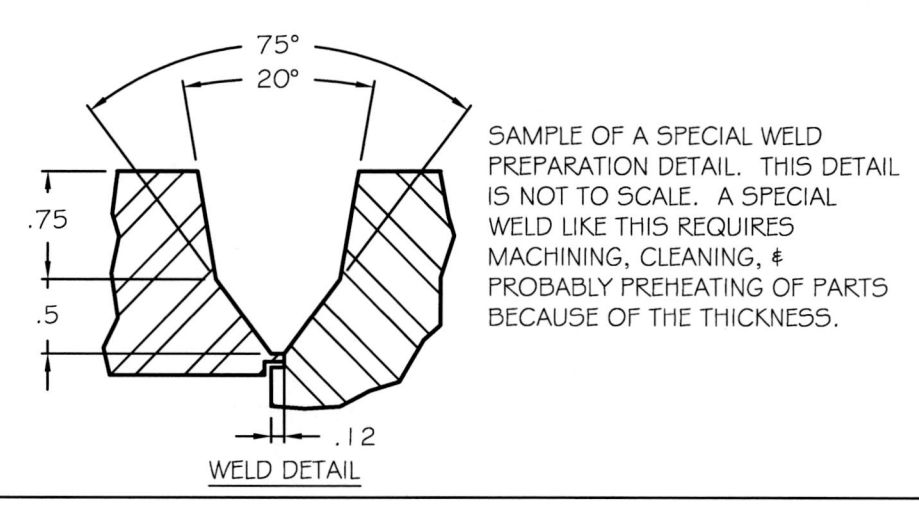

SAMPLE OF A SPECIAL WELD PREPARATION DETAIL. THIS DETAIL IS NOT TO SCALE. A SPECIAL WELD LIKE THIS REQUIRES MACHINING, CLEANING, & PROBABLY PREHEATING OF PARTS BECAUSE OF THE THICKNESS.

WELD DETAIL

LESSON 11.01
WELDING, SYMBOLS, & JOINTS

NOTE:
THE ILLUSTRATIONS BELOW DEPICT SOME OF THE MORE BASIC TYPES OF WELDING SYMBOLS.

INSTRUCTIONS:
REPRODUCE THE FOLLOWING ITEMS.

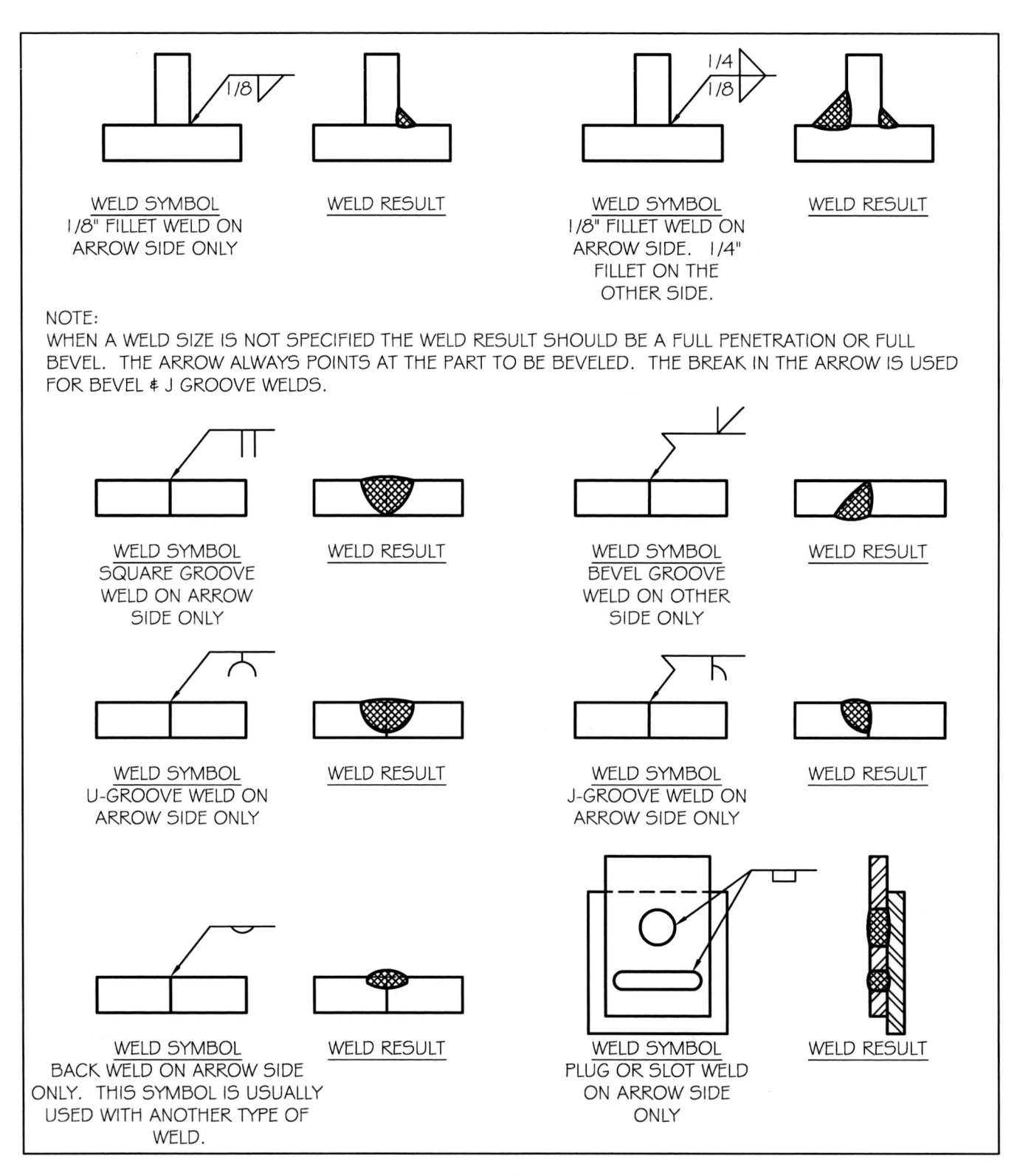

WELD SYMBOL
1/8" FILLET WELD ON
ARROW SIDE ONLY

WELD RESULT

WELD SYMBOL
1/8" FILLET WELD ON
ARROW SIDE. 1/4"
FILLET ON THE
OTHER SIDE.

WELD RESULT

NOTE:
WHEN A WELD SIZE IS NOT SPECIFIED THE WELD RESULT SHOULD BE A FULL PENETRATION OR FULL BEVEL. THE ARROW ALWAYS POINTS AT THE PART TO BE BEVELED. THE BREAK IN THE ARROW IS USED FOR BEVEL & J GROOVE WELDS.

WELD SYMBOL
SQUARE GROOVE
WELD ON ARROW
SIDE ONLY

WELD RESULT

WELD SYMBOL
BEVEL GROOVE
WELD ON OTHER
SIDE ONLY

WELD RESULT

WELD SYMBOL
U-GROOVE WELD ON
ARROW SIDE ONLY

WELD RESULT

WELD SYMBOL
J-GROOVE WELD ON
ARROW SIDE ONLY

WELD RESULT

WELD SYMBOL
BACK WELD ON ARROW SIDE
ONLY. THIS SYMBOL IS USUALLY
USED WITH ANOTHER TYPE OF
WELD.

WELD RESULT

WELD SYMBOL
PLUG OR SLOT WELD
ON ARROW SIDE
ONLY

WELD RESULT

LESSON 11.02
WELDING, SYMBOLS, & JOINTS

NOTE:
THE ILLUSTRATIONS BELOW SHOW SKIP WELDING & SOME JOINT TYPES.

INSTRUCTIONS:
REPRODUCE THE FOLLOWING ITEMS.

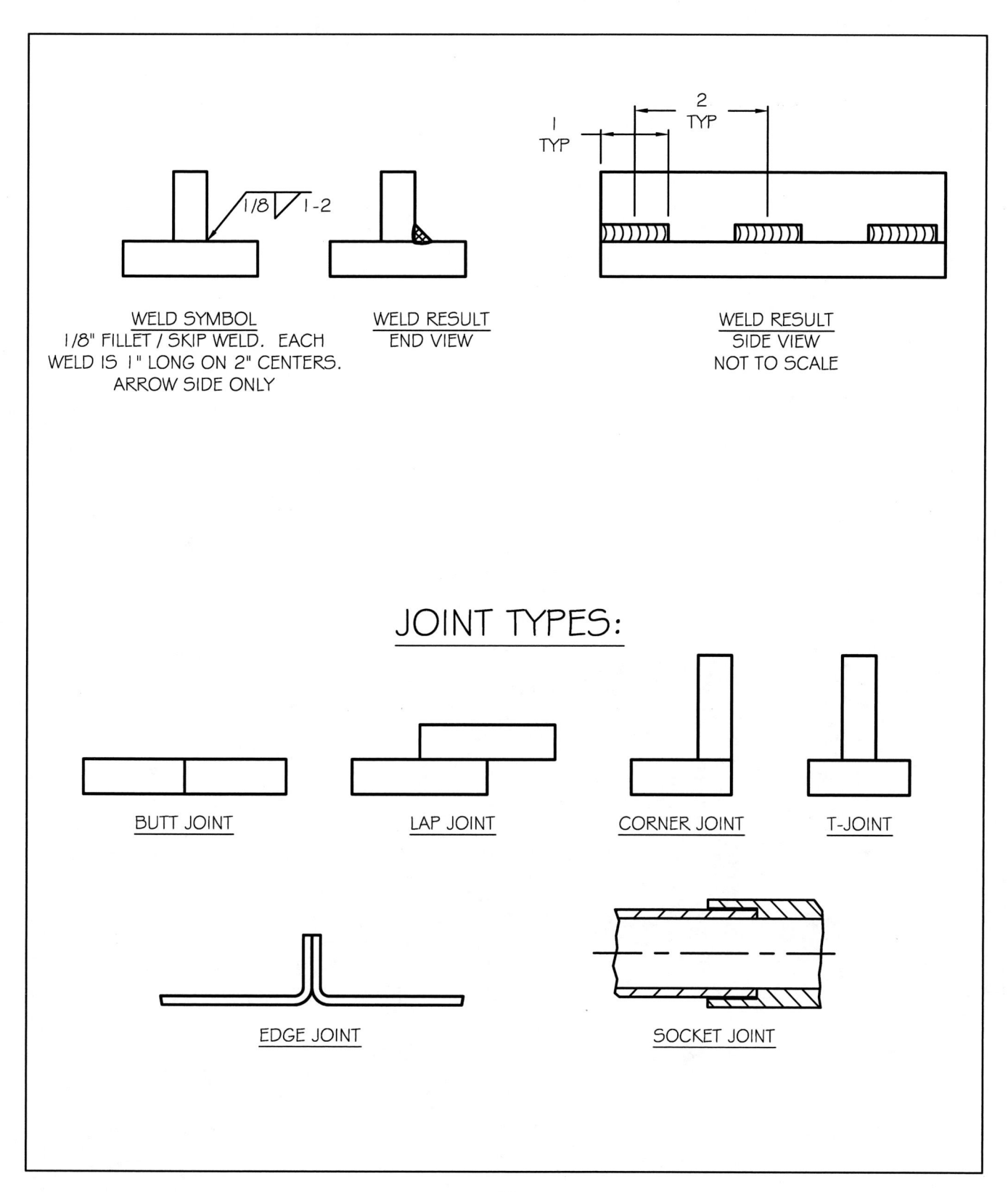

WELD SYMBOL
1/8" FILLET / SKIP WELD. EACH
WELD IS 1" LONG ON 2" CENTERS.
ARROW SIDE ONLY

WELD RESULT
END VIEW

WELD RESULT
SIDE VIEW
NOT TO SCALE

JOINT TYPES:

BUTT JOINT

LAP JOINT

CORNER JOINT

T-JOINT

EDGE JOINT

SOCKET JOINT

LESSON 12.00
SHEET METAL & PLANAR DEVELOPMENTS

NOTE:
SHEET METAL CONSTRUCTION REQUIRES THAT YOU THINK ABOUT MECHANICAL JOINTS & TABS. WITHOUT TABS OR JOINTS, THE SHEET METAL WILL NOT STAY IN THE DESIRED POSITION. BELOW ARE SEVERAL SEAM TYPES.

HANDY BEND RADIUS INFORMATION: THE NEUTRAL AXIS IS APPROXIMATELY .44 OF THE THICKNESS FROM THE INSIDE RADIUS. THIS CAN BE EXPRESSED MATHEMATICALLY AS NEUTRAL AXIS LENGTH=((.017453 X INSIDE RADIUS)+(.0078 x MATERIAL THICKNESS)) X NUMBER OF DEGREES IN BEND. THE NEUTRAL AXIS IS WHERE THE MATERIAL DOES NOT SHRINK OR STRETCH. THIS INFORMATION HELPS IN LEAVING THE CORRECT AMOUNT OF MATERIAL FOR BEND ALLOWANCES.

INSTRUCTIONS:
REPRODUCE THE FOLLOWING ITEMS.

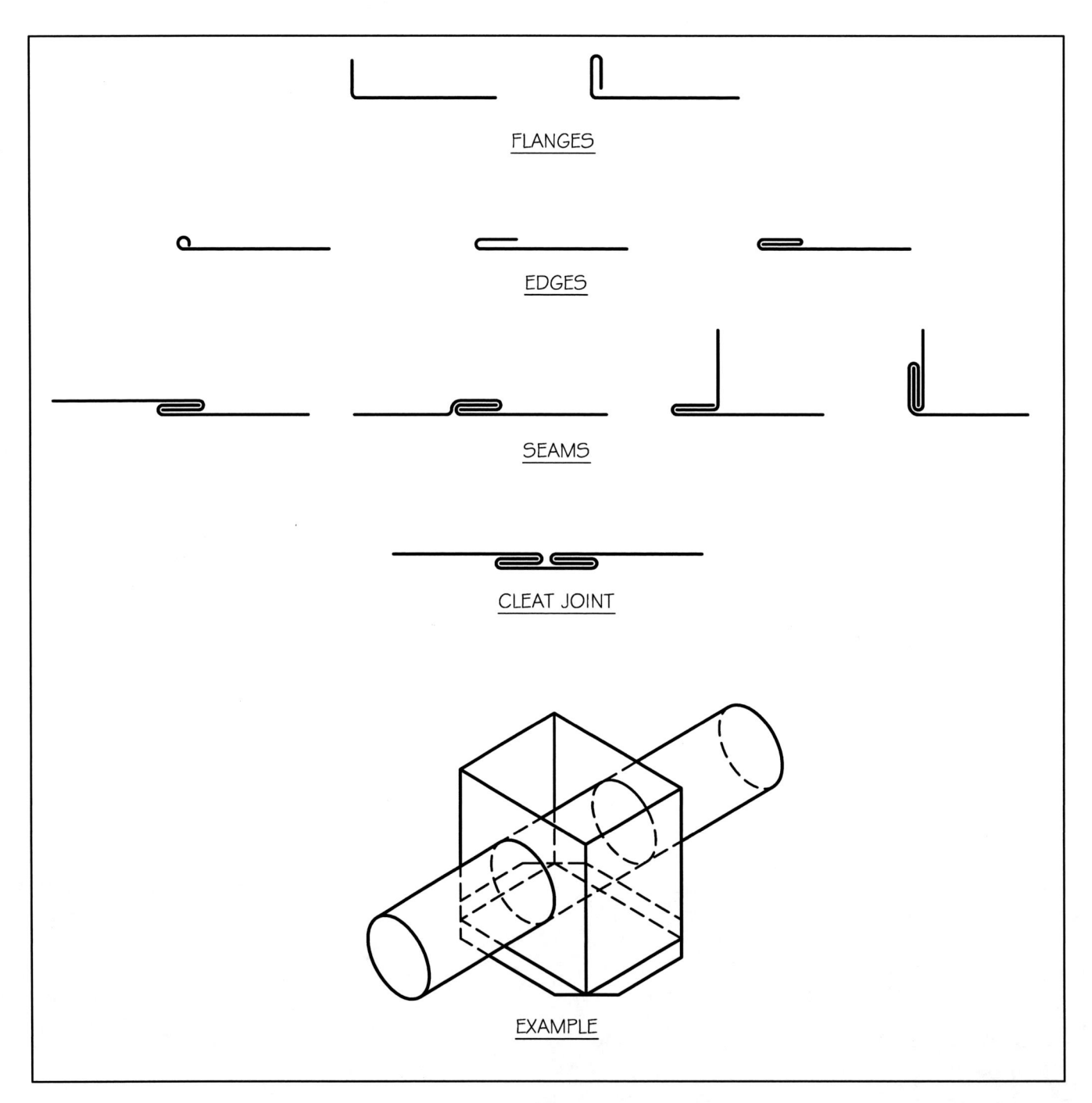

FLANGES

EDGES

SEAMS

CLEAT JOINT

EXAMPLE

LESSON 12.01
SHEET METAL & PLANAR DEVELOPMENTS

INSTRUCTIONS:
REPRODUCE THE FLAT PATTERN ITEMS, CUT THEM OUT, & ASSEMBLE PER THE ILLUSTRATIONS BELOW.

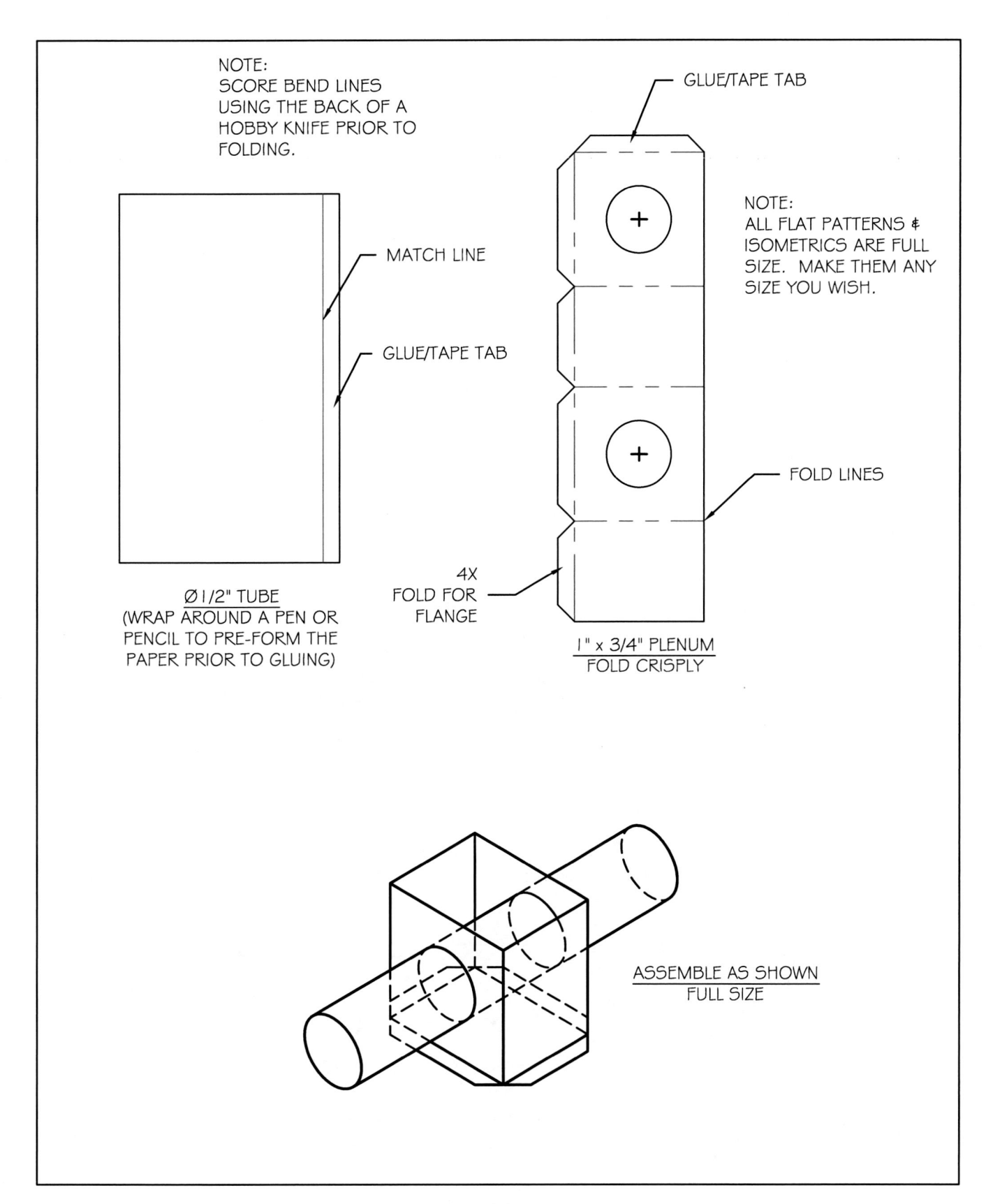

NOTE:
SCORE BEND LINES USING THE BACK OF A HOBBY KNIFE PRIOR TO FOLDING.

MATCH LINE

GLUE/TAPE TAB

Ø1/2" TUBE
(WRAP AROUND A PEN OR PENCIL TO PRE-FORM THE PAPER PRIOR TO GLUING)

GLUE/TAPE TAB

NOTE:
ALL FLAT PATTERNS & ISOMETRICS ARE FULL SIZE. MAKE THEM ANY SIZE YOU WISH.

FOLD LINES

4X
FOLD FOR FLANGE

1" x 3/4" PLENUM
FOLD CRISPLY

ASSEMBLE AS SHOWN
FULL SIZE

LESSON 12.02
SHEET METAL & PLANAR DEVELOPMENTS

INSTRUCTIONS:
REPRODUCE THE FLAT PATTERN ITEMS, CUT THEM OUT, & ASSEMBLE PER THE ILLUSTRATIONS BELOW.

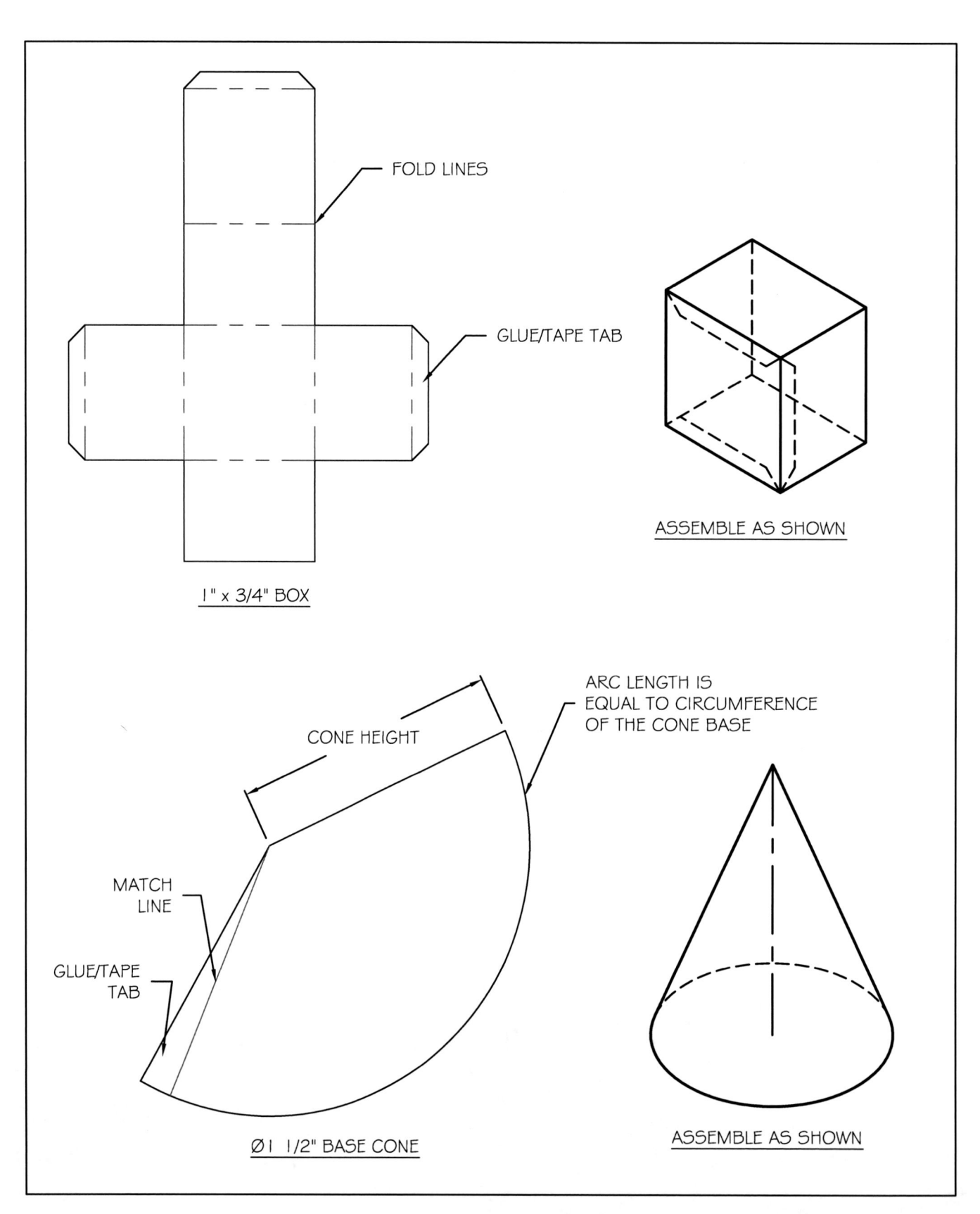

FOLD LINES

GLUE/TAPE TAB

ASSEMBLE AS SHOWN

1" x 3/4" BOX

CONE HEIGHT

ARC LENGTH IS
EQUAL TO CIRCUMFERENCE
OF THE CONE BASE

MATCH LINE

GLUE/TAPE TAB

Ø1 1/2" BASE CONE

ASSEMBLE AS SHOWN

LESSON 12.03
SHEET METAL & PLANAR DEVELOPMENTS

INSTRUCTIONS:
REPRODUCE THE FLAT PATTERN ITEMS, CUT THEM OUT, & ASSEMBLE PER THE ILLUSTRATIONS BELOW.

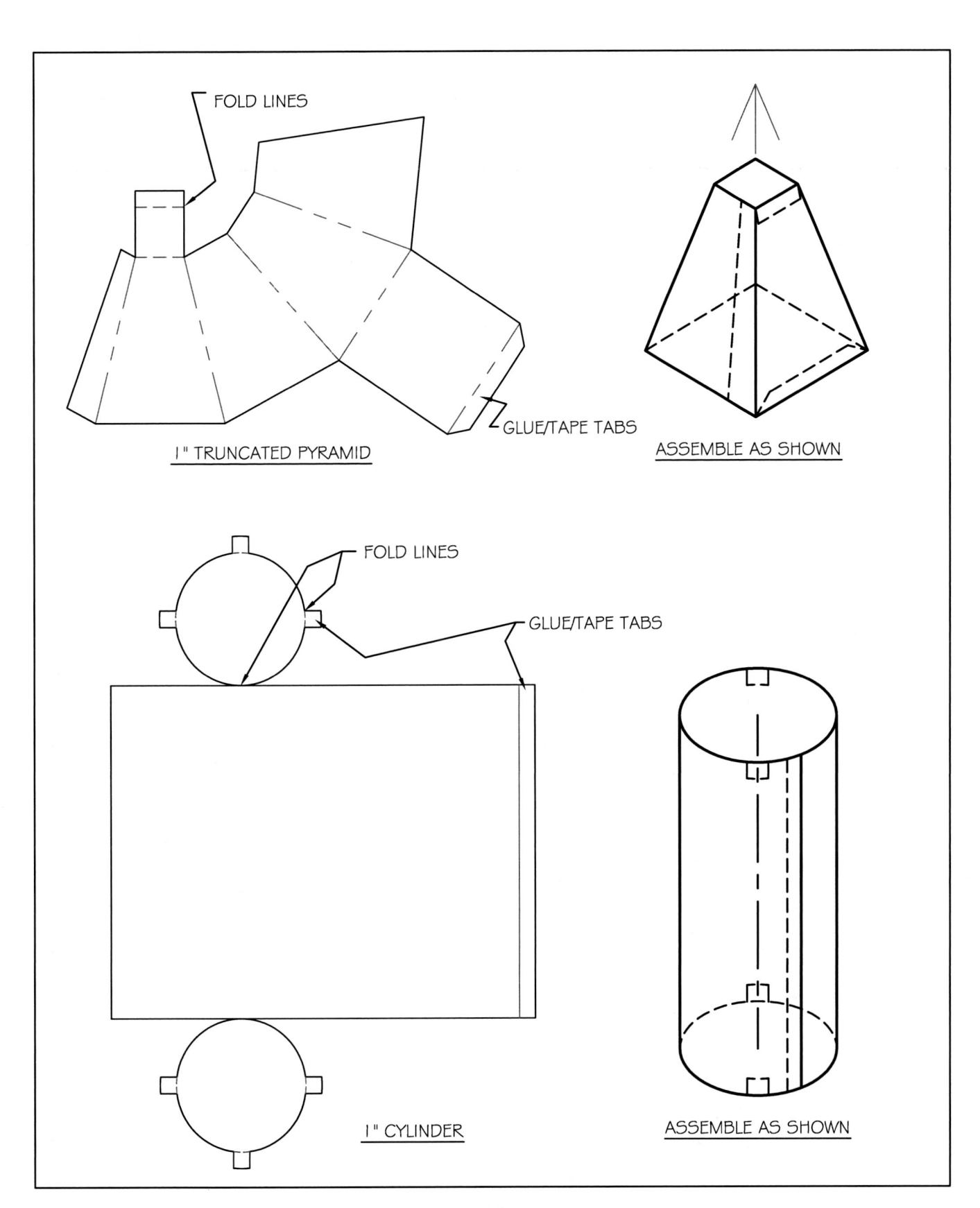

FOLD LINES

GLUE/TAPE TABS

1" TRUNCATED PYRAMID

ASSEMBLE AS SHOWN

FOLD LINES

GLUE/TAPE TABS

1" CYLINDER

ASSEMBLE AS SHOWN

LESSON 12.04
SHEET METAL & PLANAR DEVELOPMENTS

INSTRUCTIONS:
REPRODUCE THE FLAT PATTERN ITEMS, CUT THEM OUT, & ASSEMBLE PER THE ILLUSTRATIONS BELOW.

NOTE: THE EXTRA FLANGES ADD RIGIDITY.

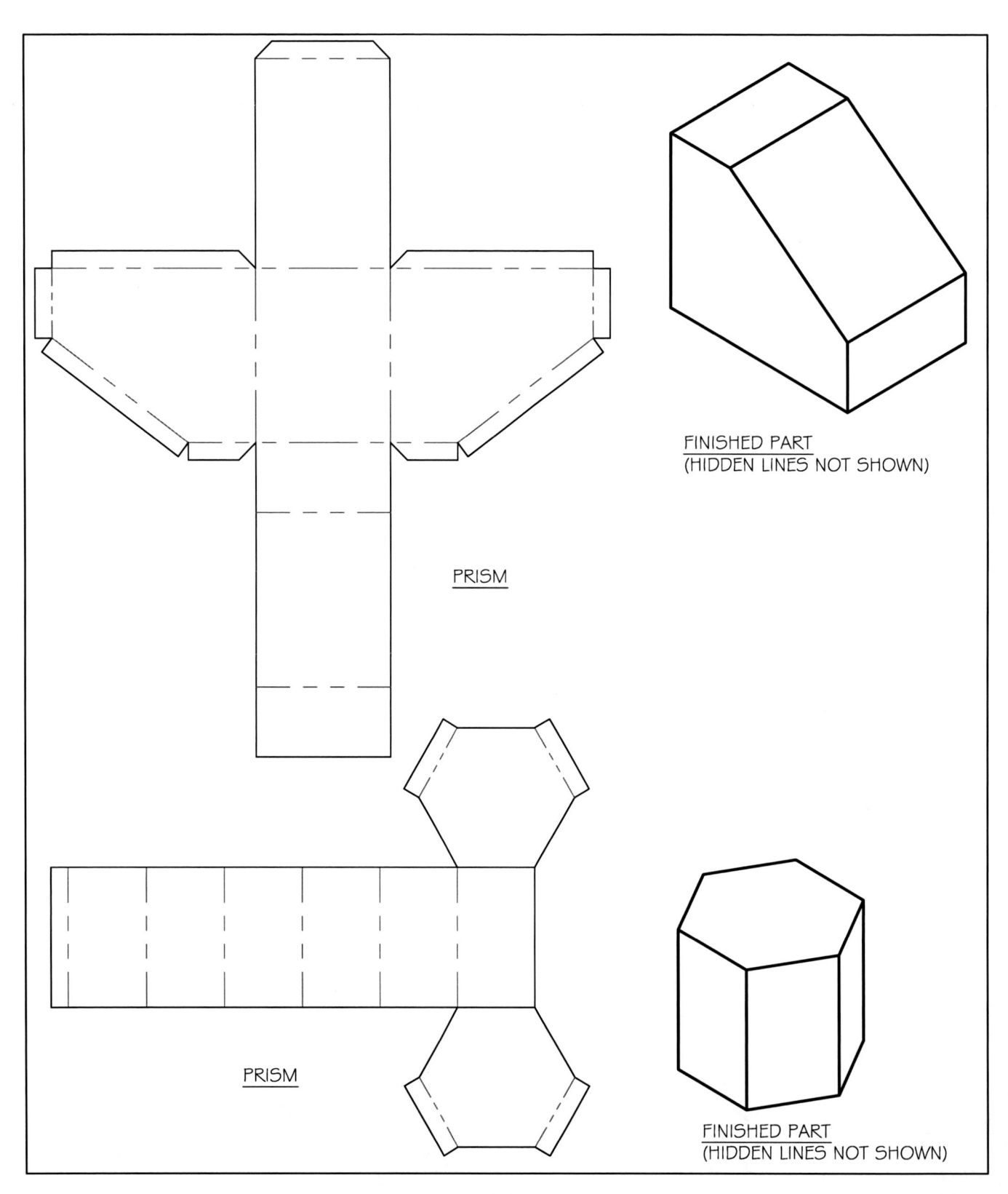

FINISHED PART
(HIDDEN LINES NOT SHOWN)

PRISM

PRISM

FINISHED PART
(HIDDEN LINES NOT SHOWN)

LESSON 12.05
SHEET METAL & PLANAR DEVELOPMENTS

INSTRUCTIONS:
REPRODUCE THE FLAT PATTERN ITEM, CUT IT OUT, & ASSEMBLE.

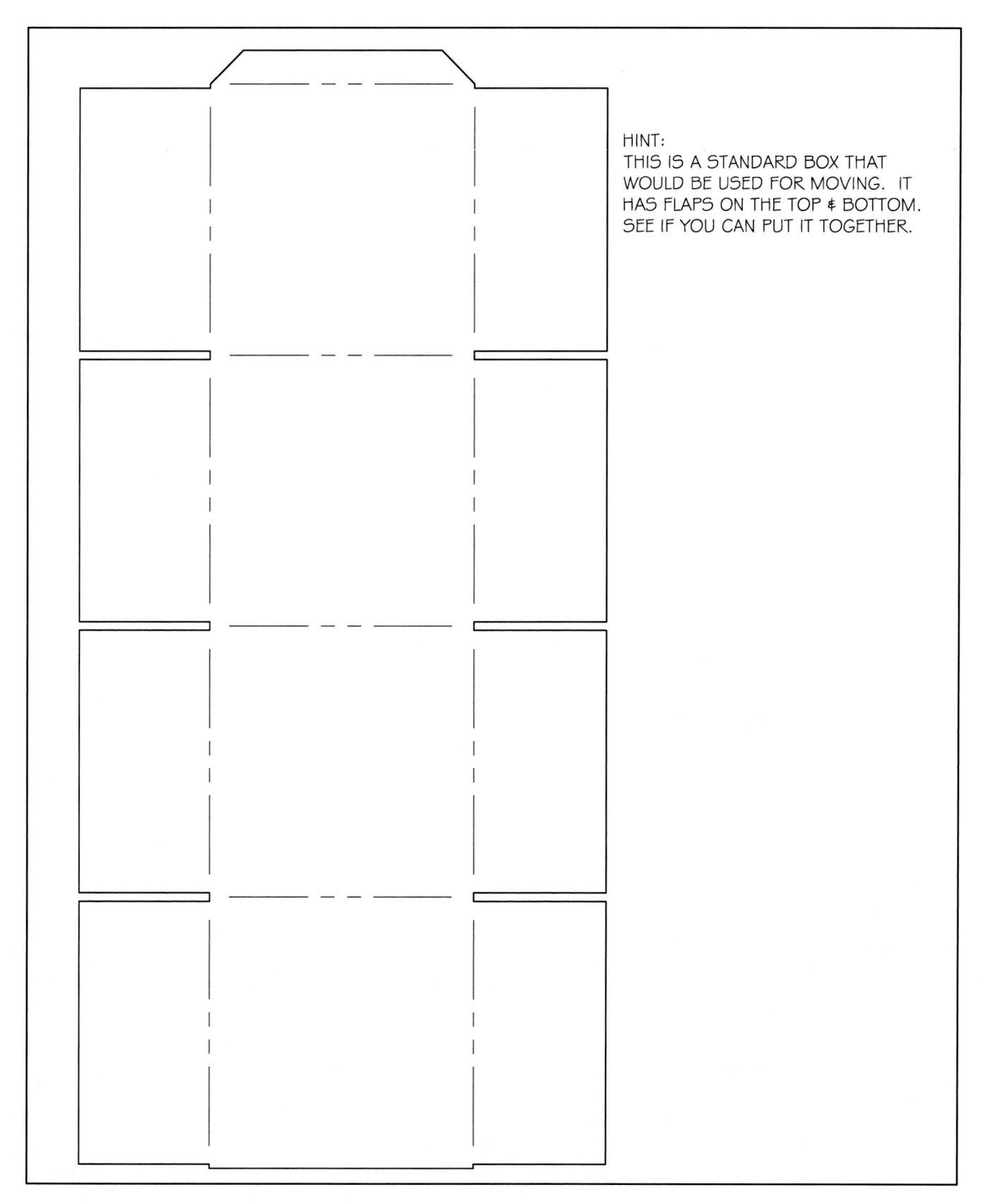

HINT:
THIS IS A STANDARD BOX THAT
WOULD BE USED FOR MOVING. IT
HAS FLAPS ON THE TOP & BOTTOM.
SEE IF YOU CAN PUT IT TOGETHER.

LESSON 12.06
SHEET METAL & PLANAR DEVELOPMENTS

INSTRUCTIONS:
REPRODUCE THE FLAT PATTERN ITEM, CUT IT OUT, & ASSEMBLE PER THE ILLUSTRATION BELOW.

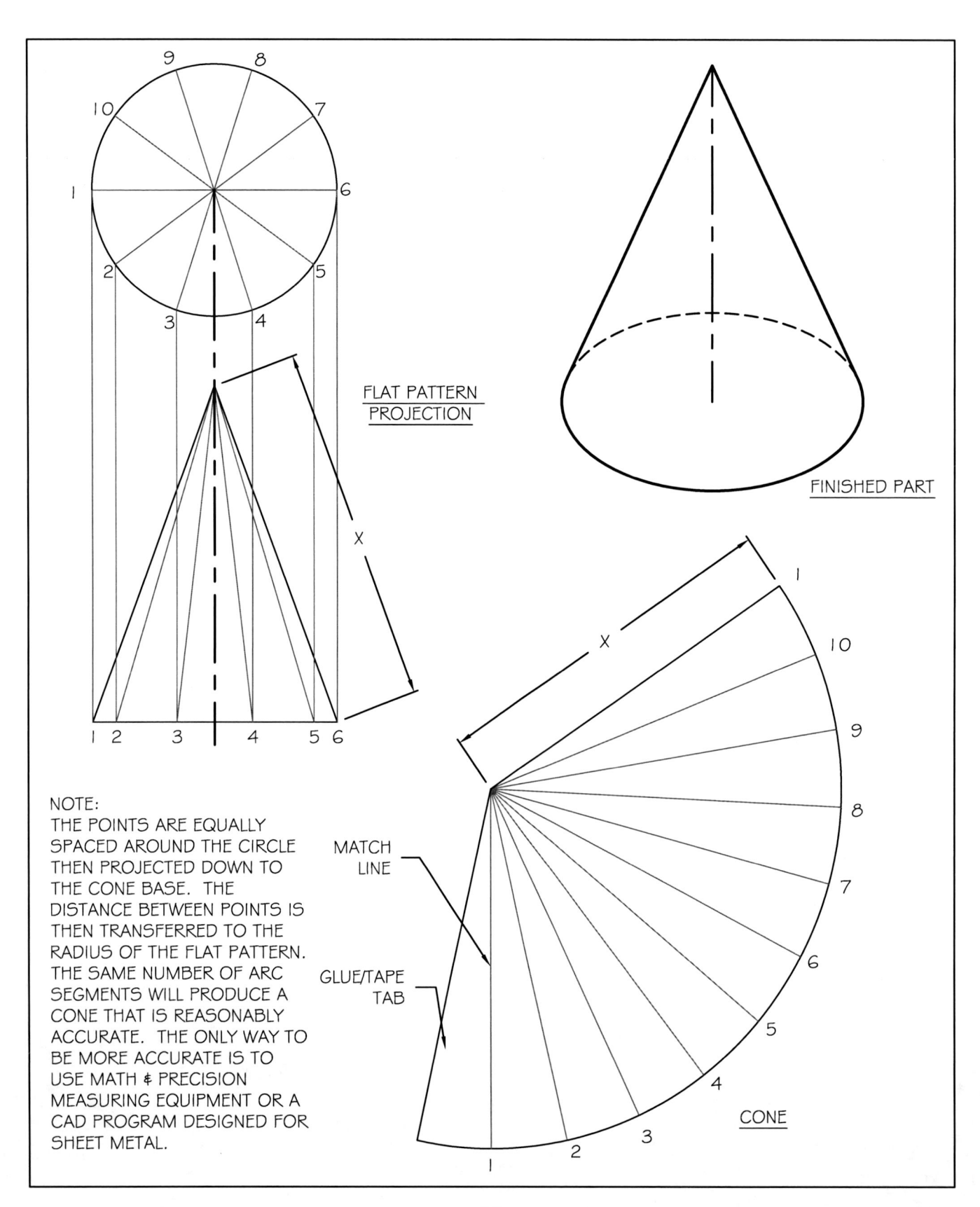

FLAT PATTERN
PROJECTION

FINISHED PART

NOTE:
THE POINTS ARE EQUALLY SPACED AROUND THE CIRCLE THEN PROJECTED DOWN TO THE CONE BASE. THE DISTANCE BETWEEN POINTS IS THEN TRANSFERRED TO THE RADIUS OF THE FLAT PATTERN. THE SAME NUMBER OF ARC SEGMENTS WILL PRODUCE A CONE THAT IS REASONABLY ACCURATE. THE ONLY WAY TO BE MORE ACCURATE IS TO USE MATH & PRECISION MEASURING EQUIPMENT OR A CAD PROGRAM DESIGNED FOR SHEET METAL.

MATCH LINE

GLUE/TAPE TAB

CONE

LESSON 13.00
GEARS

NOTE:
GEARS EXIST EVERYWHERE. PRODUCTS WITH GEARS INCLUDE CD ROM DRIVES, WATCHES, CASSETTE TAPE PLAYERS, LASER PRINTERS, GARAGE DOOR OPENERS, ETC. THERE ARE ANSI STANDARDS FOR PRODUCING STANDARD GEARS. THE PURPOSE OF THIS LESSON IS TO INTRODUCE THE MAIN FEATURES THAT MAKE UP A GEAR OR RACK. GEARS ARE A RESULT OF SEVERAL FORMULAS THAT WILL NOT BE COVERED HERE. FOR MORE INFORMATION, REFER TO THE MACHINERY'S HAND BOOK & ANSI STANDARDS.

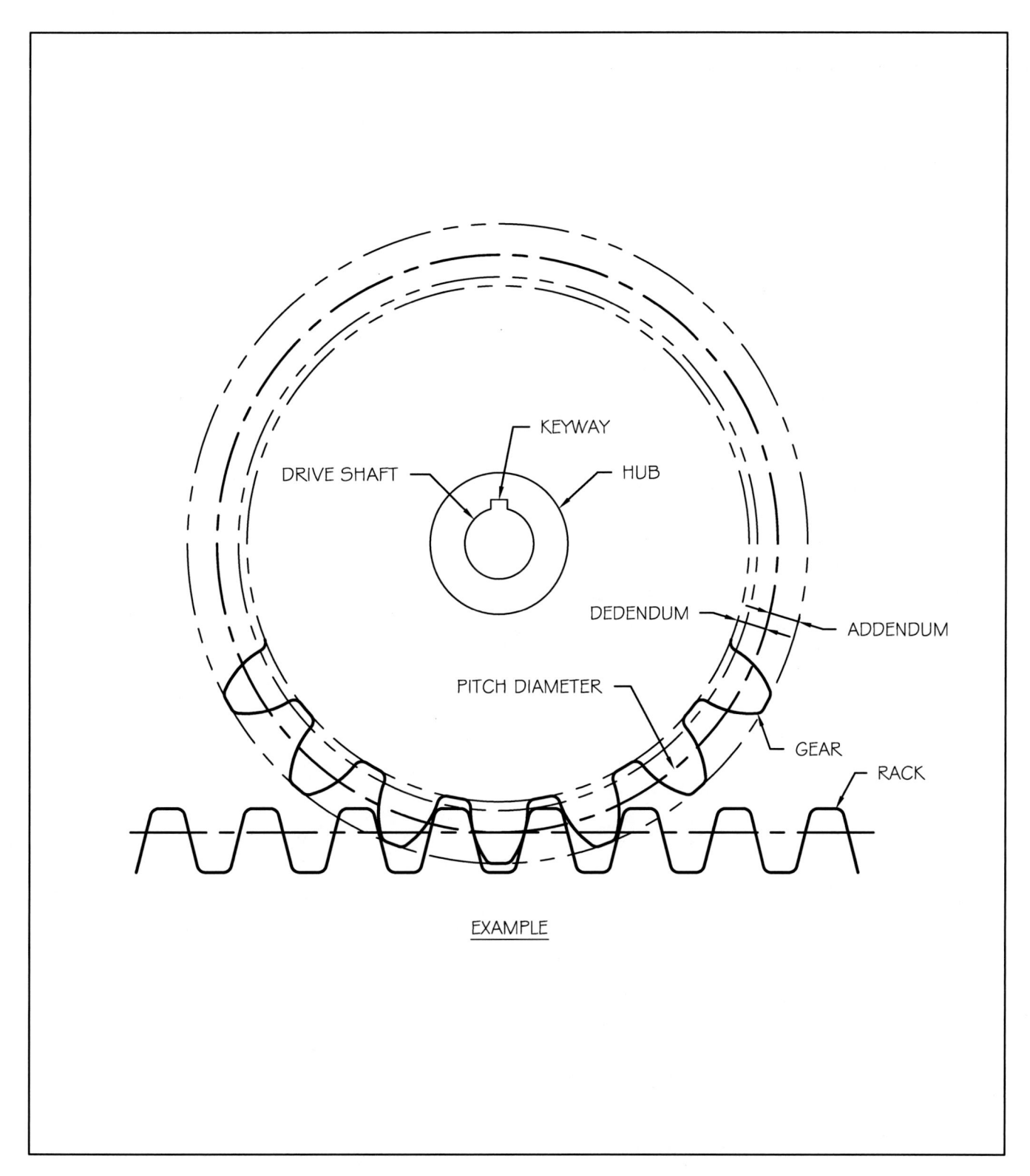

EXAMPLE

LESSON 14.00
PIPING

NOTE:
PIPING IS USED IN ALMOST EVERY INDUSTRIAL, PROFESSIONAL, & RESIDENTIAL ENVIRONMENT. THERE IS SMALL BORE PIPING (Ø6" & UNDER) AS WELL AS LARGE BORE PIPING (OVER Ø6"). SMALL BORE PIPING IS ALSO REFERRED TO AS PLUMBING, ESPECIALLY IN RESIDENTIAL & BUILDING ENVIRONMENTS. PLUMBING USUALLY REFERS TO ANY COPPER TUBING THAT IS Ø1 1/2" OR LESS THAT IS USED FOR THE SUPPLY OF WATER. PLASTIC TUBING IS ALSO USED FOR THE SUPPLY OF WATER UNDER SINKS TO MAKE THE CONNECTIONS BETWEEN THE VALVE & THE FAUCET. ON THE WASTE SIDE OF PLUMBING, THERE IS USUALLY PVC OR OTHER TYPE OF PLASTIC PIPES OF Ø6" OR LESS USED FOR DRAINS, SEWERS, & VENTS. IN INDUSTRIAL APPLICATIONS, MOST PIPING IS STEEL OR IRON. THERE ARE MANY TYPES OF MATERIALS USED IN PIPING: STEEL (PLAIN & LINED), STAINLESS STEEL (PLAIN & LINED), GLASS, CPVC, PVC, ETC. INDUSTRIAL TUBING CAN BE MADE OF IRON, COPPER, CPVC, PVC, TEFLON, NYLON, GLASS, STAINLESS STEEL, ETC. CONNECTIONS CAN BE WELDED, THREADED, GLUED, OR FLANGED.

BELOW & ON THE FOLLOWING PAGES, THERE ARE SOME EXAMPLES OF PIPING DETAILS & SCHEMATICS. FOR STANDARDS, SEE ANSI & AWS.

INSTRUCTIONS:
REPRODUCE THE SCHEMATIC BELOW TWICE AS LARGE AS ILLUSTRATED HERE.

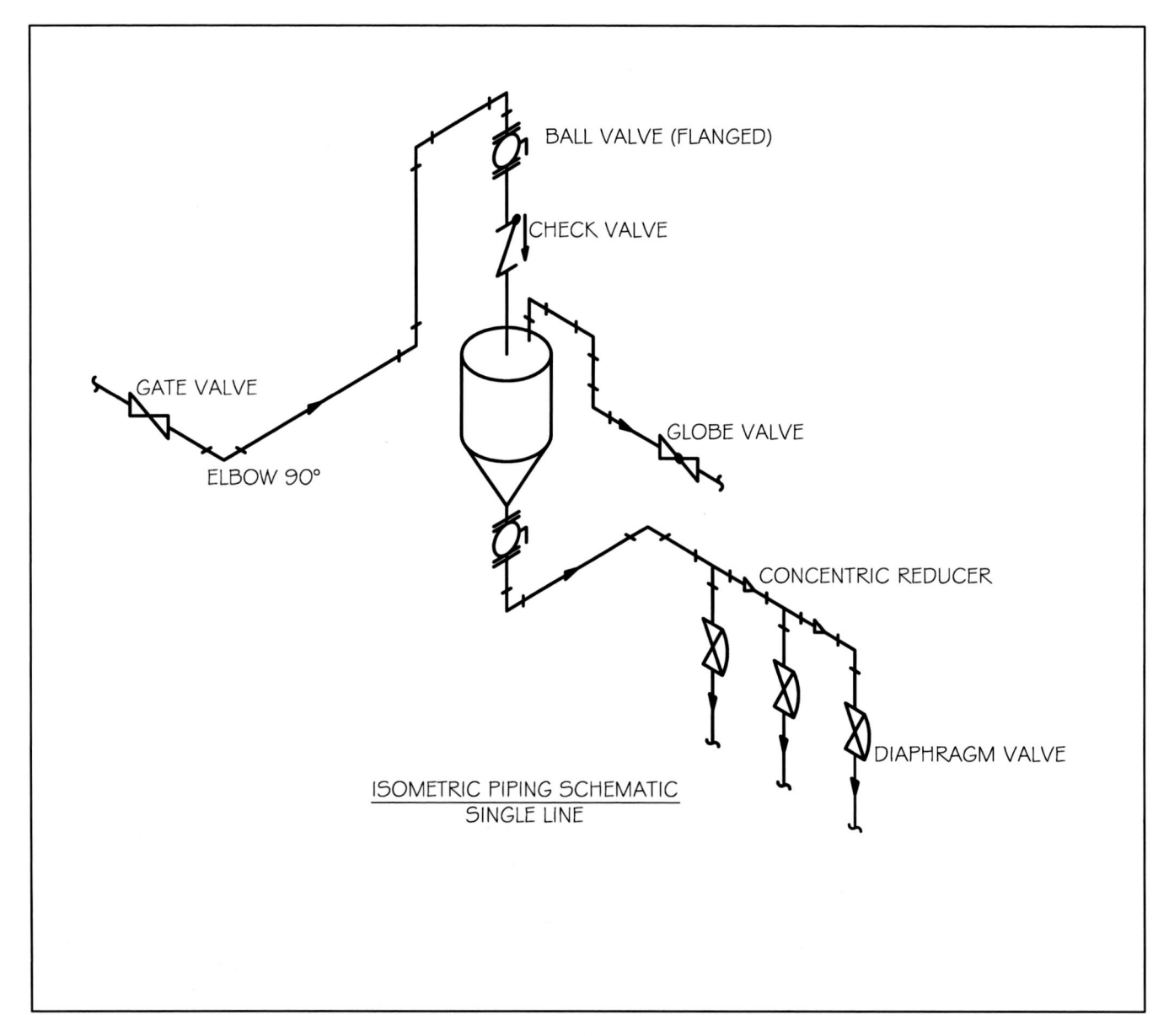

ISOMETRIC PIPING SCHEMATIC
SINGLE LINE

LESSON 14.01
PIPING

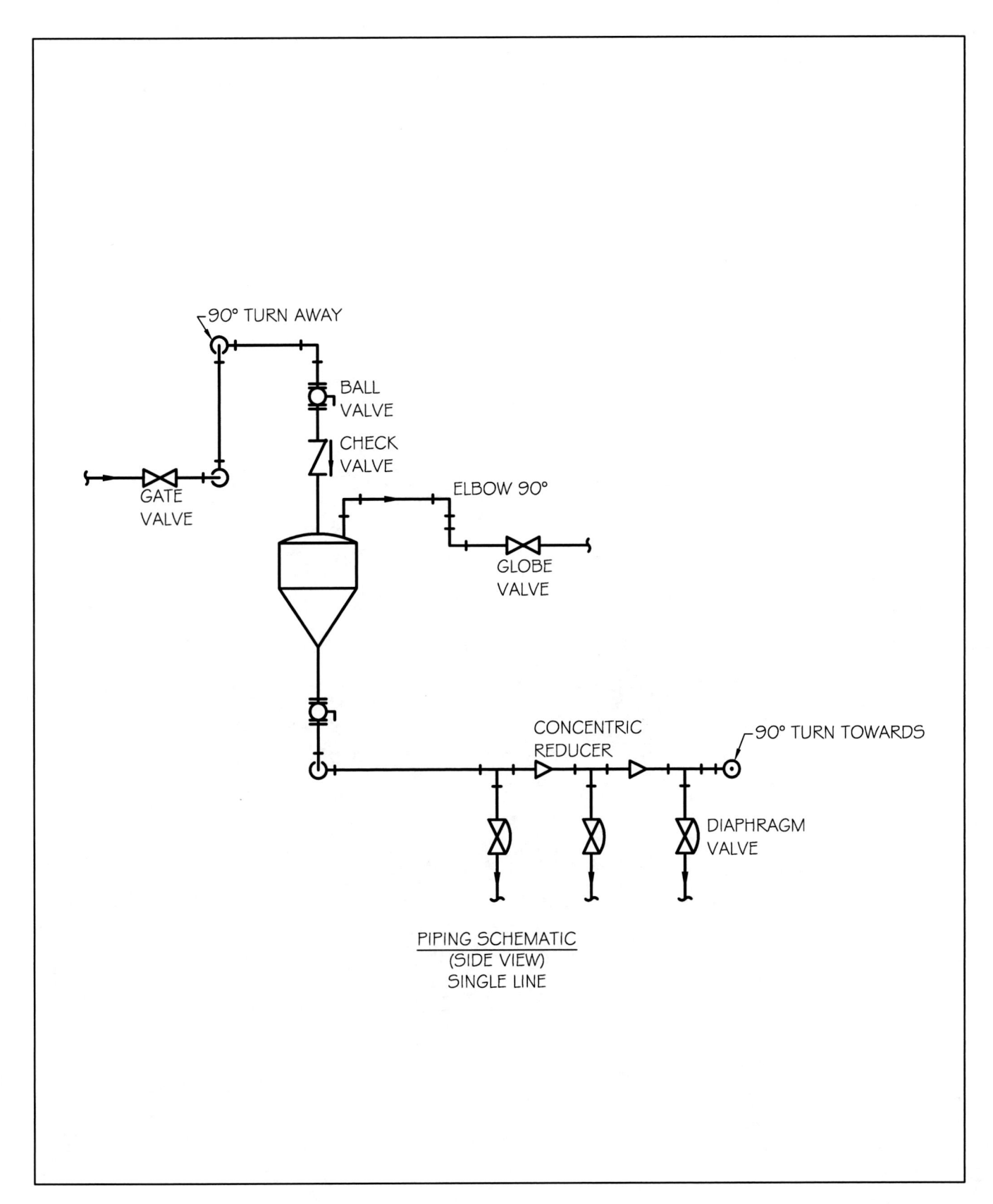

90° TURN AWAY

BALL VALVE

CHECK VALVE

GATE VALVE

ELBOW 90°

GLOBE VALVE

CONCENTRIC REDUCER

90° TURN TOWARDS

DIAPHRAGM VALVE

PIPING SCHEMATIC
(SIDE VIEW)
SINGLE LINE

LESSON 14.02
PIPING

INSTRUCTIONS:
REPRODUCE THE DRAWING BELOW TWICE THE SIZE OF THE ILLUSTRATION.

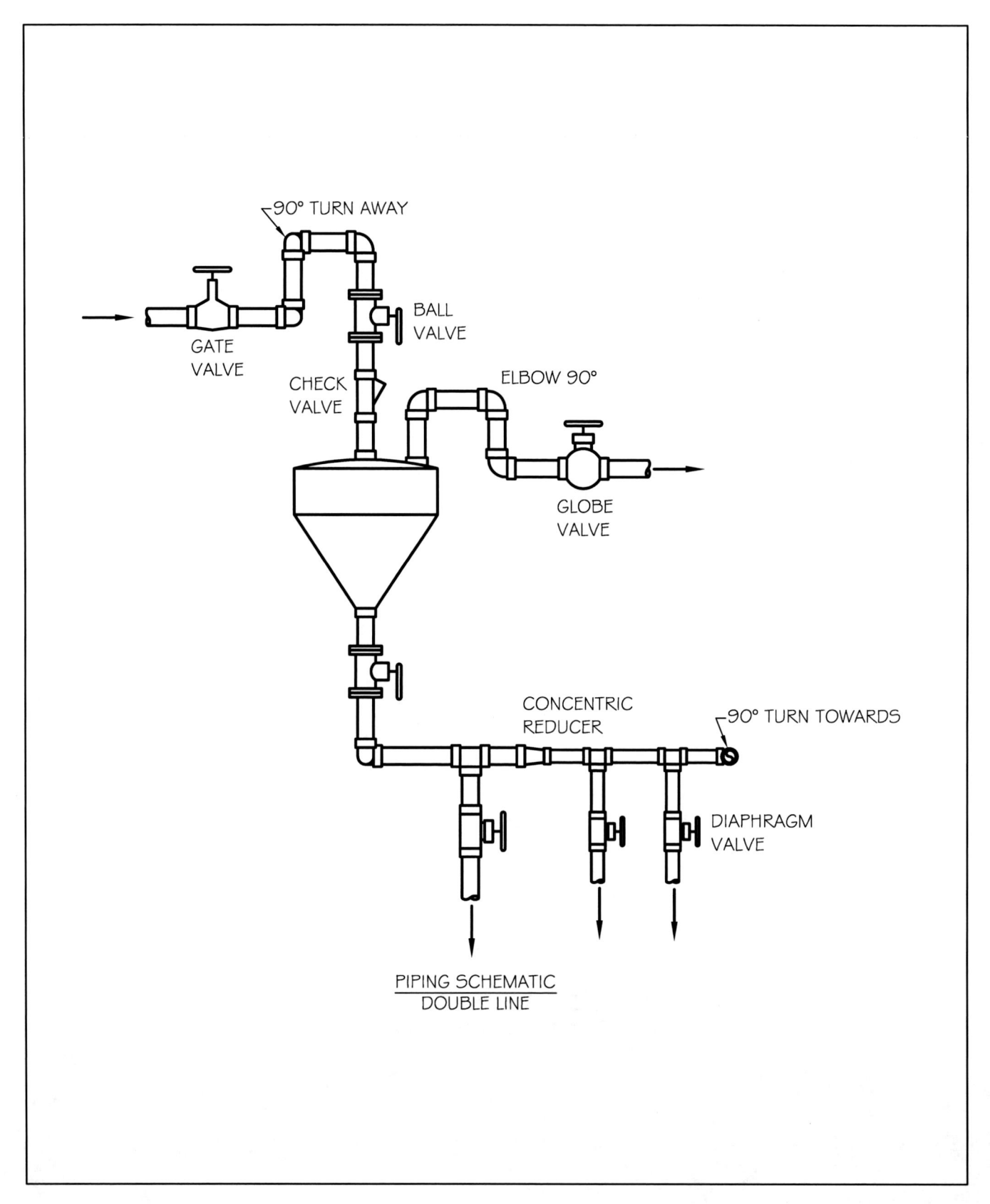

LESSON 15.00
P & I D

NOTE:

P&ID CAN MEAN DIFFERENT THINGS TO DIFFERENT ORGANIZATIONS. IT CAN BE A "PROCESS & INSTRUMENTATION DIAGRAM" OR "PIPING & INSTRUMENTATION DIAGRAM". IN BOTH CASES IT MEANS THAT THE DRAWING IS A SCHEMATIC DRAWING THAT SHOWS MECHANICAL EQUIPMENT AND/OR PIPING IN CONJUNCTION WITH ELECTRICAL SYSTEMS FOR CONTROL & MONITORING OF THE EQUIPMENT OR PROCESS. THE FOLLOWING ILLUSTRATIONS WILL SHOW SOME EXAMPLES. THE WAY A PROCESS IS SHOWN WILL BE DETERMINED BY THE REQUIRED END RESULT. A P&ID WILL USUALLY BE A PICTORIALLY SIMPLIFIED DRAWING, SHOWING SIMPLE SHAPES & BOXES TO REPRESENT EQUIPMENT & PROCESSES. P&ID'S CAN ALSO BE EXTREMELY DETAILED WITH PART NUMBERS, WIRE NUMBERS, PIPING SPECIFICATIONS, ETC., FOR A COMPLETE INFORMATION DRAWING ON ANY GIVEN SYSTEM OR PROCESS.

INSTRUCTIONS:

REPRODUCE THE SCHEMATIC BELOW AT THE SCALE OF YOUR CHOICE.

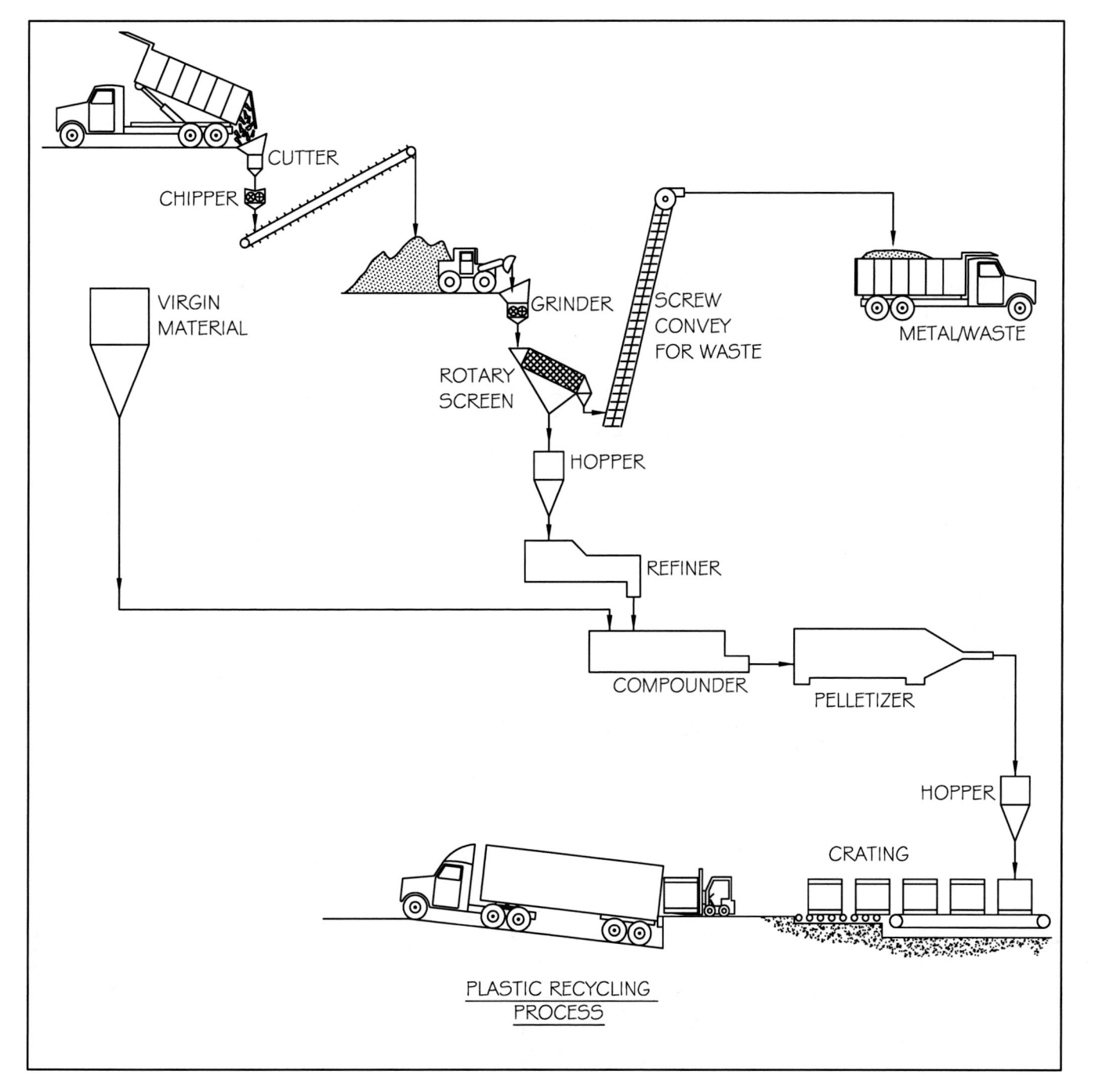

PLASTIC RECYCLING
PROCESS

LESSON 15.01
P & I D

INSTRUCTIONS:
REPRODUCE THE SCHEMATIC BELOW TWICE THE SIZE OF THE ILLUSTRATION.

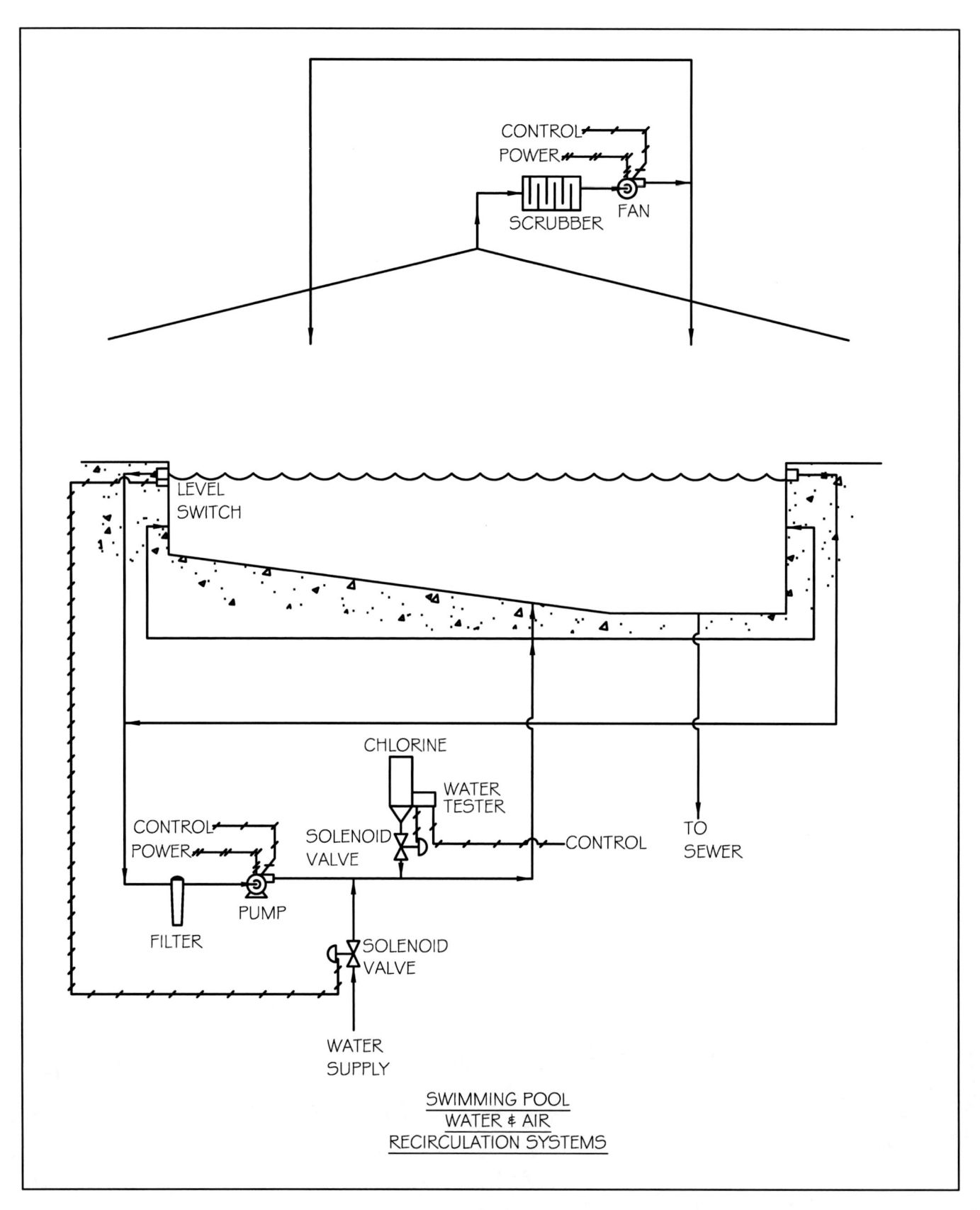

SWIMMING POOL
WATER & AIR
RECIRCULATION SYSTEMS

LESSON 16.00
ELECTRICAL

NOTE:
ELECTRICAL SYMBOLS HAVE BEEN DETERMINED BY ANSI. ELECTRICAL CODES & STANDARDS ARE DETERMINED BY THE NEC & THE IEEE. REFER TO BOOKS & DOCUMENTS ON ELECTRICAL CIRCUIT DRAFTING & DESIGN. THIS SUBJECT REQUIRES A STUDY OF ITS OWN. RADIO SHACK IS A GOOD SOURCE OF HOBBY & PROFESSIONAL REFERENCE MATERIALS.

INSTRUCTIONS:
REPRODUCE THE SCHEMATIC BELOW THE SIZE OF THE ILLUSTRATION.

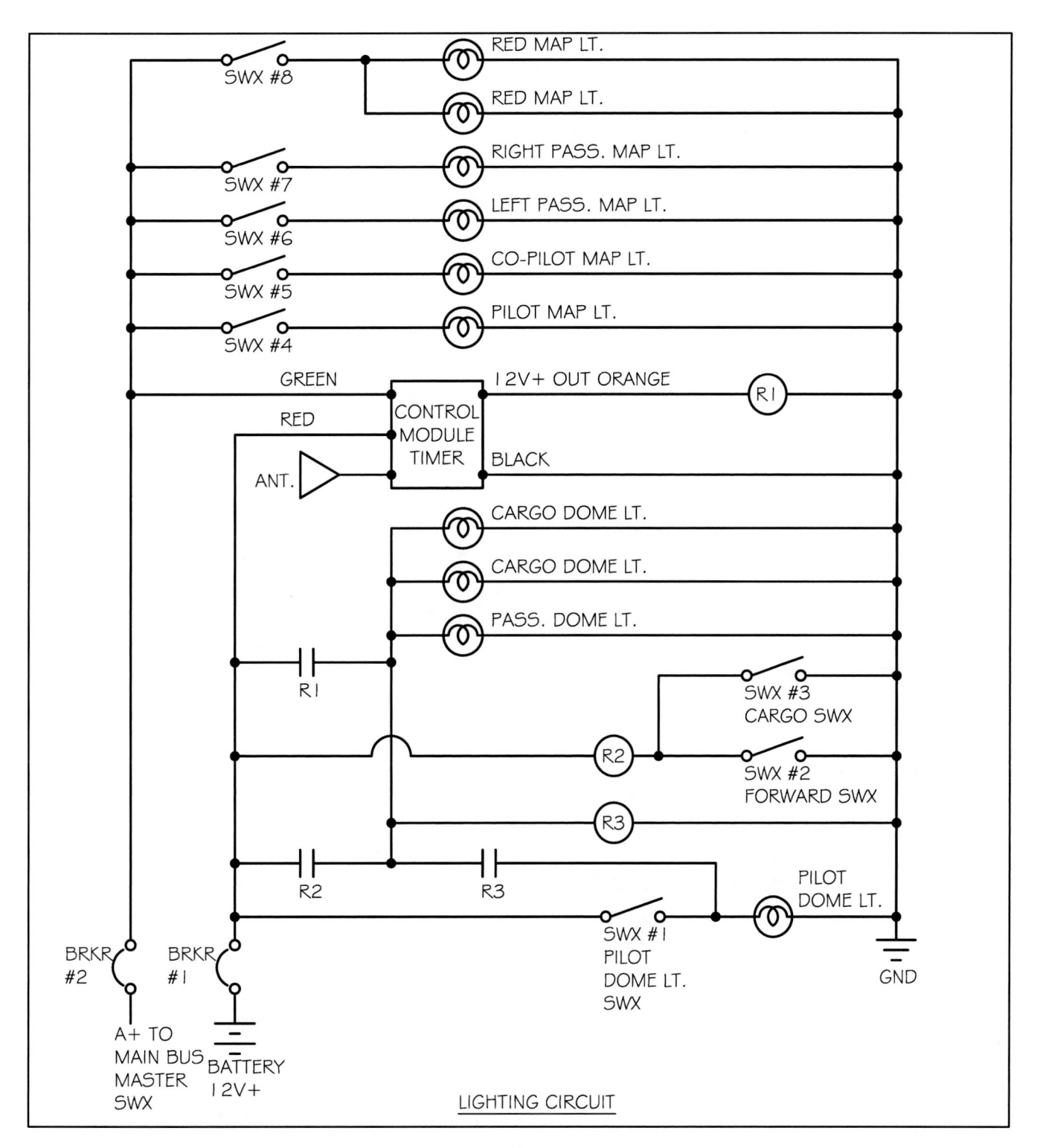

LIGHTING CIRCUIT

LESSON 17.00
PERSPECTIVE

NOTE:
A BRIEF EXPLANATION OF PERSPECTIVES: THERE ARE MANY TYPES OF PERSPECTIVES. PERSPECTIVES ARE A USEFUL METHOD FOR SHOWING DEPTH & DETAIL, SIMILAR TO THE WAY THE EYES SEE. PERSPECTIVES ARE USED IN ALL TYPES OF PRESENTATIONS; THE MOST COMMON USE IS IN THE FIELD OF ARCHITECTURE TO SHOW A DEPICTION OF A HOME OR BUILDING. FOR FURTHER STUDY, SEE ANY ENCYCLOPEDIA OR ART BOOK.

INSTRUCTIONS:
REPRODUCE THE DRAWING BELOW THE SIZE OF THE ILLUSTRATION.

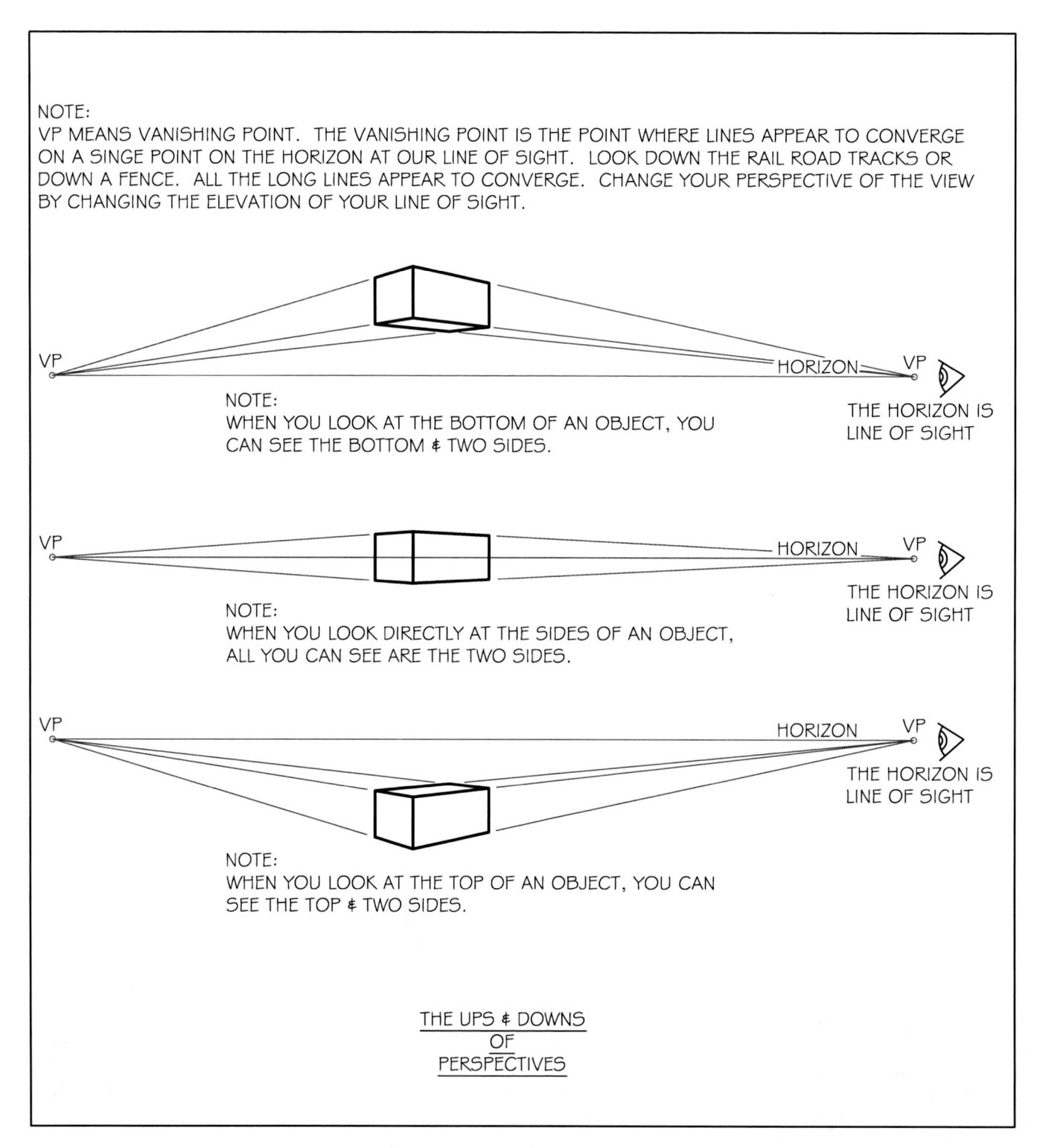

NOTE:
VP MEANS VANISHING POINT. THE VANISHING POINT IS THE POINT WHERE LINES APPEAR TO CONVERGE ON A SINGE POINT ON THE HORIZON AT OUR LINE OF SIGHT. LOOK DOWN THE RAIL ROAD TRACKS OR DOWN A FENCE. ALL THE LONG LINES APPEAR TO CONVERGE. CHANGE YOUR PERSPECTIVE OF THE VIEW BY CHANGING THE ELEVATION OF YOUR LINE OF SIGHT.

VP — HORIZON — VP
THE HORIZON IS LINE OF SIGHT

NOTE:
WHEN YOU LOOK AT THE BOTTOM OF AN OBJECT, YOU CAN SEE THE BOTTOM & TWO SIDES.

VP — HORIZON — VP
THE HORIZON IS LINE OF SIGHT

NOTE:
WHEN YOU LOOK DIRECTLY AT THE SIDES OF AN OBJECT, ALL YOU CAN SEE ARE THE TWO SIDES.

VP — HORIZON — VP
THE HORIZON IS LINE OF SIGHT

NOTE:
WHEN YOU LOOK AT THE TOP OF AN OBJECT, YOU CAN SEE THE TOP & TWO SIDES.

THE UPS & DOWNS
OF
PERSPECTIVES

LESSON 17.01
PERSPECTIVE

INSTRUCTIONS:
REPRODUCE THE DRAWING BELOW THE SIZE OF THE ILLUSTRATION.

NOTE:
THE BOOK CASE ALLOWS YOU TO SEE THE TOPS & BOTTOMS OF SHELVES AT THE SAME TIME. LOOK AT A BOOK CASE FROM THE FLOOR LEVEL, WHILE STANDING ON A CHAIR, & WHILE STANDING. NOTE THE DIFFERENCE IN PERSPECTIVE.

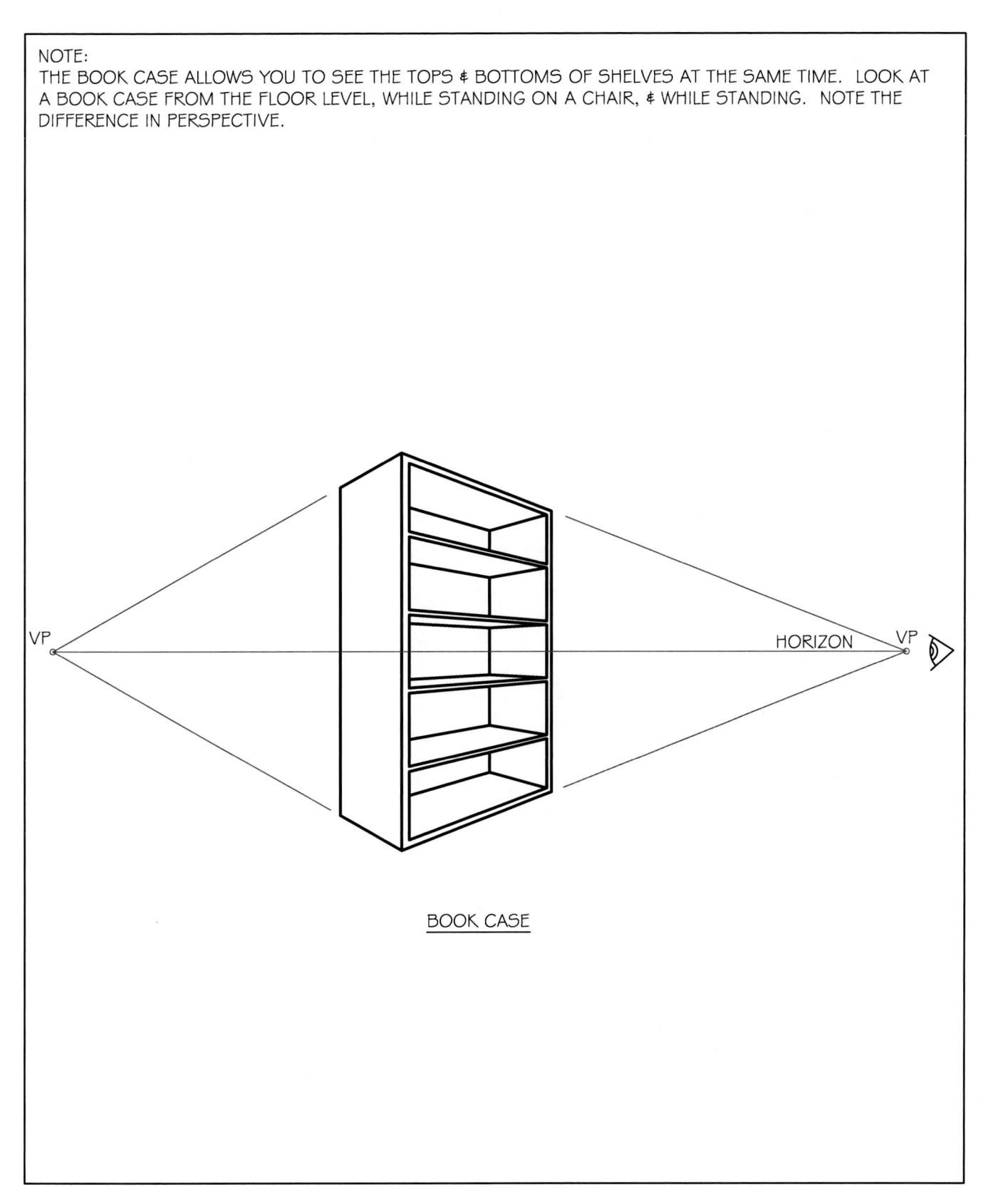

BOOK CASE

LESSON 18.00
OBLIQUE

NOTE:
A BRIEF EXPLANATION OF OBLIQUE DRAWING: OBLIQUES CAN BE PROJECTED BACK AT ANY DESIRED ANGLE. OBLIQUE DRAWINGS ARE THE SIMPLEST "3D" REPRESENTATION. THEY CAN LOOK STRANGE; HOWEVER, THEY DO HAVE THEIR PLACE IN CERTAIN APPLICATIONS LIKE SHOWING PROFILES & IN SKETCHES.

INSTRUCTIONS:
REPRODUCE THE DRAWINGS BELOW THE SIZE OF THE ILLUSTRATIONS.

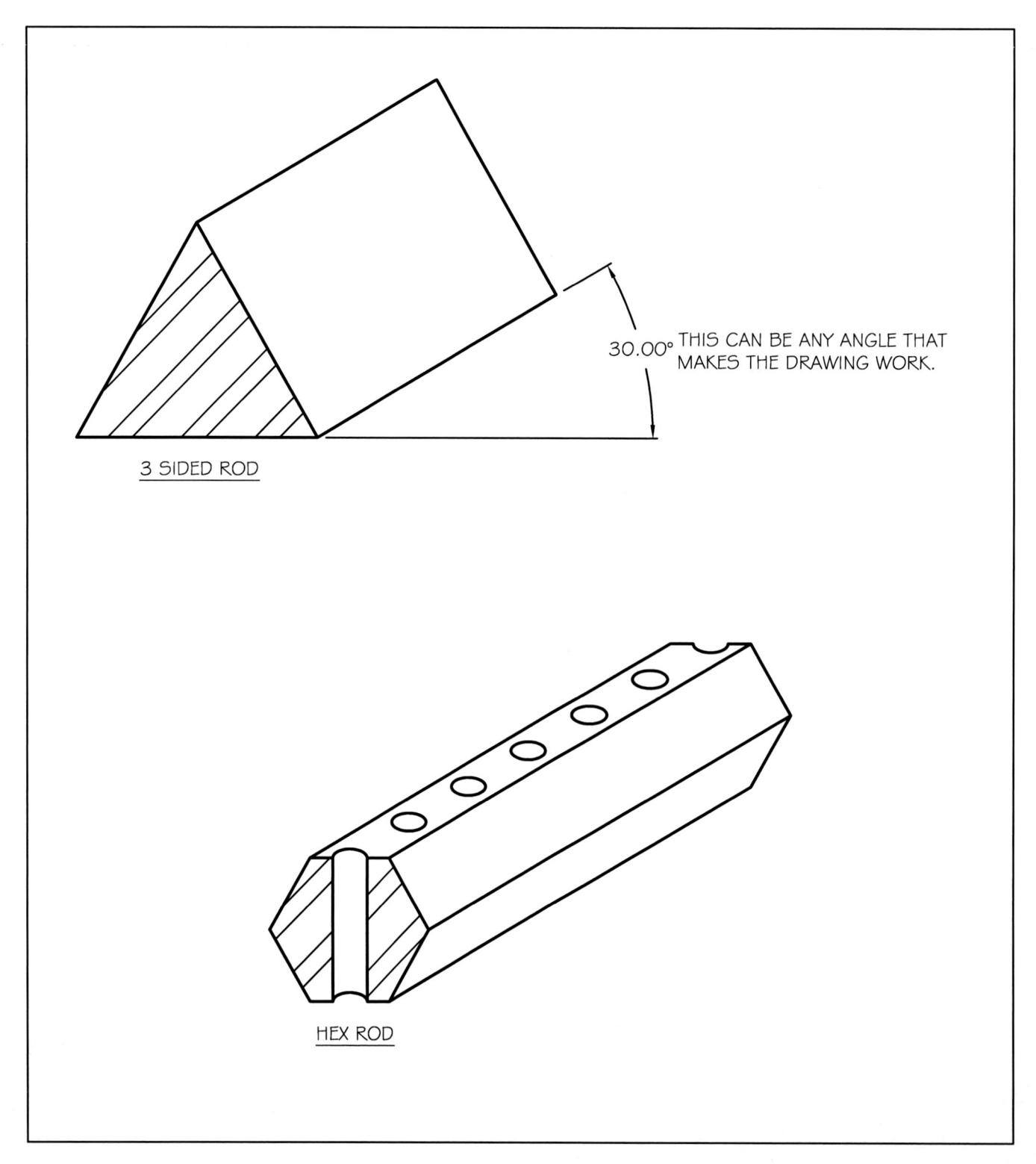

30.00° THIS CAN BE ANY ANGLE THAT MAKES THE DRAWING WORK.

3 SIDED ROD

HEX ROD

PROBLEM SOLUTIONS FOR LESSON 5.01
MULTIVIEW DRAWINGS

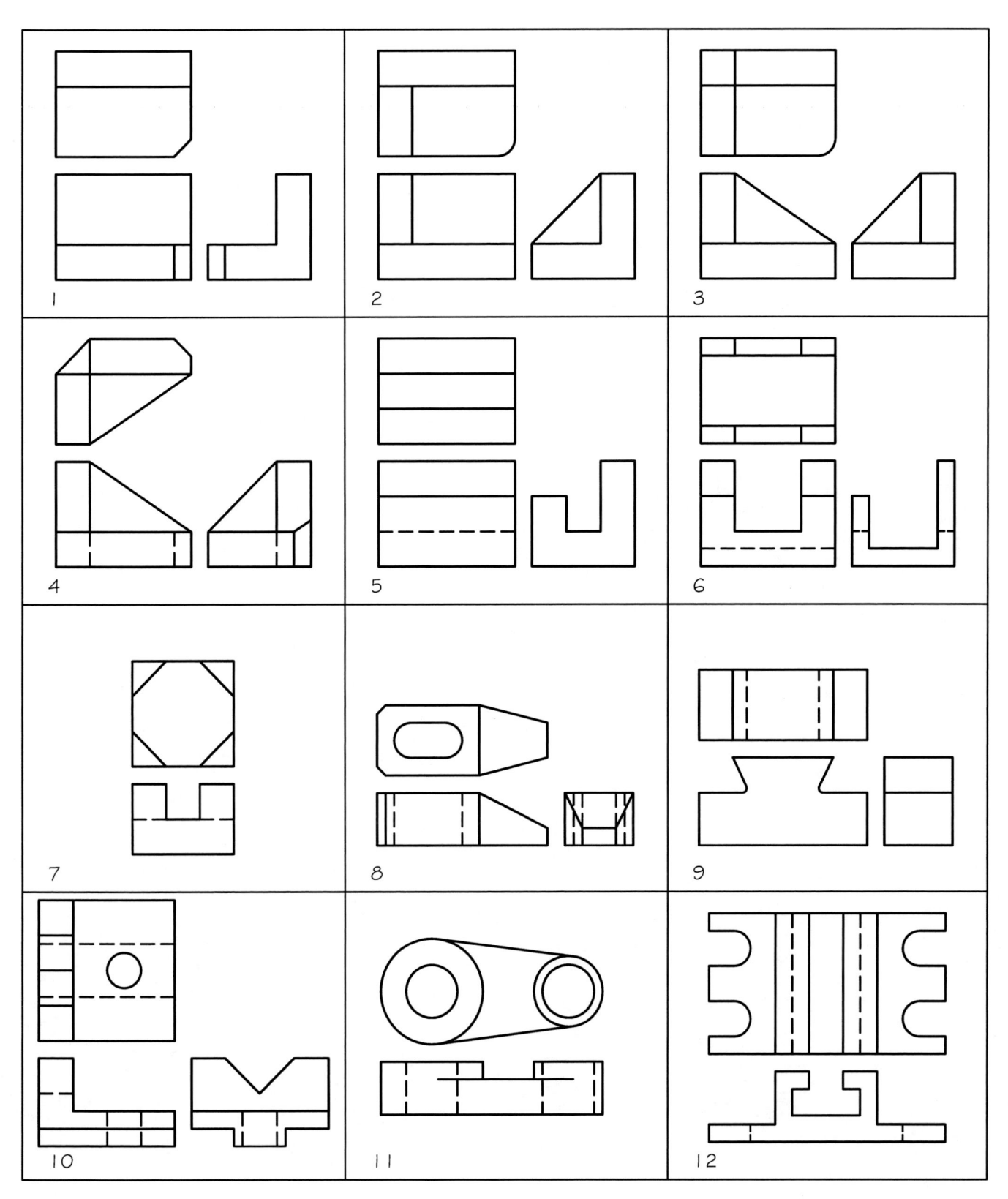

PROBLEM SOLUTIONS FOR LESSON 5.10
MULTIVIEW DRAWINGS

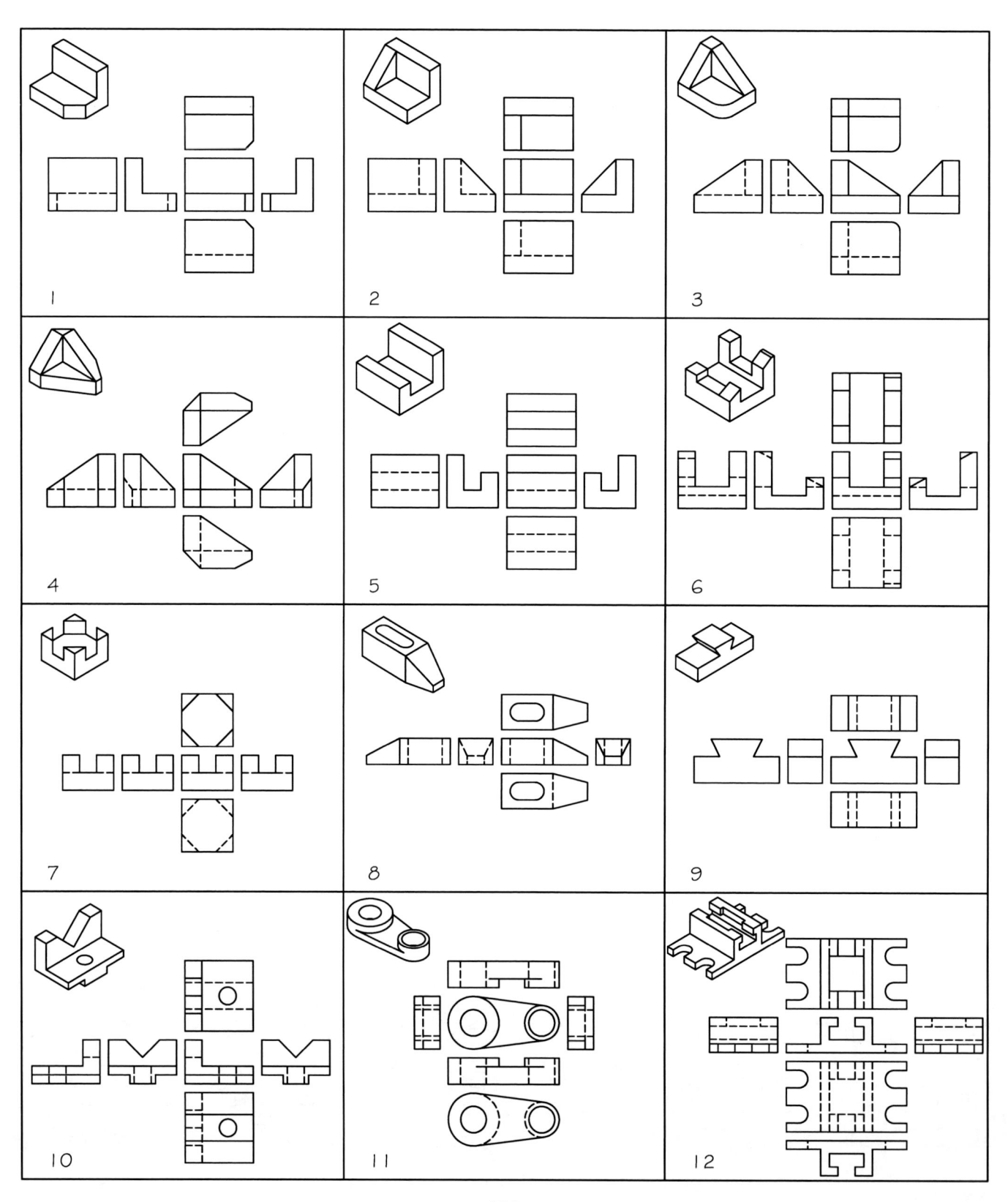

PROBLEM SOLUTIONS FOR LESSON 6.03
BREAK-AWAY VIEWS & SECTIONS

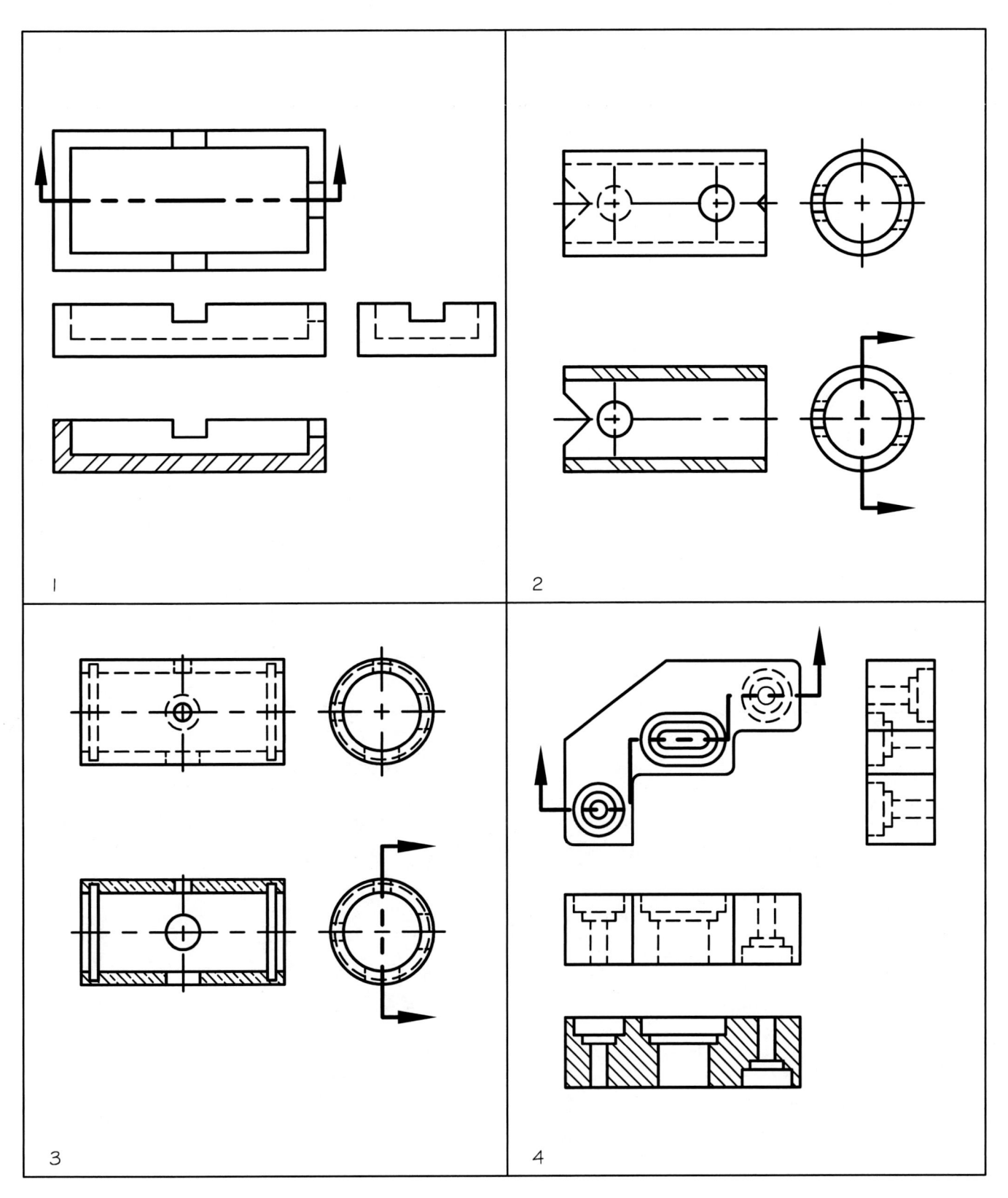

PROBLEM SOLUTIONS FOR LESSON 7.08A
DIMENSIONING & ANNOTATION

IMPORTANT NOTE:
THESE PROBLEMS CAN BE DIMENSIONED SEVERAL DIFFERENT WAYS TO ACHIEVE THE SAME END RESULT. YOU
WILL HAVE TO JUDGE FOR YOURSELF IF YOUR DRAWINGS ARE COMPLETE.

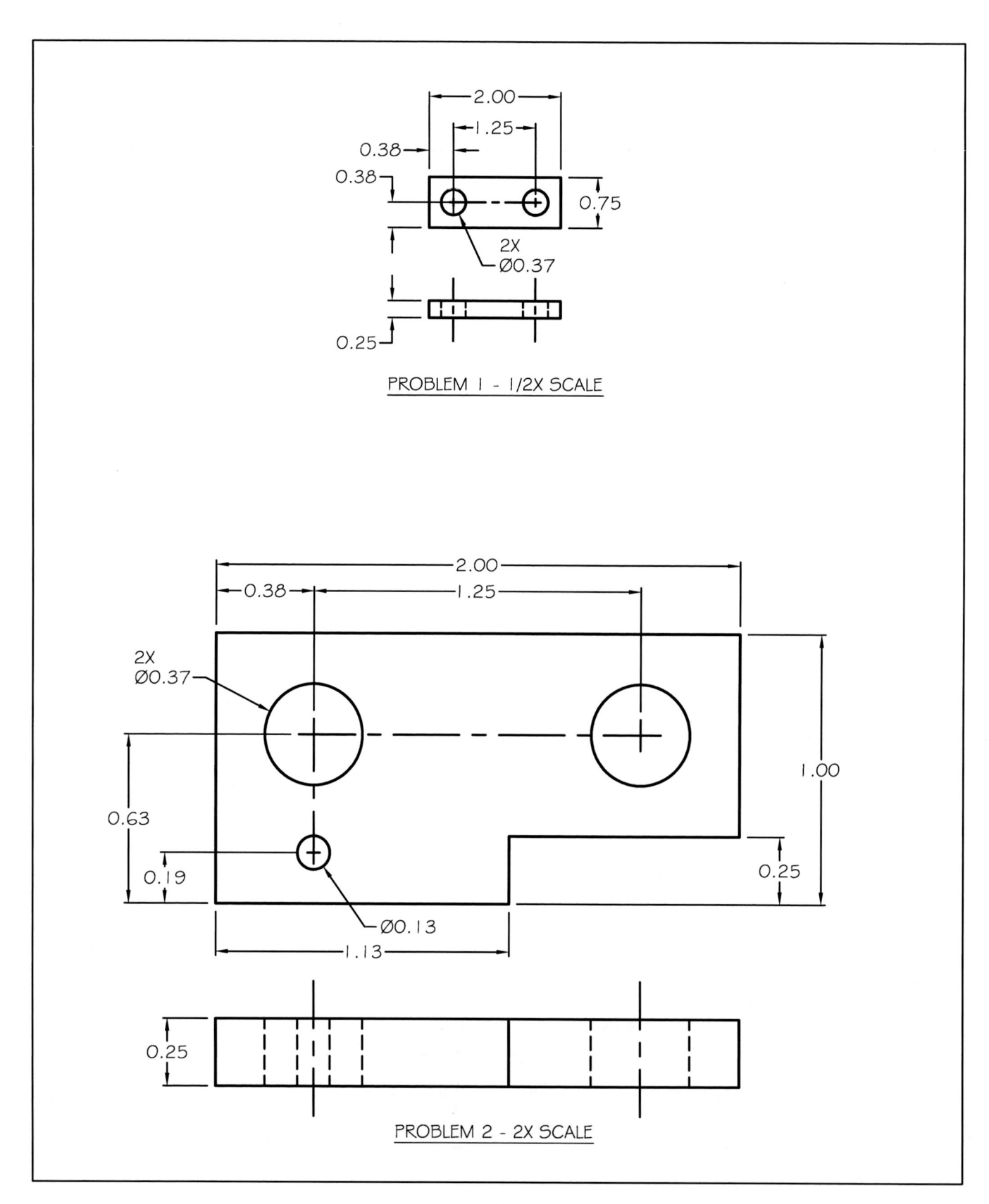

PROBLEM 1 - 1/2X SCALE

PROBLEM 2 - 2X SCALE

PROBLEM SOLUTIONS FOR LESSON 7.08B
DIMENSIONING & ANNOTATION

IMPORTANT NOTE:
THESE PROBLEMS CAN BE DIMENSIONED SEVERAL DIFFERENT WAYS TO ACHIEVE THE SAME END RESULT. YOU WILL
HAVE TO JUDGE FOR YOURSELF IF YOUR DRAWINGS ARE COMPLETE.

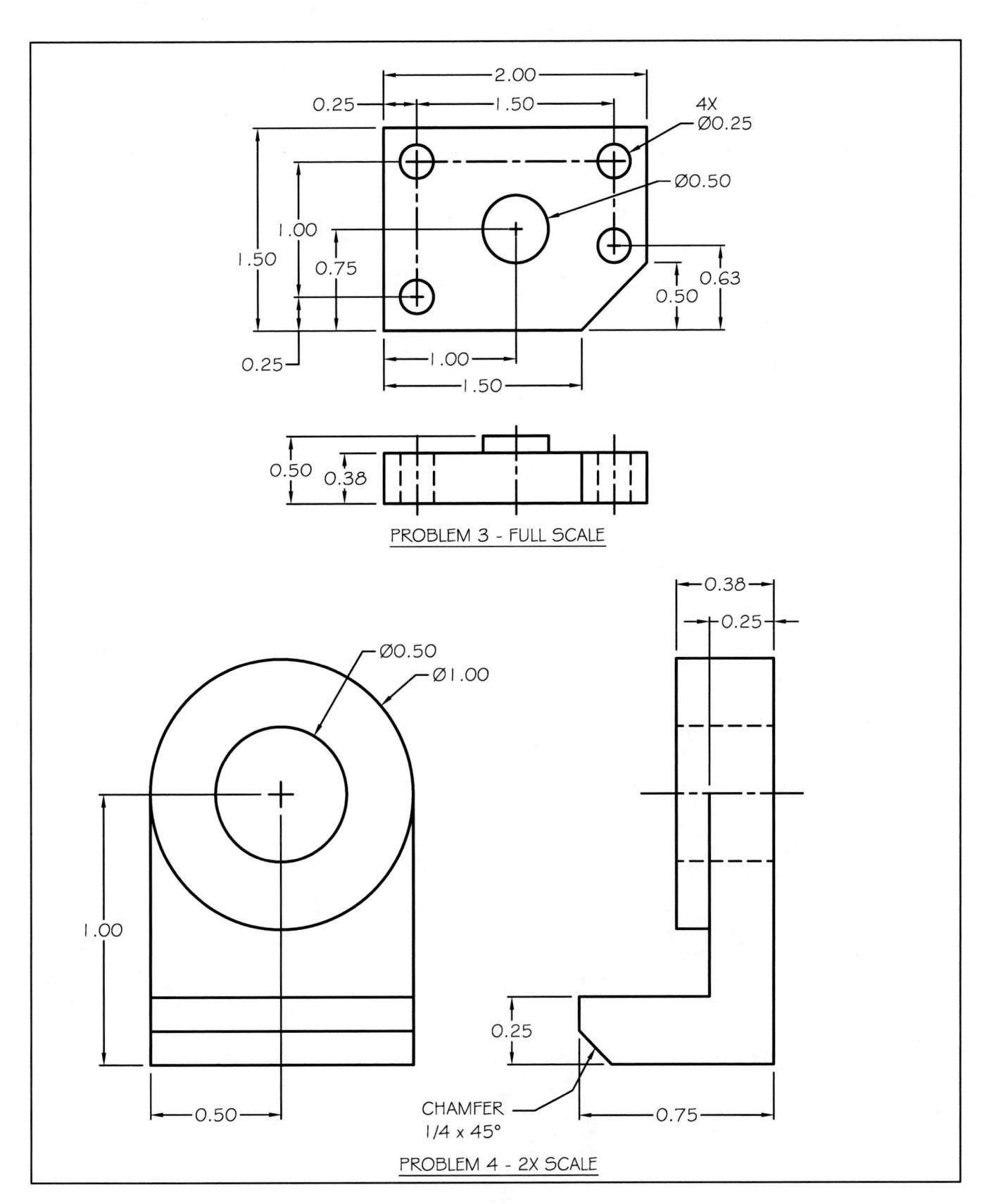

PROBLEM 3 - FULL SCALE

PROBLEM 4 - 2X SCALE

PROBLEM SOLUTIONS FOR LESSON 7.08C
DIMENSIONING & ANNOTATION

IMPORTANT NOTE:
THESE PROBLEMS CAN BE DIMENSIONED SEVERAL DIFFERENT WAYS TO ACHIEVE THE SAME END RESULT. YOU WILL HAVE TO JUDGE FOR YOURSELF IF YOUR DRAWINGS ARE COMPLETE.

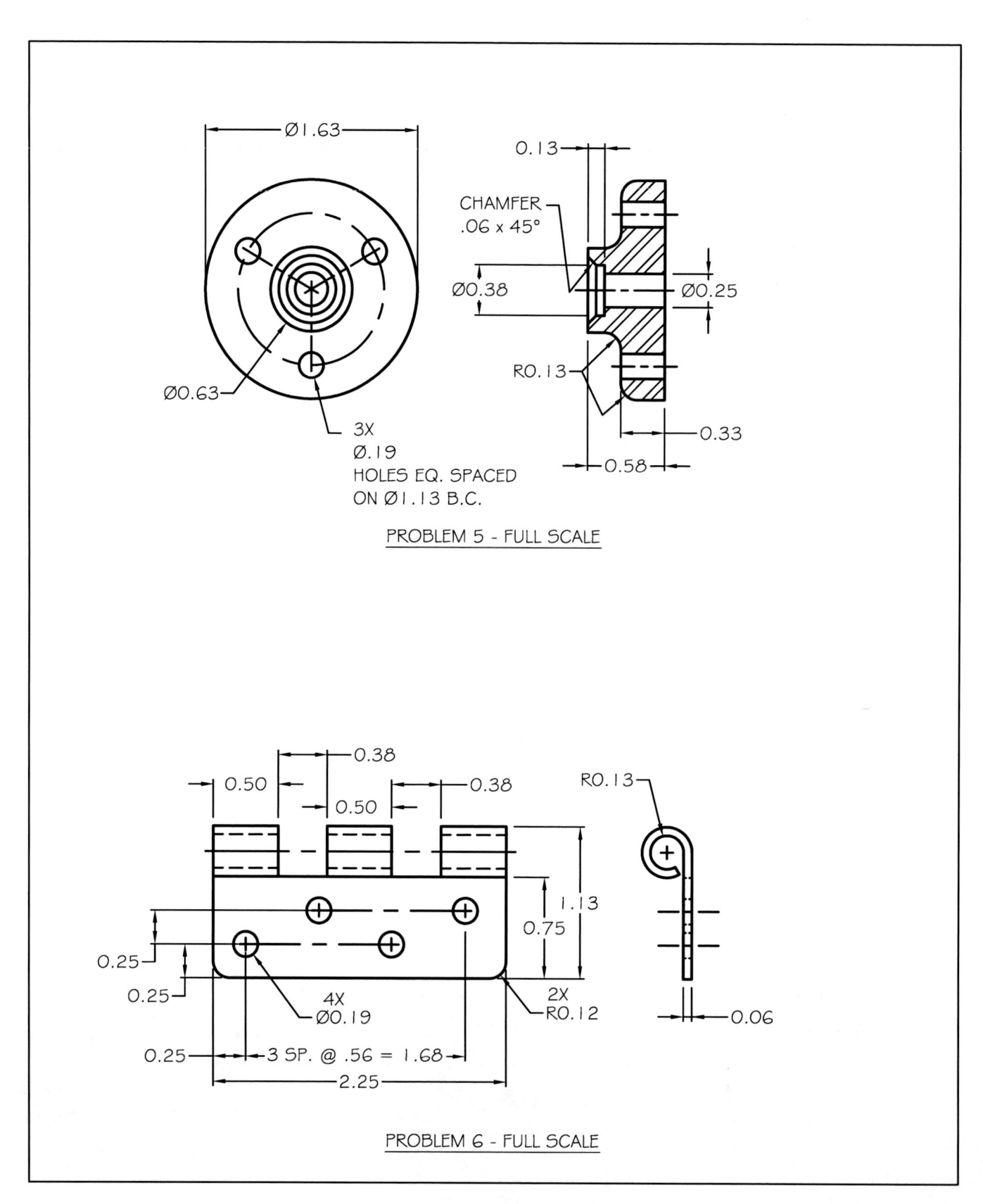

PROBLEM 5 - FULL SCALE

PROBLEM 6 - FULL SCALE

REFERENCE - CONTENTS

Books

This is only a partial list to get you started. Contact any good book store and they can point you in the right direction. Libraries are also a great resource. Also, look for books and subjects on the World Wide Web.

Insight™ Technical Education Complete-A-Sketch™ Series
By: Melvin G. Peterman

Technical Drawing
By: F.E. Giesecke, A. Mitchell, H.C. Spencer, I.L. Hill, J.T. Dygon
Macmillan Publishing Co., Inc.

Descriptive Geometry
By: E.G. Pare', R.O. Loving, I.L. Hill
Macmillan Publishing Co., Inc.

Machinery's Handbook
By: E. Oberg, F.D. Jones, H.L. Horton
Industrial Press Inc.

American National Standards Institute, Inc.
11 West 42nd Street, New York, NY 10036
       Publishes books on the following subjects:
            Bolts & Screws
            Dimensioning and Surface Finish
            Drafting Manual
            Gears
            Graphic Symbols
            Keys & Pins
            Piping
            Rivets
            Small Tools and Machine Tool Elements
            Threads
            Washers

Electrical & Electronic Drawing
By: C.J. Baer
McGraw-Hill Inc.

Subjects:

Architectural drawing	Blue print reading	Cams
Electrical drawing	Electrical design	Graphical computation
Illustration	Machine design	Map drawing
Mechanisms	Perspective	Pipe design
Sheet metal design	Shop processes	Tool design
Topography	Welding	

My favorite independent bookseller is a source of new, used, out of print, and hard to find books of every kind. The main store fills a full city block with a second store just for technical books.

Powell's City of Books
1005 W Burnside
Portland, OR 97209
USA
503-228-4651
800-878-7323
Fax: 503-228-4631
TDD: 503-226-2475
www.powells.com

STANDARD PRESSURE & FLOW RATE CONVERSIONS

Multiply	By	To Obtain
CCM	0.0000353	CFM
CFM	28,317	CCM
CFM	28.317	SLM
SLM	0.0353	CFM
IHG	13.6091	IWC
IWC	0.07348	IHG

STANDARD PRESSURE & FLOW RATE DESIGNATIONS

Acronym	Meaning
Pressure	
PSI	Pounds per Square Inch
PSIG	Pounds per Square Inch Gauge
Vacuum	
IWC	Inches of Water Column
IHg	Inches of Mercury
Flow Rate	
CFM	Cubic Feet per Minute
SCFM	Standard Cubic Feet per Minute
LPM	Liters Per Minute
SLPM	Standard Liters Per Minute
CCM	Cubic Centimeters per Minute
SCCM	Standard Cubic Centimeters per Minute
GPM	Gallons Per Minute

Note that "STANDARD" refers to a standard temperature & atmospheric pressure as a base line (i.e. 70°F at sea level). This standard can be whatever it needs to be for the organization as its own standard.

USEFUL MULTIPLIERS

Multiply	By	To Obtain
Acres	43,560	Square feet
Acres	4047	Square meters
Acres	1.562 x 0.001	Square miles
Acres	4840	Square yards
Acre-feet	43,560	Cubic feet
Acre-feet	325,851	Gallons
Acre-feet	1233.49	Cubic meters
Atmospheres	76.0	Centimeters of mercury
Atmospheres	29.92	Inches of mercury
Atmospheres	33.90	Feet of water
Atmospheres	10,333	Kilograms/square meter
Atmospheres	14.70	Pounds/square inch
Atmospheres	1.058	Tons/square foot
Barrels-oil	42	Gallons-oil
Barrels-cement	376	Pounds-cement
Bags or sacks-cement	94	Pounds-cement
Board feet	144 square inch x 1 inch	Cubic inches
British Thermal Units	0.2520	Kilogram-calories
British Thermal Units	777.5	Foot-pounds
British Thermal Units	3.927 x 0.0001	Horsepower-hours
British Thermal Units	107.5	Kilogram-meters
British Thermal Units	2.928 x 0.0001	Kilowatt-hours
British Thermal Units/minute	12.96	Foot-pounds/second
British Thermal Units/minute	0.02356	Horsepower
British Thermal Units/minute	0.01757	Kilowatts
British Thermal Units/minute	17.57	Watts
Centares (Centiares)	1	Square meters
Centigrams	0.01	Grams
Centiliters	0.01	Liters
Centimeters	0.3937	Inches
Centimeters	0.01	Meters
Centimeters	10	Millimeters
Centimeters of mercury	0.01316	Atmospheres
Centimeters of mercury	0.4461	Feet of water
Centimeters of mercury	136.0	Kilograms/square meter
Centimeters of mercury	27.85	Pounds/square foot
Centimeters of mercury	0.1934	Pounds/square inch
Centimeters/second	1.969	Feet/minute
Centimeters/second	0.03281	Feet/second
Centimeters/second	0.036	Kilometers/hour
Centimeters/second	0.6	Meters/minute
Centimeters/second	0.02237	Miles/hour
Centimeters/second	3.728 x 0.0001	Miles/minute
Centimeters/second/second	0.03281	Feet/second/second
Cubic centimeters	3.531 x 0.00001	Cubic feet
Cubic centimeters	6.102 x 0.01	Cubic inches
Cubic centimeters	0.000001	Cubic meters
Cubic centimeters	1.308 x 0.000001	Cubic yards
Cubic centimeters	2.642 x 0.0001	Gallons
Cubic centimeters	0.001	Liters
Cubic centimeters	2.113 x 0.001	Pints (liquid)
Cubic centimeters	1.057 x 0.001	Quarts (liquid)
Cubic feet	2.832 x 10,000	Cubic centimeters
Cubic feet	1728	Cubic inches
Cubic feet	0.02832	Cubic meters
Cubic feet	0.03704	Cubic yards
Cubic feet	7.48052	Gallons

Multiply	By	To Obtain
Cubic feet	28.32	Liters
Cubic feet	59.84	Pints (liquid)
Cubic feet	29.92	Quarts (liquid)
Cubic feet/minute	472.0	Cubic centimeters/second
Cubic feet/minute	0.1247	Gallons/second
Cubic feet/minute	0.4720	Liters/second
Cubic feet/minute	62.43	Pounds of water/minute
Cubic feet/second	0.646317	Millions gallons/day
Cubic feet/second	448.831	Gallons/minute
Cubic inches	16.39	Cubic centimeters
Cubic inches	5.787 x 0.0001	Cubic feet
Cubic inches	1.639 x 0.00001	Cubic meters
Cubic inches	2.143 x 0.00001	Cubic yards
Cubic inches	4.329 x 0.001	Gallons
Cubic inches	1.639 x 0.01	Liters
Cubic inches	0.03463	Pints (liquid)
Cubic inches	0.01732	Quarts (liquid)
Cubic meters	1,000,000	Cubic centimeters
Cubic meters	35.31	Cubic feet
Cubic meters	61.023	Cubic inches
Cubic meters	1.308	Cubic yards
Cubic meters	264.2	Gallons
Cubic meters	1,000	Liters
Cubic meters	2113	Pints (liquid)
Cubic meters	1057	Quarts (liquid)
Cubic yards	7.646 x 100,000	Cubic centimeters
Cubic yards	27	Cubic feet
Cubic yards	46,656	Cubic inches
Cubic yards	0.7646	Cubic meters
Cubic yards	202.0	Gallons
Cubic yards	764.6	Liters
Cubic yards	1616	Pints (liquid)
Cubic yards	807.9	Quarts (liquid)
Cubic yards/minute	0.45	Cubic feet/second
Cubic yards/minute	3.367	Gallons/second
Cubic yards/minute	12.74	Liters/second
Decigrams	0.1	Grams
Deciliters	0.1	Liters
Decimeters	0.1	Meters
Degrees (angle)	60	Minutes
Degrees (angle)	0.01745	Radians
Degrees (angle)	3600	Seconds
Degrees/second	0.01745	Radians/second
Degrees/second	0.1667	Revolutions/minute
Degrees/second	0.002778	Revolutions/second
Dekagrams	10	Grams
Dekaliters	10	Liters
Dekameters	10	Meters
Drams	27.34375	Grains
Drams	0.0625	Ounces
Drams	1.771845	Grams
Fathoms	6	Feet
Feet	30.48	Centimeters
Feet	12	Inches
Feet	0.3048	Meters
Feet	304.8	Millimeters
Feet	0.333333	Yards
Feet of water	0.02950	Atmospheres
Feet of water	0.8826	Inches of mercury

Multiply	By	To Obtain
Feet of water	304.8	Kilograms/square meter
Feet of water	62.43	Pounds/square foot
Feet of water	0.4335	Pounds/square inch
Feet/minute	0.5080	Centimeters/second
Feet/minute	0.01667	Feet/second
Feet/minute	0.01829	Kilometers/hour
Feet/minute	0.3048	Meters/minute
Feet/minute	0.01136	Miles/hour
Feet/second	30.48	Centimeters/second
Feet/second	1.097	Kilometers/hour
Feet/second	0.5921	Knots
Feet/second	18.29	Meters/minute
Feet/second	0.6818	Miles/hour
Feet/second	0.01136	Miles/minute
Feet/second/second	30.48	Centimeters/second/second
Feet/second/second	0.3048	Meters/second/second
Foot-pounds	1.286 x 0.001	British Thermal Units
Foot-pounds	5.050 x 0.0000001	Horsepower-hours
Foot-pounds	3.241 x 0.0001	Kilogram-calories
Foot-pounds	0.1383	Kilogram-meters
Foot-pounds	3.766 x 0.0000001	Kilowatt-hours
Foot-pounds/minute	1.286 x 0.001	British Thermal Units/minute
Foot-pounds/minute	0.01667	Foot-pounds/second
Foot-pounds/minute	3.030 x 0.00001	Horsepower
Foot-pounds/minute	3.241 x 0.0001	Kg.-calories/minute
Foot-pounds/minute	2.260 x 0.00001	Kilowatts
Foot-pounds/second	7.717 x 0.01	British Thermal Units/minute
Foot-pounds/second	1.818 x 0.001	Horsepower
Foot-pounds/second	1.945 x 0.01	Kg.-calories/minute
Foot-pounds/second	1.356 x 0.001	Kilowatts
Gallons	3785	Cubic centimeters
Gallons	0.1337	Cubic feet
Gallons	231	Cubic inches
Gallons	3.785 x 0.001	Cubic meters
Gallons	4.951 x 0.001	Cubic yards
Gallons	3.785	Liters
Gallons	8	Pints (liquid)
Gallons	4	Quarts (liquid)
Gallons-Imperial	1.20095	U.S. gallons
Gallons-U.S.	0.83267	Imperial gallons
Gallons water	8.3453	Pounds of water
Gallons/minute	2.228 x 0.001	Cubic feet/second
Gallons/minute	0.06308	Liters/second
Gallons/minute	8.0208	Cubic feet/hour
Grains (troy)	0.06480	Grams
Grains (troy)	0.04167	Pennyweights (troy)
Grains (troy)	2.0833 x 0.001	Ounces (troy)
Grains/U.S. gallon	17.118	Parts/million
Grains/U.S. gallon	142.86	Pounds/million gallons
Grains/Imperial gallon	14.254	Parts/million
Grams	980.7	Dynes
Grams	15.43	Grains
Grams	0.001	Kilograms
Grams	1,000	Milligrams
Grams	0.03527	Ounces
Grams	0.03215	Ounces (troy)
Grams	2.205 x 0.001	Pounds
Grams/centimeter	5.600 x 0.001	Pounds/inch
Grams/cubic centimeter	62.43	Pounds/cubic foot

Multiply	By	To Obtain
Grams/cubic centimeter	0.03613	Pounds/cubic inch
Grams/liter	58.417	Grains/gallon
Grams/liter	8.345	Pounds/1000 gallons
Grams/liter	0.062427	Pounds/cubic foot
Grams/liter	1000	Parts/million
Hectares	2.471	Acres
Hectares	1.076 x 100,000	Square feet
Hectograms	100	Grams
Hectoliters`	100	Liters
Hectometers	100	Meters
Hectowatts	100	Watts
Horsepower	42.44	British Thermal Units/minute
Horsepower	33,000	Foot-pounds/minute
Horsepower	550	Foot-pounds/second
Horsepower	1.014	Horsepower (metric)
Horsepower	10.70	Kg.-calories/minute
Horsepower	0.7457	Kilowatts
Horsepower	745.7	Watts
Horsepower (boiler)	33,479	British Thermal Units/hour
Horsepower (boiler)	9.803	Kilowatts
Horsepower-hours	2547	British Thermal Units
Horsepower-hours	1.98 x 1,000,000	Foot-pounds
Horsepower-hours	641.7	Kilogram-calories
Horsepower-hours	2.737 x 100,000	Kilogram-meters
Horsepower-hours	0.7457	Kilowatt-hours
Inches	2.540	Centimeters
Inches of mercury	0.03342	Atmospheres
Inches of mercury	1.133	Feet of water
Inches of mercury	345.3	Kilograms/square meter
Inches of mercury	70.73	Pounds/square foot
Inches of mercury	0.4912	Pounds/square inch
Inches of water	0.002458	Atmospheres
Inches of water	0.07355	Inches of mercury
Inches of water	25.40	Kilograms/square meter
Inches of water	0.5781	Ounces/square inch
Inches of water	5.202	Pounds/square foot
Inches of water	0.03613	Pounds/square inch
Kilograms	980,665	Dynes
Kilograms	2.205	Pounds
Kilograms	1.102 x 0.001	Tons (short)
Kilograms	1,000	Grams
Kilograms-calories	3.968	British Thermal Units
Kilograms-calories	3086	Foot-pounds
Kilograms-calories	1.558 x 0.001	Horsepower-hours
Kilograms-calories	1.162 x 0.001	Kilowatt-hours
Kilogram-calories/minute	51.43	Foot-pounds/second
Kilogram-calories/minute	0.09351	Horsepower
Kilogram-calories/minute	0.06972	Kilowatts
Kilograms/meter	0.6720	Pounds/foot
Kilograms/square meter	9.678 x 0.00001	Atmospheres
Kilograms/square meter	3.281 x 0.001	Feet of water
Kilograms/square meter	2.896 x 0.001	Inches of mercury
Kilograms/square meter	0.2048	Pounds/square foot
Kilograms/square meter	1.422 x 0.001	Pounds/square inch
Kilograms/square millimeter	1,000,000	Kilograms/square meter
Kiloliters	1,000	Liters
Kilometers	100,000	Centimeters
Kilometers	3281	Feet
Kilometers	1,000	Meters

Multiply	By	To Obtain
Kilometers	0.6214	Miles
Kilometers	1094	Yards
Kilometers/hour	27.78	Centimeters/second
Kilometers/hour	54.68	Feet/minute
Kilometers/hour	0.9113	Feet/second
Kilometers/hour	0.5396	Knots
Kilometers/hour	16.67	Meters/minute
Kilometers/hour	0.6214	Miles/hour
Kms./hour/second	27.78	Centimeters/second/second
Kms./hour/second	0.9113	Feet/second/second
Kms./hour/second	0.2778	Meters/second/second
Kilowatts	56.92	British Thermal Units/minute
Kilowatts	4.425 x 10,000	Foot-pounds/minute
Kilowatts	737.6	Foot-pounds/second
Kilowatts	1.341	Horsepower
Kilowatts	14.34	Kilogram-calories/minute
Kilowatts	1,000	Watts
Kilowatt-hours	3415	British Thermal Units
Kilowatt-hours	2.655 x 1,000,000	Foot-pounds
Kilowatt-hours	1.341	Horsepower-hours
Kilowatt-hours	860.5	Kilogram-calories
Kilowatt-hours	3.671 x 100,000	Kilogram-meters
Liters	1,000	Cubic centimeters
Liters	0.03531	Cubic feet
Liters	61.02	Cubic inches
Liters	0.001	Cubic meters
Liters	1.308 x 0.001	Cubic yards
Liters	0.2642	Gallons
Liters	2.113	Pints (liquid)
Liters	1.057	Quarts (liquid)
Liters/minute	5.886 x 0.0001	Cubic feet/second
Liters/minute	4.403 x 0.001	Gallons/second
Lumber Width (inch) x Thickness (inch) ÷ 12	Length (feet)	Board feet
Meters	100	Centimeters
Meters	3.281	Feet
Meters	39.37	Inches
Meters	0.001	Kilometers
Meters	1,000	Millimeters
Meters	1.094	Yards
Meters/minute	1.667	Centimeters/second
Meters/minute	3.281	Feet/minute
Meters/minute	0.05468	Feet/second
Meters/minute	0.06	Kilometers/hour
Meters/minute	0.03728	Miles/hour
Meters/second	196.8	Feet/minute
Meters/second	3.6	Kilometers/hour
Meters/second	0.06	Kilometers/minute
Meters/second	2.237	Miles/hour
Meters/second	0.03728	Miles/minute
Microns	0.000001	Meters
Miles	1.609 x 100,000	Centimeters
Miles	5280	Feet
Miles	1.609	Kilometers
Miles	1760	Yards
Miles/hour	44.70	Centimeters/second
Miles/hour	88	Feet/minute
Miles/hour	1.467	Feet/second
Miles/hour	1.609	Kilometers/hour
Miles/hour	0.8684	Knots

Multiply	By	To Obtain
Miles/hour	26.82	Meters/minute
Miles/minute	2682	Centimeters/second
Miles/minute	88	Feet/second
Miles/minute	1.609	Kilometers/minute
Miles/minute	60	Miles/hour
Milligrams	0.001	Grams
Milliliters	0.001	Liters
Millimeters	0.1	Centimeters
Millimeters	0.03937	Inches
Milligrams/liter	1	Parts/million
Million gallons/day	1.54723	Cubic feet/second
Minutes (angle)	2.909 x 0.0001	Radians
Ounces	16	Drams
Ounces	437.5	Grains
Ounces	0.0625	Pounds
Ounces	28.349527	Grams
Ounces	0.9115	Ounces (troy)
Ounces	2.790 x 0.00001	Tons (long)
Ounces	2.835 x 0.00001	Tons (metric)
Ounces (troy)	480	Grains
Ounces (troy)	20	Pennyweights (troy)
Ounces (troy)	0.08333	Pounds (troy)
Ounces (troy)	31.103481	Grams
Ounces (troy)	1.09714	Ounces (avoir.)
Ounces (fluid)	1.805	Cubic inches
Ounces (fluid)	0.02957	Liters
Ounces/square inch	0.0625	Pounds/square inch
Overflow rate (feet/hour)	0.12468 x area (square feet)	Gallons/minute
Parts/million	0.0584	Grains/U.S. gallon
Parts/million	0.07016	Grains/Imperial gallon
Parts/million	8.345	Pounds/million gallons
Pennyweights (troy)	24	Grains
Pennyweights (troy)	1.55517	Grams
Pennyweights (troy)	0.05	Ounces (troy)
Pennyweights (troy)	4.1667 x 0.001	Pounds (troy)
Pounds	16	Ounces
Pounds	256	Drams
Pounds	7000	Grains
Pounds	0.0005	Tons (short)
Pounds	453.5924	Grams
Pounds	1.21528	Pounds (troy)
Pounds	14.5833	Ounces (troy)
Pounds (troy)	5760	Grains
Pounds (troy)	240	Pennyweights (troy)
Pounds (troy)	12	Ounces (troy)
Pounds (troy)	373.24177	Grams
Pounds (troy)	3.6735 x 0.0001	Tons (long)
Pounds (troy)	4.1143 x 0.0001	Tons (short)
Pounds (troy)	3.7324 x 0.0001	Tons (metric)
Pounds of water	0.01602	Cubic feet
Pounds of water	27.68	Cubic inches
Pounds of water	0.1198	Gallons
Pounds of water/minute	2.670 x 0.0001	Cubic feet/second
Pounds/cubic foot	0.01602	Grams/cubic centimeter
Pounds/cubic foot	16.02	Kilograms/cubic meters
Pounds/cubic foot	5.787 x 0.0001	Pounds/cubic inch
Pounds/cubic inch	27.68	Grams/cubic centimeter
Pounds/cubic inch	2.768 x 10,000	Kilograms/cubic meter
Pounds/cubic inch	1728	Pounds/cubic foot

Multiply	By	To Obtain
Pounds/foot	1.488	Kilograms/meter
Pounds/inch	178.6	Grams/centimeter
Pounds/square foot	0.01602	Feet of water
Pounds/square foot	4.883	Kilograms/square meter
Pounds/square foot	6.945 x 0.001	Pounds/square inch
Pounds/square inch	0.06804	Atmospheres
Pounds/square inch	2.307	Feet of water
Pounds/square inch	2.036	Inches of mercury
Pounds/square inch	703.1	Kilograms/square meter
Quadrants (angle)	90	Degrees
Quadrants (angle)	5400	Minutes
Quadrants (angle)	1.571	Radians
Quarts (dry)	67.20	Cubic inches
Quarts (liquid)	57.75	Cubic inches
Quintal, Metric	220.46	Pounds
Quires	25	Sheets
Radians	57.30	Degrees
Radians	3438	Minutes
Radians	0.637	Quadrants
Radians/second	57.30	Degrees/second
Radians/second	0.1592	Revolutions/second
Radians/second	9.549	Revolutions/minute
Radians/second/second	573.0	Revolutions/minute/minute
Radians/second/second	0.1592	Revolutions/second/second
Reams	500	Sheets
Revolutions	360	Degrees
Revolutions	4	Quadrants
Revolutions	6.283	Radians
Revolutions/minute	6	Degrees/second
Revolutions/minute	0.1047	Radians/second
Revolutions/minute	0.01667	Revolutions/second
Revolutions/minute/minute	1.745 x 0.001	Radians/second/second
Revolutions/minute/minute	2.778 x 0.0001	Revolutions/second/second
Revolutions/second	360	Degrees/second
Revolutions/second	6.283	Radians/second
Revolutions/second	60	Revolutions/minute
Revolutions/second/second	6.283	Radians/second/second
Revolutions/second/second	3600	Revolutions/minute/minute
Seconds (angle)	4.848 x 0.000001	Radians
Square centimeters	1.076 x 0.001	Square feet
Square centimeters	0.1550	Square inches
Square centimeters	0.0001	Square meters
Square centimeters	100	Square millimeters
Square feet	2.296 x 0.00001	Acres
Square feet	929.0	Square centimeters
Square feet	144	Square inches
Square feet	0.09290	Square meters
Square feet	3.587 x 0.00000001	Square miles
Square feet	0.111111	Square yards
Square inches	6.452	Square centimeters
Square inches	6.944 x 0.001	Square feet
Square inches	645.2	Square millimeters
Square kilometers	247.1	Acres
Square kilometers	10.76 x 1,000,000	Square feet
Square kilometers	1,000,000	Square meters
Square kilometers	0.3861	Square miles
Square kilometers	1.196 x 1,000,000	Square yards
Square meters	2.471 x 0.0001	Acres
Square meters	10.76	Square feet

Multiply	By	To Obtain
Square meters	3.861 x 0.0000001	Square miles
Square meters	1.196	Square yards
Square miles	640	Acres
Square miles	27.88 x 1,000,000	Square feet
Square miles	2.590	Square kilometers
Square miles	3.098 x 1,000,000	Square yards
Square millimeters	0.01	Square centimeters
Square millimeters	1.550 x 0.001	Square inches
Square yards	2.066 x 0.0001	Acres
Square yards	9	Square feet
Square yards	0.8361	Square feet
Square yards	3.228 x 0.0000001	Square miles
Temperature ($°$C.) + 273	1	Absolute Temperature ($°$C.)
Temperature ($°$C.) + 17.78	1.8	Temperature ($°$F.)
Temperature ($°$F.) + 460	1	Absolute Temperature ($°$F.)
Temperature ($°$F.) – 32	0.555555	Temperature ($°$C.)
Tons (long)	1016	Kilograms
Tons (long)	2240	Pounds
Tons (long)	1.12000	Tons (short)
Tons (metric)	1,000	Kilograms
Tons (metric)	2205	Pounds
Tons (short)	2000	Pounds
Tons (short)	32,000	Ounces
Tons (short)	907.18486	Kilograms
Tons (short)	2430.56	Pounds (troy)
Tons (short)	0.89287	Tons (long)
Tons (short)	29166.66	Ounces (troy)
Tons (short)	0.90718	Tons (metric)
Watts	0.05692	British Thermal Units/minute
Watts	44.26	Foot-pounds/minute
Watts	0.7376	Foot-pounds/second
Watts	1.341 x 0.001	Horsepower
Watts	0.01434	Kilogram-calories/minute
Watts	0.001	Kilowatts
Watt-hours	3.415	British Thermal Units
Watt-hours	2655	Foot-pounds
Watt-hours	1.341 x 0.001	Horsepower-hours
Watt-hours	0.8605	Kilogram-calories
Watt-hours	367.1	Kilogram-meters
Watt-hours	0.001	Kilowatt-hours
Yards	91.44	Centimeters
Yards	3	Feet
Yards	36	Inches
Yards	0.9144	Meters

COMMON MEASURES

Volume		
60 Drops = 1 Teaspoon	1 Ounce = 1/8 Cup	2 Pints = 1 Quart
3 Teaspoons = 1 Tablespoon	8 Ounces = 1 Cup	4 Quarts = 1 Gallon
2 Tablespoons = 1 Fluid Ounce	2 Cups = 1 Pint	
Weight		
16 Ounces = 1 Pound		

WEB SITES

Please Note: The following web pages are just for reference. This is not an endorsement of any kind. Web page addresses change on a regular basis and the listed URLs may or may not exist. The Internet has many inherent risks. Beware.

MELVIN G. PETERMAN / INSIGHT™

www.sixbranches.com - or - www.insighttechnicaleducation.com

ASSOCIATIONS / STANDARDS / CODES

www.4spe.org/links.html -- Society of Plastics Engineers, Inc.
www.aaes.org -- American Association of Engineering Societies (AAES)
www.aia.org – American Institute of Architects (AIA)
www.aisc.org – American Institute of Steel Construction, Inc. (AISC)
www.aise.org -- Association of Iron and Steel Engineers (AISE)
www.amweld.org -- American Welding Society (AWS)
www.ansi.org – American National Standards Institute, Inc. (ANSI)
www.asce.org -- American Society of Civil Engineers (ASCE)
www.ashrae.org -- American Society of Heating, Refrig. & Air-Cond. (ASHRAE)
www.asme.org -- American Society of Mechanical Engineers (ASME)
www.idis.com/aime/ -- Amer. Inst. of Mining, Metallurgical, & Petroleum Eng.
www.idis.com/aime/iss.htm – Iron & Steel Society (ISS)
www.ieee.com -- Institute of Electrical and Electronics Engineers, Inc. (IEEE)
www.iienet.org -- Institute of Industrial Engineers (IIE)
www.iso.ch -- International Organization for Standardization (ISO)
www.nema.org -- National Electrical Manufacturers Association (NEMA)
www.nfpa.com -- National Fluid Power Association (NFPA)
www.sae.org -- Society of Automotive Engineers (SAE)
www.tms.org – American Institute of Mining Engineering (AIME)

BOOKS

www.industrialpress.com – industrial press Inc.
www.powells.com

CAD (COMPUTER AIDED DESIGN)

FREE CAD*

* www.cadstd.com -- John Apperson (free cad software)
* www.completelyfreesoftware.com
www.ansys.com – ANSYS, Inc.
www.ashlar.com – Ashlar, Inc.
www.Autodesk.com – Autodesk Inc.
www.bentley.com – Bently Systems Incorporated
www.cadalog.com – CAD stuff
www.cadam.com -- Dassault Systemes (IBM)
www.cadkey.com – Baystate Technologies
www.cadshack.com – CAD stuff
www.catia.com -- Dassault Systemes (IBM)
www.division.com – Division Inc.
www.i-deas.com – Structural Dynamics Research Corporation
www.imsisoft.com -- TurboCAD
www.ironcad.com – Iron CAD
www.kurta.com – ALTEK Corporation
www.ptc.com – Parametric Technology Corporation
www.sdrc.com -- Structural Dynamics Research Corporation
www.solidworks.com – SolidWorks Corporation
www.ugsolutions.com – Unigraphics Solutions, Inc
www.visio.com – Visio Corporation

CAM (Computer Aided Manufacturing)
www.featuremill.com -- Engineering Geometry Systems
www.mastercam.com – cnc software, inc.
www.sdrc.com – SmartCAM -- Structural Dynamics Research Corporation
www.turboguide.com/cdprod1/swhrec/016/612.shtml – smartcam

Computers & Printers
www.compaq.com -- Compaq Computer Corporation
www.dec.com – Digital Equipment Corporation
www.epson.com – Epson America, Inc.
www.hp.com – Hewlett Packard Company
www.ibm.com – International Business Machines Corporation
www.sgi.com – Silicon Graphics Inc.
www.sun.com – Sun Microsystems Inc.
www.xerox.com – Xerox Corporation

Digital Cameras
www.agfa.com -- Agfa-Gevaert
www.kodak.com -- Eastman Kodak Company
www.canon.com -- Canon U.S.A., Inc.
www.minolta.com -- Minolta Co., Ltd.
www.nikon.com -- Nikon Corporation
www.olympus.com -- Olympus America Inc.,

FEA (Finite Element Analysis)
www.algor.com -- Algor, Inc.
www.noraneng.com -- NE/Nastran / NASA
www.cosmosm.com -- Structural Research & Analysis Corp.
www.hks.com -- Hibbitt, Karlsson & Sorensen, Inc.

Hardware (Parts, Fasteners)
tda.carrlane.com – Carr Lane Manufacturing Company
www.appliedindustrial.com – Applied Industrial Technologies
www.kaman.com – Kaman Corporation
www.emhart.com – Emhart Industries Inc.
www.spstech.com -- SPS Technologies Inc.
www.circlip.com -- Rotor Clip Company, Inc.
www.parker.com -- Parker Hannifin Corporation
www.chicago-rawhide.com -- Chicago Rawhide
www.skf.com -- SKF USA Inc.
www.camcar.textron.com – Camcar Textron Inc.

Interesting / Miscellaneous
www.livelink.com/sumeria/free – free energy
www,mikeholt.com
www.castlegate.net/swapshop/tradepost.htm#sublinks
www.timberdoodle.com
www.thehomeschool.com
www.englib.cornell.edu/ice/ice-index.html

Jobs
www.ceweekly.com -- Jobs
www.dice.com – Jobs
www.headhunter.net – Jobs
www.monster.com – Jobs

Magazines

www.manufacturing.net/magazine/dn/webex/webtoc.html – Design News
www.winmag.com – CMP Media Inc.
www.penton.com – Penton Media Inc.

Material Safety Data Sheets (MSDS) information / Chemistry

www.ilpi.com/msds/index.chtml
chemlab.pc.maricopa.edu/periodic/periodic.html
www.periodictable.com/Pages/3ptDisp.html
mwanal.lanl.gov/CST/imagemap/periodic/periodic.html

Models

www.plasticmodels.com
www.revell-monogram.com
www.testors.com – The Testor Corporation

Rapid Prototyping

www.solidconcepts.com -- Solid Concepts Inc.,
www.sibcoinc.com – Sibco Inc.
www.dtm-corp.com – DTM Corporation

Reference / Information

ww2.itoday.com/jobs-careers/plastics/infolinks.html
www.hotbot.com – search engine
www.infoseek.com – search engine
www.lcweb.loc.gov/copyright – U.S. copyright office
www.go2net.com – search engine
www.thomasregister.com – Thomas Register
www.ucc.ie/cgi-bin/acronym
www.uspto.gov – U.S. patent office

Simulation

www.krev.com – Knowledge Revolution

WWW Search Words

Architectural
Chemical Engineering
Civil Engineering
Computer Engineering
Electrical Engineering
Environmental Engineering
Environmental Science
Fluid Power
Hydraulics
Mechanical Engineering
Plant Engineering
Plastics Engineering
Pneumatics
Structural Engineering

DECIMAL CHART

	INCH	mm			INCH	mm
1/64	.015625	0.3969		33/64	.515625	13.0969
1/32	.03125	0.7937		17/32	.53125	13.4937
3/64	.046875	1.1906		35/64	.546875	13.8906
1/16	.0625	1.5875		9/16	.5625	14.2875
5/64	.078125	1.9844		37/64	.578125	14.6844
3/32	.09375	2.3812		19/32	.59375	15.0812
7/64	.109375	2.7781		39/64	.609375	15.4781
1/8	.125	3.1750		5/8	.625	15.8750
9/64	.140625	3.5719		41/64	.640625	16.2719
5/32	.15625	3.9687		21/32	.65625	16.6687
11/64	.171875	4.3656		43/64	.671875	17.0656
3/16	.1875	4.7625		11/16	.6875	17.4625
13/64	.203125	5.1594		45/64	.703125	17.8594
7/32	.21875	5.5562		23/32	.71875	18.2562
15/64	.234375	5.9531		47/64	.734375	18.6531
1/4	.25	6.3500		3/4	.75	19.0500
17/64	.265625	6.7469		49/64	.765625	19.4469
9/32	.28125	7.1437		25/32	.78125	19.8437
19/64	.296875	7.5406		51/64	.796875	20.2406
5/16	.3125	7.9375		13/16	.8125	20.6375
21/64	.328125	8.3344		53/64	.828125	21.0344
11/32	.34375	8.7312		27/32	.84375	21.4312
23/64	.359375	9.1281		55/64	.859375	21.8281
3/8	.375	9.5250		7/8	.875	22.2250
25/64	.390625	9.9219		57/64	.890625	22.6219
13/32	.40625	10.3187		29/32	.90625	23.0187
27/64	.421875	10.7156		59/64	.921875	23.4156
7/16	.4375	11.1125		15/16	.9375	23.8125
29/64	.453125	11.5094		61/64	.953125	24.2094
15/32	.46875	11.9062		31/32	.96875	24.6062
31/64	.484375	12.3031		63/64	.984375	25.0031
1/2	.5	12.7000		1	1	25.4001

ELECTRICAL SYMBOLS

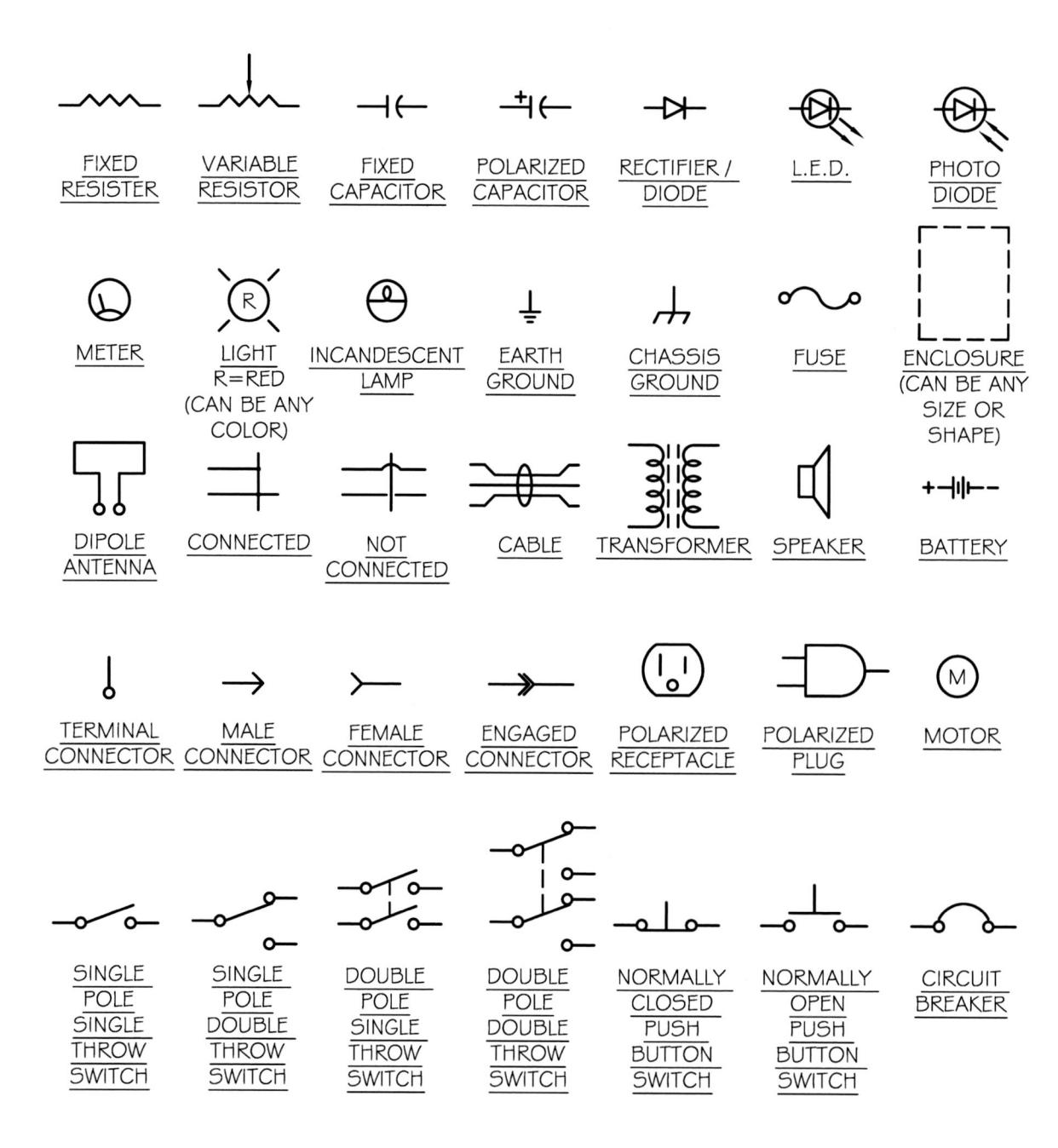

FIXED RESISTER

VARIABLE RESISTOR

FIXED CAPACITOR

POLARIZED CAPACITOR

RECTIFIER / DIODE

L.E.D.

PHOTO DIODE

METER

LIGHT R=RED (CAN BE ANY COLOR)

INCANDESCENT LAMP

EARTH GROUND

CHASSIS GROUND

FUSE

ENCLOSURE (CAN BE ANY SIZE OR SHAPE)

DIPOLE ANTENNA

CONNECTED

NOT CONNECTED

CABLE

TRANSFORMER

SPEAKER

BATTERY

TERMINAL CONNECTOR

MALE CONNECTOR

FEMALE CONNECTOR

ENGAGED CONNECTOR

POLARIZED RECEPTACLE

POLARIZED PLUG

MOTOR

SINGLE POLE SINGLE THROW SWITCH

SINGLE POLE DOUBLE THROW SWITCH

DOUBLE POLE SINGLE THROW SWITCH

DOUBLE POLE DOUBLE THROW SWITCH

NORMALLY CLOSED PUSH BUTTON SWITCH

NORMALLY OPEN PUSH BUTTON SWITCH

CIRCUIT BREAKER

NOTE:
THIS IS ONLY A SMALL SAMPLE OF THE MOST COMMON SYMBOLS. FOR MORE INFORMATION SEE ANSI & IEEE STANDARDS. A GOOD RESOURCE FOR OTHER MATERIALS & INFORMATION IS YOUR LOCAL ELECTRONICS HOBBY SHOP OR RADIO SHACK.

FASTENER, RETAINER, & KEY IDENTIFICATION

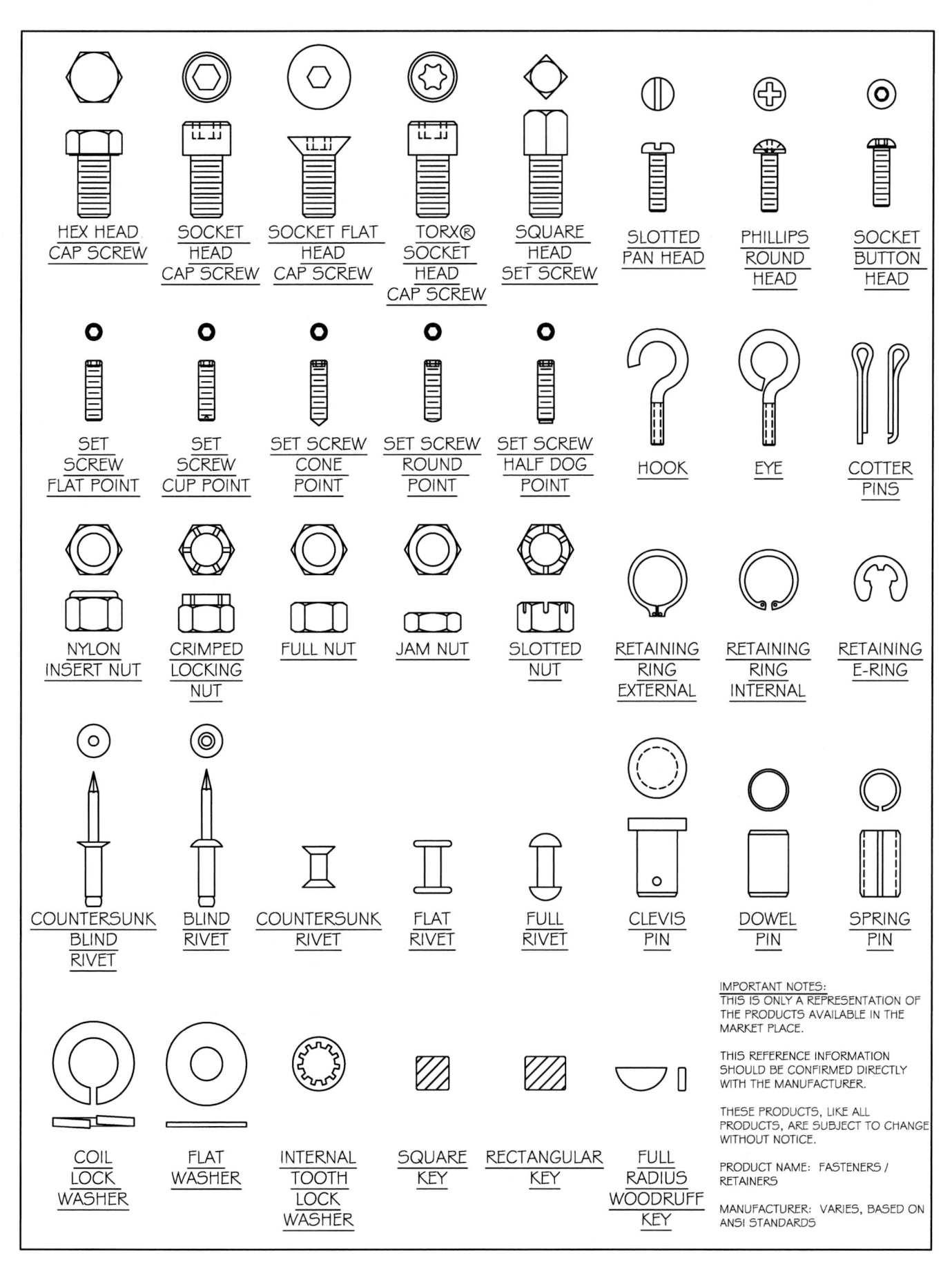

HEX HEAD
CAP SCREW

SOCKET
HEAD
CAP SCREW

SOCKET FLAT
HEAD
CAP SCREW

TORX®
SOCKET
HEAD
CAP SCREW

SQUARE
HEAD
SET SCREW

SLOTTED
PAN HEAD

PHILLIPS
ROUND
HEAD

SOCKET
BUTTON
HEAD

SET
SCREW
FLAT POINT

SET
SCREW
CUP POINT

SET SCREW
CONE
POINT

SET SCREW
ROUND
POINT

SET SCREW
HALF DOG
POINT

HOOK

EYE

COTTER
PINS

NYLON
INSERT NUT

CRIMPED
LOCKING
NUT

FULL NUT

JAM NUT

SLOTTED
NUT

RETAINING
RING
EXTERNAL

RETAINING
RING
INTERNAL

RETAINING
E-RING

COUNTERSUNK
BLIND
RIVET

BLIND
RIVET

COUNTERSUNK
RIVET

FLAT
RIVET

FULL
RIVET

CLEVIS
PIN

DOWEL
PIN

SPRING
PIN

COIL
LOCK
WASHER

FLAT
WASHER

INTERNAL
TOOTH
LOCK
WASHER

SQUARE
KEY

RECTANGULAR
KEY

FULL
RADIUS
WOODRUFF
KEY

IMPORTANT NOTES:
THIS IS ONLY A REPRESENTATION OF
THE PRODUCTS AVAILABLE IN THE
MARKET PLACE.

THIS REFERENCE INFORMATION
SHOULD BE CONFIRMED DIRECTLY
WITH THE MANUFACTURER.

THESE PRODUCTS, LIKE ALL
PRODUCTS, ARE SUBJECT TO CHANGE
WITHOUT NOTICE.

PRODUCT NAME: FASTENERS /
RETAINERS

MANUFACTURER: VARIES, BASED ON
ANSI STANDARDS

GEOMETRIC & GENERAL DIMENSION SYMBOLS

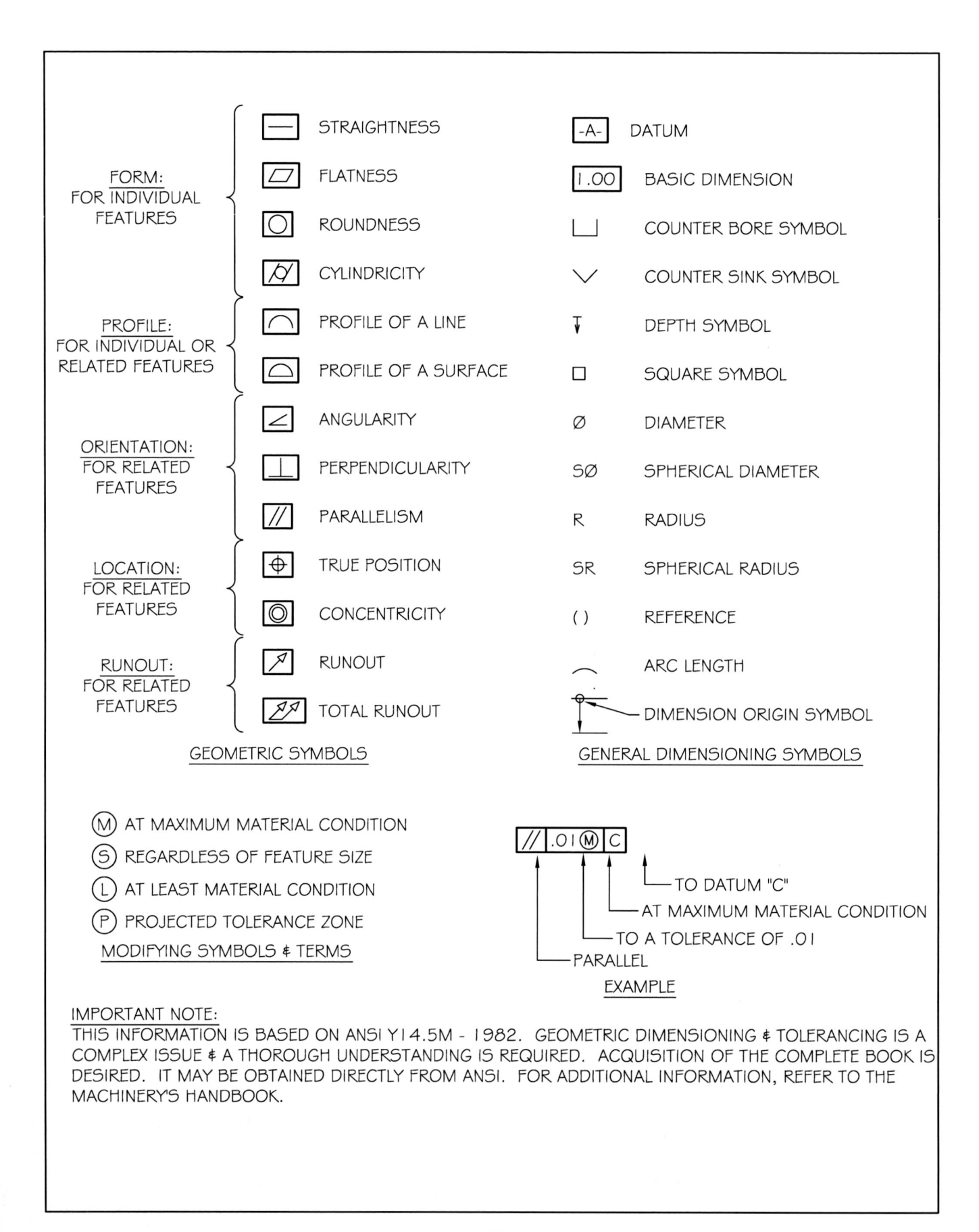

IMPORTANT NOTE:
THIS INFORMATION IS BASED ON ANSI Y14.5M - 1982. GEOMETRIC DIMENSIONING & TOLERANCING IS A COMPLEX ISSUE & A THOROUGH UNDERSTANDING IS REQUIRED. ACQUISITION OF THE COMPLETE BOOK IS DESIRED. IT MAY BE OBTAINED DIRECTLY FROM ANSI. FOR ADDITIONAL INFORMATION, REFER TO THE MACHINERY'S HANDBOOK.

METAL FRAMING SHAPES - KINDORF

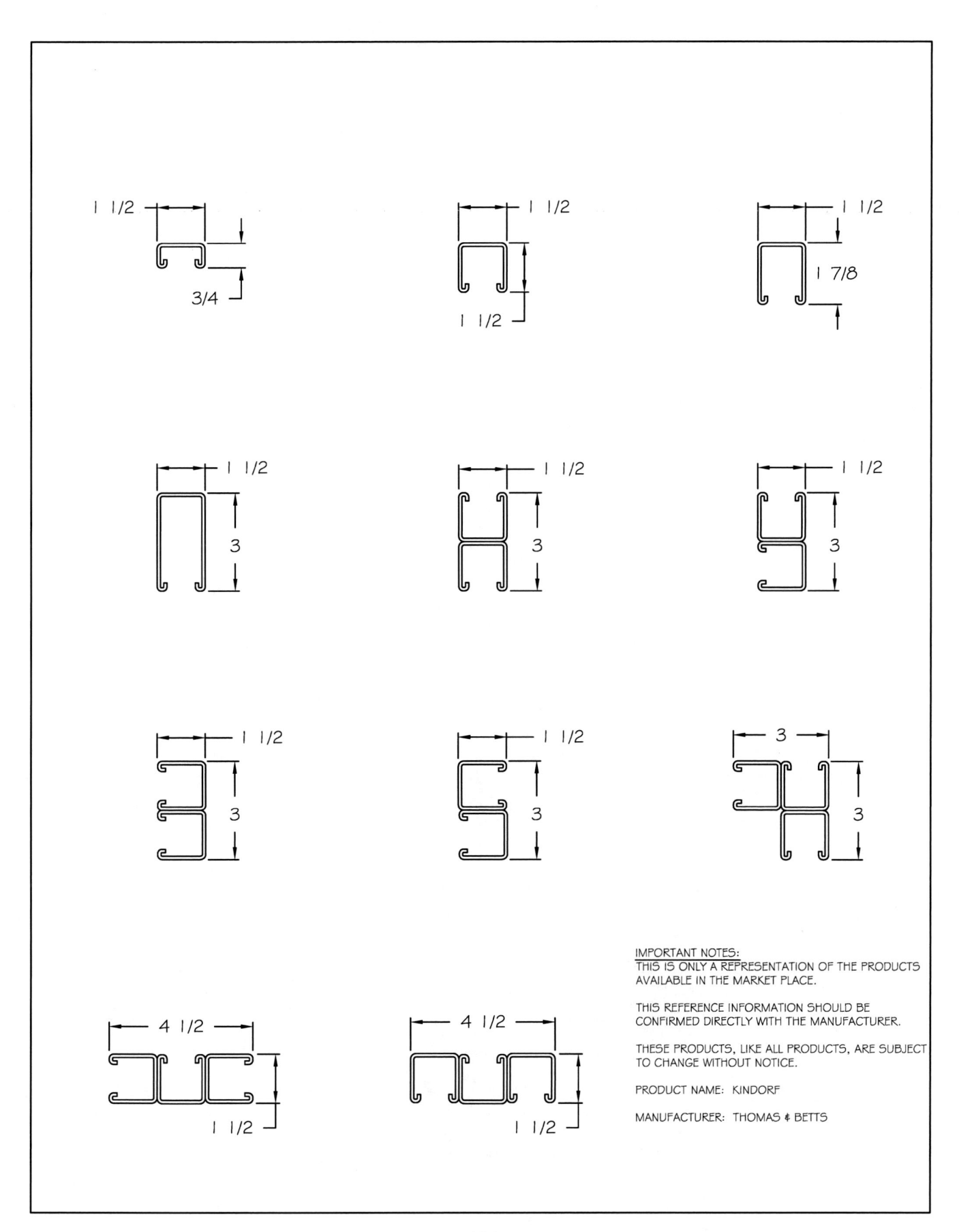

IMPORTANT NOTES:
THIS IS ONLY A REPRESENTATION OF THE PRODUCTS
AVAILABLE IN THE MARKET PLACE.

THIS REFERENCE INFORMATION SHOULD BE
CONFIRMED DIRECTLY WITH THE MANUFACTURER.

THESE PRODUCTS, LIKE ALL PRODUCTS, ARE SUBJECT
TO CHANGE WITHOUT NOTICE.

PRODUCT NAME: KINDORF

MANUFACTURER: THOMAS & BETTS

METAL FRAMING SHAPES - UNISTRUT

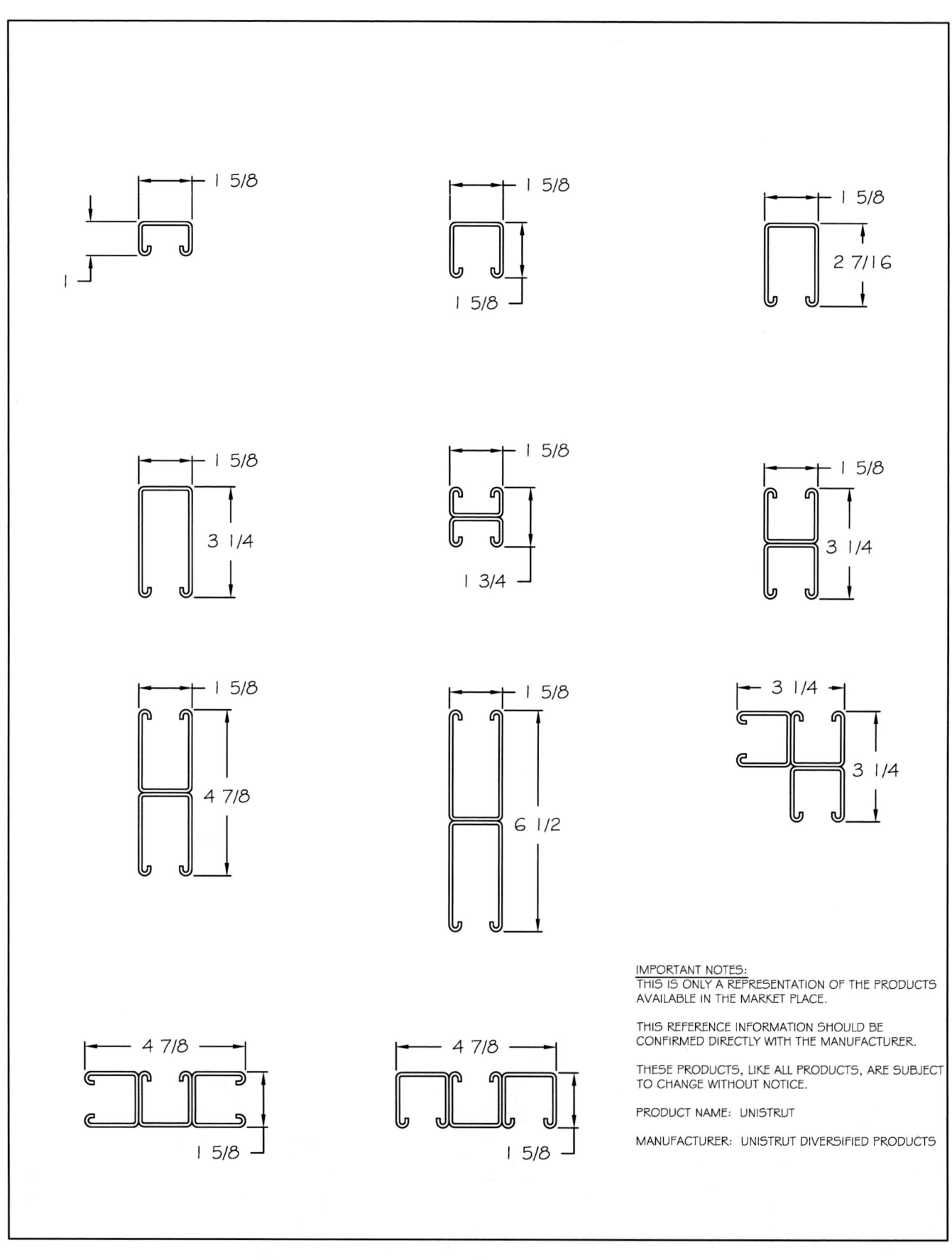

PIPING SYMBOLS

JOINT TYPES	SCREWED	FLANGED	WELDED
STRAIGHT			
ELBOW, 90°			
ELBOW, 90°, REDUCING			
ELBOW, 90°, TOWARDS			
ELBOW, 90°, AWAY			
ELBOW, 45°			
TEE			
TEE, AWAY			
TEE, TOWARDS			
CROSS			
REDUCER, CONCENTRIC			
REDUCER, ECCENTRIC			
Y			
VALVE, GATE			
VALVE, GLOBE			
VALVE, CHECK			
VALVE, DIAPHRAGM			
VALVE, BALL			
VALVE, SOLENOID			
UNION			

NOTE:
THIS IS ONLY A SMALL SAMPLE OF THE MOST COMMON SYMBOLS. FOR MORE INFORMATION
SEE ANSI STANDARDS.

COMMON STEEL SHAPES (PROFILES)

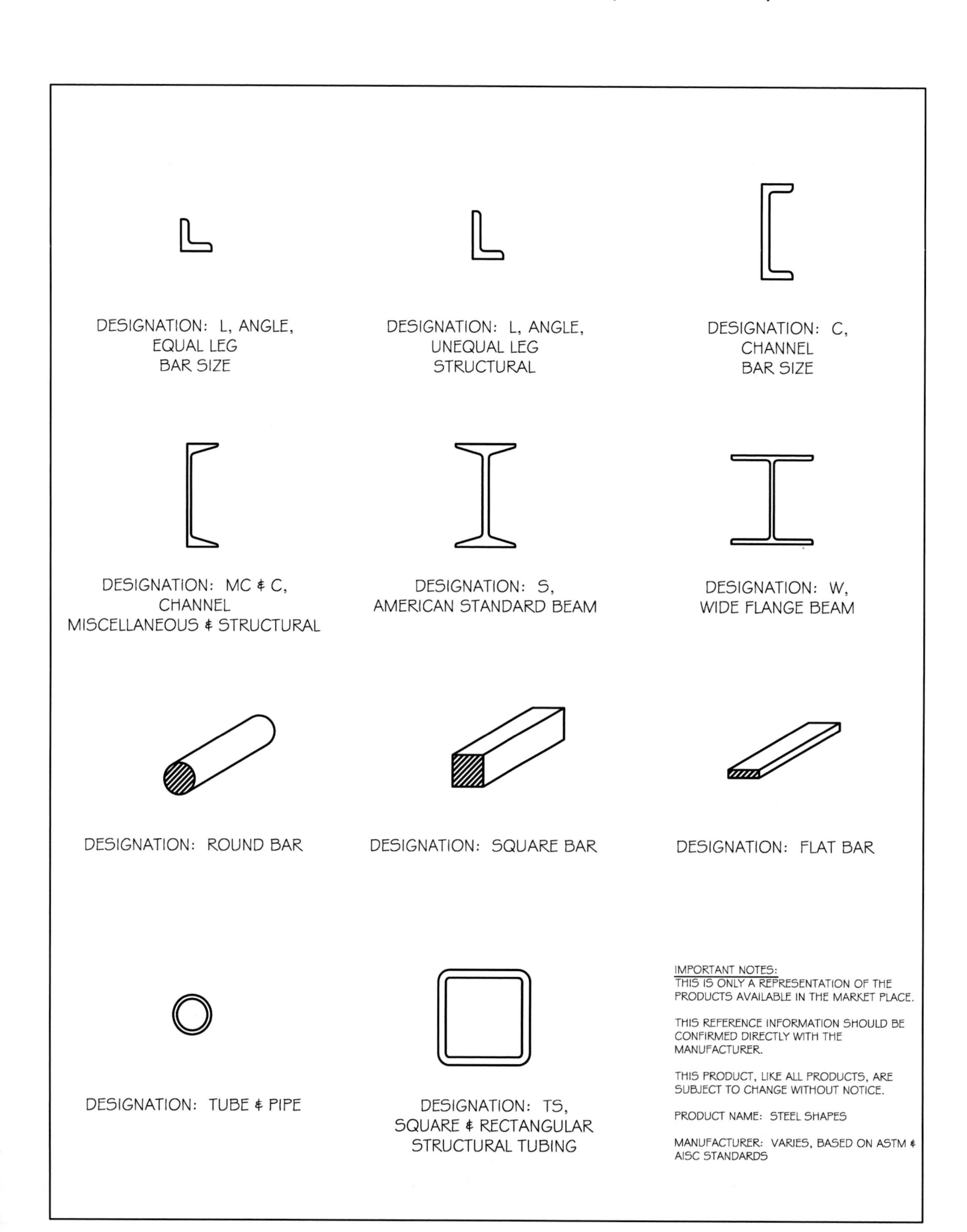

DESIGNATION: L, ANGLE,
EQUAL LEG
BAR SIZE

DESIGNATION: L, ANGLE,
UNEQUAL LEG
STRUCTURAL

DESIGNATION: C,
CHANNEL
BAR SIZE

DESIGNATION: MC & C,
CHANNEL
MISCELLANEOUS & STRUCTURAL

DESIGNATION: S,
AMERICAN STANDARD BEAM

DESIGNATION: W,
WIDE FLANGE BEAM

DESIGNATION: ROUND BAR

DESIGNATION: SQUARE BAR

DESIGNATION: FLAT BAR

DESIGNATION: TUBE & PIPE

DESIGNATION: TS,
SQUARE & RECTANGULAR
STRUCTURAL TUBING

IMPORTANT NOTES:
THIS IS ONLY A REPRESENTATION OF THE
PRODUCTS AVAILABLE IN THE MARKET PLACE.

THIS REFERENCE INFORMATION SHOULD BE
CONFIRMED DIRECTLY WITH THE
MANUFACTURER.

THIS PRODUCT, LIKE ALL PRODUCTS, ARE
SUBJECT TO CHANGE WITHOUT NOTICE.

PRODUCT NAME: STEEL SHAPES

MANUFACTURER: VARIES, BASED ON ASTM &
AISC STANDARDS

SURFACE TEXTURE

 BASIC SURFACE TEXTURE SYMBOL. PRODUCED BY ANY METHOD.

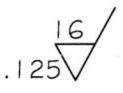 MATERIAL REMOVAL BY MACHINING IS REQUIRED.

MATERIAL REMOVAL BY MACHINING IS REQUIRED. THE AMOUNT OF MATERIAL TO BE REMOVED IS SPECIFIED.

 NO MATERIAL REMOVAL ALLOWED. SURFACE MUST BE PRODUCED BY OTHER METHODS SUCH AS CASTING.

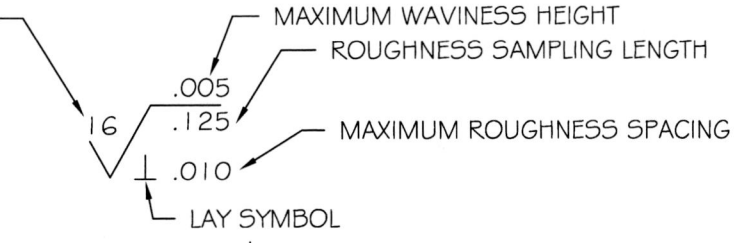

SURFACE FINISH IN μin — MAXIMUM WAVINESS HEIGHT — ROUGHNESS SAMPLING LENGTH — MAXIMUM ROUGHNESS SPACING — LAY SYMBOL

RECOMMENDED FINISHES	
μin	μm
1	.025
2	.050
4	.075
8	.10
16	.20
32	.40
63	.80
125	1.60
250	3.2
500	6.3
1000	12.5
	25

⊥ = PERPENDICULAR LAY TO INDICATED SURFACE
= = PARALLEL LAY TO INDICATED SURFACE
X = ANGULAR CROSS PATTERN
M = MULTIDIRECTIONAL LAY, ALL DIRECTIONS, NO PATTERN
C = CIRCULAR LAY, CIRCULAR PATTERN
R = RADIAL LAY
P = PARTICULATE, NON-DIRECTIONAL LAY

COMPARISON OF SURFACE TEXTURES		
SAMPLE PROCESS	ROUGHNESS AVERAGE	
	μin	μm
FLAME CUT	1000-500	25 - 12.5
SAWING	1000-250	25 - 6.3
DRILLING	250 - 63	6.3 - 1.6
MILLING	250 - 32	6.3 - .80
LASER	250 - 32	6.3 - .80
BROACHING	125 - 32	3.2 - .80
GRINDING	63 - 4	1.6 - .10
LAPPING	16 - 2	.40 - .05
SAND CASTING	1000 - 500	25 - 12.5
HOT ROLLING	1000 - 500	25 - 12.5
INVESTMENT CASTING	125 - 63	3.2 - 1.6
COLD ROLLED	125 - 32	3.2 - .80

IMPORTANT NOTE:
THIS INFORMATION IS BASED ON ANSI Y14.36 - 1978. NOTING SURFACE TEXTURES IS A COMPLEX ISSUE & A THOROUGH UNDERSTANDING IS REQUIRED. ACQUISITION OF THE COMPLETE BOOK IS DESIRED. IT MAY BE OBTAINED DIRECTLY FROM ANSI.

WELDING SYMBOLS

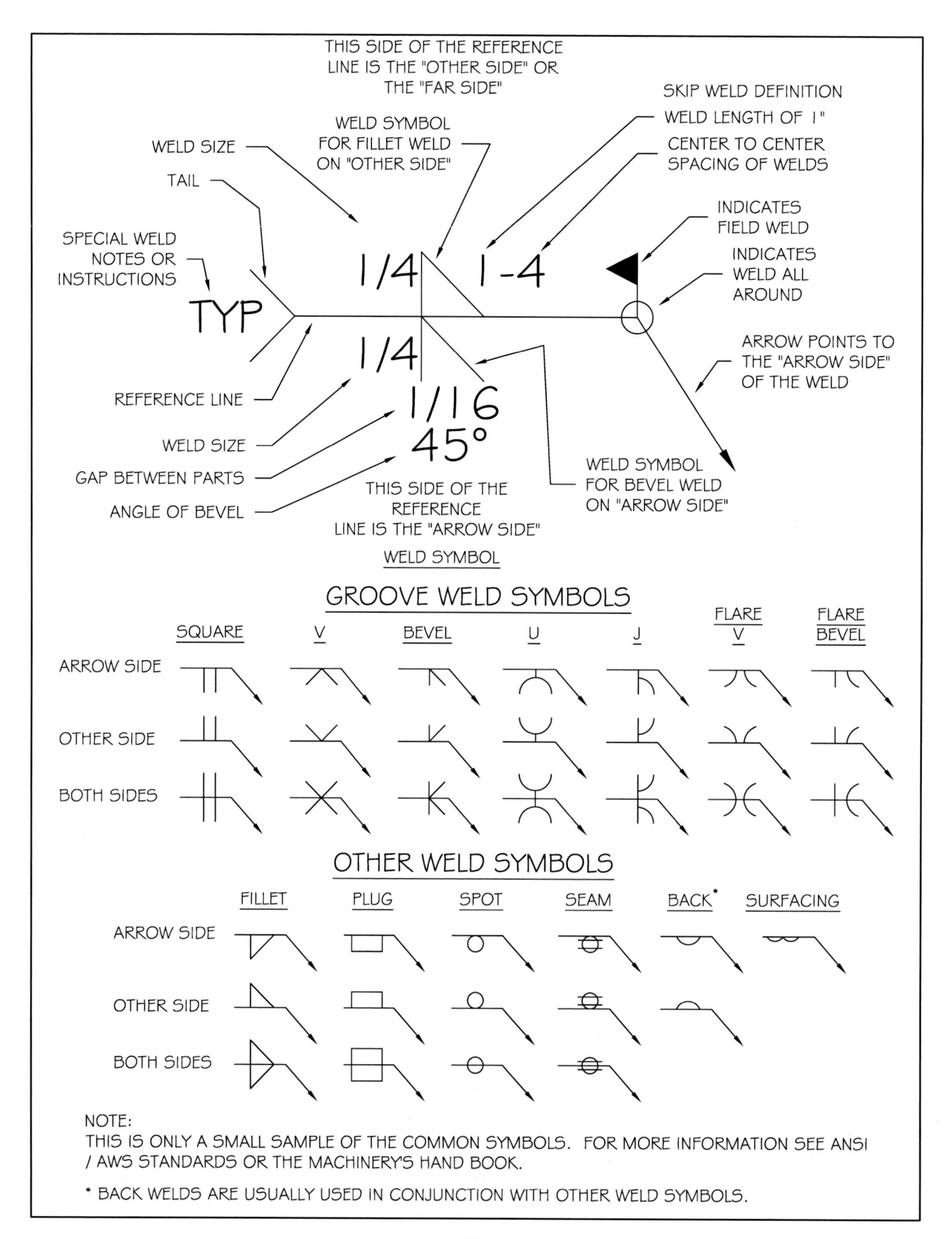

GROOVE WELD SYMBOLS

OTHER WELD SYMBOLS

NOTE:
THIS IS ONLY A SMALL SAMPLE OF THE COMMON SYMBOLS. FOR MORE INFORMATION SEE ANSI / AWS STANDARDS OR THE MACHINERY'S HAND BOOK.

* BACK WELDS ARE USUALLY USED IN CONJUNCTION WITH OTHER WELD SYMBOLS.

Thank you for purchasing this book!

We hope that you have enjoyed this book and that it has helped you in meeting your goals and that what you have learned will benefit you in your life pursuits.

Our complete line of books:

COMPLETE-A-SKETCH™ VOLUME 1 - ORTHOGAPHIC
COMPLETE-A-SKETCH™ VOLUME 2 - ISOMETRIC
COMPLETE-A-SKETCH™ VOLUME 3 - PERSPECTIVE
COMPLETE-A-SKETCH™ VISION - DEXTERITY - FOCUS™
PRACTICAL DRAFTING™
PRACTICAL GRAPHIC DESIGN™
PRACTICAL ACCOUNTING FUNDAMENTALS™

We are always working on new books, so please feel free to visit our website to see what new topics we may have added.

All the best,
Mel Peterman, Publisher
Insight Technical Education
www.insightteched.com
877.640.2256